URP GCOE DOCUMENT 9

International Symposium:
Urban Regeneration through Cultural Creativity and
Social Inclusion

The 1st International Roundtable Meeting
Towards the Century of Cities

大阪市立大学 都市研究プラザ
Urban Research Plaza, Osaka City University

© 2011 Urban Research Plaza, Osaka City University

All rights reserved. No part of this publication may be reproduced, stored in a retrieval system, or transmitted, in any form or by any means, electronic, mechanical, photocopying, recording, or otherwise, without the prior written permission of the publisher.

URP GCOE DOCUMENT 9
International Symposium:
Urban Regeneration through Cultural Creativity and Social Inclusion
Editors: Masayuki Sasaki, Toshio Mizuuchi
Editorial Committee: Hong Gyu Jeon, Yumi Sato, Shinichi Takaoka, Kazuya Sakurada,
Tomonaga Horiguchi, Nobu Amenomori, Tomoko Hayashi, Hannu Kurunsaari, Yu Cui, Shinya Kitagawa,
Geerhardt Kornatowski, Hideaki Sasajima

Published by Urban Research Plaza, Osaka City University
3-3-138, Sugimoto, Sumiyoshi-ku, Osaka, 558-8585 JAPAN
Tel:+81-6-6605-2071
Fax:+81-6-6605-2069
www.ur-plaza.osaka-cu.ac.jp

ISBN 978-4-904010-10-5
Printed in Japan

Contents

Advisers, Organizing Committee, Executive Committee

Welcome Remarks
 Toshio Mizuuchi
 Yoshiki Nishizawa
 Kunio Hiramatsu

Opening Address
 Masayuki Sasaki

Session 1. Keynote Addresses: Urban Regeneration through Cultural Creativity and Social Inclusion 19
 1-0. Opening Remarks
  Toshio Mizuuchi
 1-1. Public Art: Tracing the Life Cycle of New York's Creative Districts
  Sharon Zukin
 1-2. "Precariousness" in the Creative Economy: Implications for Economic Planning in Singapore
  Lily Kong
 1-3. Power and Openness: Appropriating City Space for Re-creating "the Urban"
  Takashi Machimura

Session 2. Perspectives from the New Journal *'City, Culture and Society'* 61
 2-0. Opening Remarks
  Hiroshi Okano
 2-1. Elsevier – Open to Accelerate Science
  Ritsuko Miki
 2-2. Academic Research in Arts Management
  François Colbert
 2-3. Journals in the Age of Limited Attention Span
  Andy C Pratt
 2-4. The Rise of China Inc. and Challenges for the Next Generation of Urban Scholars
  Hyun Bang Shin
 2-5. Some Thoughts on Urban Studies Towards the Century of Cities
  Jung Duk Lim
 2-6. Discussion

Session 3. Rethinking Urban Creativity 103
 3-0. Opening Remarks
  Kenkichi Nagao
 3-1. Technological Innovation in Creative Clusters: The Case of Laser Technology in the Conservation of Artworks in Florence
  Luciana Lazzeretti

3-2. Redundancy, "Creative" Innovation and Agglomeration: Japanese Home Videogame and Television Program Production Industries
   Seiji Hanzawa

3-3. Rethinking Urban Creativity: Lessons Learned from Barcelona and Montréal
   Patrick Cohendet

3-4. The Cultural Contradictions of the Creative City
   Andy C Pratt

3-5. Discussion

Session 4. "Networking the Asian Urban Studies" Overseas Sub-Centers 151
   4-0. Opening Remarks
       Shin Nakagawa
   4-1. Hybridization Can Create Strong Species
       Jong Gyun Seo
   4-2. Help Systems of Housing / Residence Life in Shanghai: Our Survey and Ideas
       Ying-Fang Chen
   4-3. Cultural Practices, Urban Redevelopment and the Marginalized Urban Poor in Taipei
       Liling Huang
   4-4. Networking within Asian Urban Studies: An Inside-out Perspective
       Wing Shing Tang
   4-5. Deepening Urban Culture Research through the Exchange Program between Bangkok and Osaka
       Bussakorn Binson
   4-6. Struggle for Inclusion: Residents and Citizenship in Urban Marginalized Neighborhoods
       Nicolaas Warouw
   4-7. Is Social Inclusion Everyone's Business?
       Suzy Goldsmith
   4-8. Discussion

Session 5. Presentations by URP Research Fellows 203
   5-0. Opening Remarks
       Hong Gyu Jeon
   5-1. Audience Development and Successor Training in Japanese Traditional Performing Arts
       Chisako Takashima
   5-2. Accounting in Recycling Network Enterprises : Reflections on Capability-building
       Hannu Kurunsaari
   5-3. The Experimental Investigation between Social Enterprise and Community-based Art
       Sunsik Kim
   5-4. Problem of Mismatch between the Process of Securing Permanent Housing and Housing Policy for Single Mother Households in Japan
       Lisa Kuzunishi

Session 6. Perspectives of the AUC and its Prospects 235
    Masayuki Sasaki
    Toshio Kamo

ADVISERS

Yoshiki Nishizawa	President, Osaka City University
Kenichi Nagata	President, Osaka International House Foundation

ORGANIZING COMMITTEE

Chairman

Masayuki Sasaki	Director, Urban Research Plaza, Professor, Graduate School for Creative Cities, Osaka City University

Vice-Chairman

Hiroki Hashimoto	Senior Executive Director, Osaka International House Foundation
Hiroshi Okano	Vice-Director, Urban Research Plaza, Professor, Graduate School of Business, Osaka City University

Members

Toshio Mizuuchi	Vice-Director Urban Research Plaza, Professor, Department of Geography, Osaka City University
Michio Miyano	Vice-President, Osaka City University
Hong Gyu Jeon	Associate Professor, Urban Research Plaza, Osaka City University
Tsuneo Tomita	Vice-Director, Urban Research Plaza, Osaka City University
Tateo Arahori	Director, Planning and Communications Division, Osaka International House Foundation
Takashi Yamazaki	Professor, Graduate School of Literature and Human Sciences, Osaka City University
Shin Nakagawa	Professor, Graduate School of Literature and Human Sciences, Osaka City University
Kenkichi Nagao	Professor, Graduate School of Economics, Osaka City University
Katsuhiro Miyamoto	Professor, Graduate School of Engineering, Osaka City University
Naoki Tani	Professor, Graduate School of Human Life Science, Osaka City University
Hiroshi Yahagi	Professor, Graduate School for Creative Cities, Osaka City University
Franz Waldengerger	Professor, Japan Center, Faculty of Business, Ludwig Maximilian University of Munich

EXECUTIVE COMMITTEE

Chairman

Toshio Mizuuchi	Vice-Director, Urban Research Plaza, Professor, Department of Geography, Osaka City University

Chief of the Secretariat

Hong Gyu Jeon	Associate Professor, Urban Research Plaza, Osaka City University

Vice-Chief of the Secretariat

Tomonaga Horiguchi	Adjunct Lecturer, Urban Research Plaza, Osaka City University
Manami Kimura	Senior Staff Officer, Planning and Communications Division, Osaka International House Foundation

Members

Masayuki Sasaki	Director, Urban Research Plaza, Professor, Graduate School for Creative Cities, Osaka City University
Hiroshi Okano	Vice-Director, Urban Research Plaza, Professor, Graduate School of Business, Osaka City University
Tsuneo Tomita	Vice-Director, Urban Research Plaza, Osaka City University
Mayumi Asamatsu	Staff Officer, Planning and Communications Division, Osaka International House Foundation
Shin Nakagawa	Professor, Graduate School of Literature and Human Sciences, Osaka City University
Takashi Uchida	Associate Professor, Graduate School of Engineering, Osaka City University
Sachiko Kawaida	Adjunct Lecturer, Urban Research Plaza, Osaka City University
Kazuya Sakurada	Adjunct Lecturer, Urban Research Plaza, Osaka City University
Yumi Sato	Adjunct Lecturer, Urban Research Plaza, Osaka City University
Shinichi Takaoka	Adjunct Lecturer, Urban Research Plaza, Osaka City University
Shinya Kitagawa	GCOE Postdoctoral Research Fellow, Urban Research Plaza, Osaka City University
Hannu Kurunsaari	GCOE Postdoctoral Research Fellow, Urban Research Plaza, Osaka City University
Fumitake Meno	URP Postdoctoral Research Fellow, Urban Research Plaza, Osaka City University

Maho Shimizu	GCOE Postdoctoral Research Fellow (former), Urban Research Plaza, Osaka City University
Sunsik Kim	GCOE Postdoctoral Research Fellow, Urban Research Plaza, Osaka City University
Chisako Takashima	GCOE Postdoctoral Research Fellow, Urban Research Plaza, Osaka City University
Yu Cui	GCOE Postdoctoral Research Fellow, Urban Research Plaza, Osaka City University
Geerhardt Kornatowski	Ph.D. Candidate, Urban Research Plaza, Osaka City University
Junichi Kondo	Administrative Staff, Urban Research Plaza, Osaka City University
Takako Nishida	Administrative Staff, Urban Research Plaza, Osaka City University

Welcome Remarks

Toshio Mizuuchi

Vice-Director, Urban Research Plaza,
Professor, Department of Geography,
Osaka City University

Ladies and gentlemen, I would like to now begin our international symposium on 'Urban Regeneration through Cultural Creativity and Social Inclusion' as part of the First International Roundtable Conference, entitled 'Towards the Century of Cities.'

My name is Toshio Mizuuchi. I am a Vice-Director of Osaka City University's Urban Research Plaza and I will be acting as the moderator for the first session. I humbly ask for your cooperation. I would like to offer my sincere thanks to all the professors and researchers, city officials and students who have taken the time from their busy schedules to attend today's conference. I also wish to thank the Mayor of Osaka and the President of Osaka City University who are also with us today. This year's academic symposium is one of a series of international symposiums held every year at Osaka City University. In particular, our Urban Research Plaza was specifically established in order to conduct strategic research on urban problems and issues facing Osaka City. We are now in our fifth year.

In commemorating this milestone, we are honored to welcome to this conference participants from 15 different nations and regions. We have planned a program in which to discuss how to deal with the many different problems of various cities in Japan, Asia, Europe, and the rest of the world, and what suggestions we should make. Throughout the morning today, and then, after breaking for lunch, in the afternoon, we will have sessions which will present groundbreaking urban research from New York, Singapore, and Tokyo, and also suggest how we should deal with issues of the city. However, before we begin, I would like to call upon Dr. Yoshiki Nishizawa, the president of Osaka City University, to make a welcoming statement on behalf of the organizers and sponsors of the conference.

Welcome Remarks

Yoshiki Nishizawa

President of Osaka City University

I am Yoshiki Nishizawa, the president of Osaka City University. I would like to thank all of you for participating in this symposium on 'Urban Regeneration through Cultural Creativity and Social Inclusion' as part of the First International Roundtable, 'Towards the Century of Cities.' As a representative of the sponsors of the conference, I would like to offer you a word of welcome.

This symposium is being jointly sponsored by Osaka City University and Osaka International House Foundation. In the beginning, planning for an international roundtable was initiated by Osaka International House, which then requested assistance from our university's Urban Research Plaza, and as a result they jointly sponsored the conference. In other words, I believe it can be said that planning for this project resulted from a cooperative linkage between Osaka International House Foundation, which is the center for international exchange in Osaka, and Osaka City University, whose mission is the dissemination of information based on academic scholarship.

This year Osaka City University is celebrating its 130th anniversary since its founding in 1880 as the Osaka Commercial Training Institute. Our university has a history of evolving together with the citizens against the background of the City of Osaka and a spirit and mission of scholarship, and because we believe it must be a university of which the citizens can be proud, we hope to continue to move forward towards an ever newer university that contributes to the life of the city and its citizens.

The Urban Research Plaza which has organized today's symposium was established in April, 2006 as a forum for urban research with the goal of working for the development of the city through activities in urban research and making policy proposals. In 2007 it became a Global Center of Excellence program, taking on the regenerating of the city through cultural creativity and social inclusion, and it is an institution that has attracted attention throughout the nation.

In international society, the 21st century has been called the 'Century of Cities,' a number of different concepts such as global cities, creative cities, and sustainable cities have arisen, and a reexamination of cities has become a pressing issue. The engine of growth for cities is in the process of changing, from heretofore being manufacturing industries or finance, into advanced knowledge industries or the creative industries, whose core is made up of the arts and culture. At the same time as promoting the creative economy of the 21st century, I believe it is the duty of Osaka City University, which is a part of the City of Osaka, to contribute to building and sustaining a more livable city where a safety net is amply provided by the city government and by local communities.

In this sense, the principal theme that the Urban Research Plaza addresses, the perspective of using the creative energy of culture for inclusive urban social policies, is an extremely important issue, and I look forward to their ever deeper involvement in it. And, responding positively to these research themes of the Urban Research Plaza, and in order to seek policy solutions to the many difficult problems that cities are confronting, a number of truly outstanding scholars and urban researchers from countries around the world have gathered together here in Osaka.

I am truly delighted that this symposium is being held and that many researchers from both Japan and abroad are participating in it. Also, in relation to the theme of this symposium, the Urban Research Plaza is publishing the inaugural issue of a new international journal, *City, Culture and Society*. I believe that this ambitious undertaking will serve to enhance the prestige of Osaka City University internationally. Once again let me say that this symposium, entitled 'Urban Regeneration through Cultural Creativity and Social Inclusion,' has been planned in order to put forth experiments for multifaceted renewal of the city and to provide an opportunity for the world's researchers to come together and meet and discuss the various problems confronting the city.

I hope we can use this occasion to disseminate knowledge from Osaka that will contribute to development in culture, the economy, and in industries. And I would like to conclude my remarks by asking for the continuing understanding and support of all the citizens in the future. Thank you very much.

Welcome Remarks

Kunio Hiramatsu

Mayor of Osaka

Good morning, everyone. My name is Hiramatsu, and I am the Mayor of Osaka. I want to express my delight that the international symposium on 'Urban Regeneration through Cultural Creativity and Social Inclusion' which raises the curtain of the First International Roundtable Conference on 'Towards the Century of Cities' has so successfully opened, and as Mayor of Osaka and representative of the citizens of Osaka, I want to offer a warm welcome to everyone who has come here from far and wide.

The urban population of the world approximately 100 years ago was no more than about 10 per cent of the total world population, but today it is said to have reached more than half, and in that sense the 21st century has truly become the century of cities. On the other hand, the world's great cities have seen the collapse of communities, and are facing many difficulties such as large scale unemployment. In the City of Osaka as well, there is an ongoing trend towards fewer children and more old people, the bonds between people have weakened, utilitarianism has been pushed too far, the awareness and the behavior of people mutually supporting each other have been halted due to competitive market ideologies, and each day problems that are intimately linked to people's livelihoods become more apparent. In the midst of this, the fact that the world's top class urban researchers have been invited here and are discussing the direction that Osaka and the world's other large cities should be headed towards, and the policy principles and guidelines they need to look for, is something that I feel is truly of great significance. I wish to express my deep gratitude to everyone who has given their energies to the opening of this conference, beginning with Osaka City University and Osaka International House Foundation.

In Osaka City, currently we are addressing a new reform of city governance from the viewpoint of changing our posture, starting from the local areas. We are trying to protect people's livelihoods and communities by restoring the power of the local areas and building a new local social community where the people who live there support each other mutually. At the same time, because we are the City of Osaka, we believe that we must pull all of the Kansai Region along with us and act as the engine of development for the Kansai Region as a whole. Culture imbues the form we should aim for; it was positioned in and expressed the community in the urban core. I have great confidence that Osaka is an appropriate place to discuss 'Reviving the City through Cultural Creativity and Social Inclusion.' I look forward to these international conferences continuing to be held here, and for the results to be disseminated from Osaka to the world.

Today's symposium coincides with the inaugural publication of the international academic journal *'City, Culture and Society'* that is attracting worldwide attention, and is one of the commemorative events of Osaka City University's 130th anniversary, and I look forward to Osaka City making even broader contributions to the world with Osaka City University continuing as a base for opening up a splendorous century of cities. With sincere wishes that this symposium is fruitful, that Osaka City University and Osaka International House Foundation continue to prosper, and that all of you will be healthy and productive, I offer my welcome. Thank you very much.

Opening Address

Masayuki Sasaki

Director, Urban Research Center,
Professor, Graduate School for Creative Cities,
Osaka City University

Thank you all very much for coming out to the conference hall. I would also like to express my thanks to those who have come from around the world in order to help make our symposium a success. Actually, this is the fourth time that I have myself opened a conference at this Center for International Exchange. The symposium we held in 2004 included leading exponents of the creative city: Sir Peter Hall, Charles Landry, and Allen Scott. The second time, we invited a number of researchers including Andy Pratt who is with us here today. At the time, I wished that we could invite even more researchers from around the world, but my energy and my financial resources were inadequate.

Thinking that if it were possible I would like to put on a more fruitful conference, this time, unexpectedly, I have been given an extremely good opportunity thanks to the energies of Mayor Hiramatsu of Osaka, President Nishizawa of Osaka City University, and everyone else, including in particular Mr. Nagata, chairman of the board of Osaka International House Foundation. It was with the support of these people that we were able to hold the conference. Additionally, we had the cooperation of the university staff, and so we were able to bring this occasion to fruition. I think we have been very fortunate.

We are just ten years into the 21st century. For us it is unlike the 20th century in which there were world wars in which many people were sacrificed, and the earth's environment was severely degraded in the midst of heavy industrial development. The 20th was a century in which there were positive aspects, but there were many negative aspects as well. However, in the 21st century we were looking forward to a new century in which the environment is beautified and culture and the arts flourish.

Regrettably, however, after the passing of 10 years, it has become all too clear that the 21st century so far has not been rosy. In particular, since the Lehman Brothers shock in September 2008, the world economy has met with its greatest crisis in 80 years. In the midst of this, Osaka and other large cities of the world are confronting many different problems including large scale unemployment, the collapse of communities, and the deterioration of the environment.

In order to seek for solutions to all these problems that cities are facing, we at the Urban Research Plaza and Osaka International House Foundation in cooperation together decided to initiate a new series of international roundtable conferences 'towards the century of cities.' And so, for the first such meeting we are able to intensively discuss over a period of three days 'Urban Regeneration through Cultural Creativity and Social I nclusion'.

As President Nishizawa has said, we at Osaka City University this year are observing the 130th year since our founding. The mayor of Osaka at the time of the opening of the university was Hajime Seki who had been a professor at Hitotsubashi University and then transferred here to become Osaka's deputy mayor. He was a researcher of social policies. At the founding of Osaka City University, he offered up the motto, "the university should grow with the city, and the city should grow with the university." In Japan there are firstrate universities that the national government has created such as Tokyo University and Kyoto University, but Osaka City University was the first in Japan that a city had established.

Consequently, as a university created by the city, it is expected to scientifically research the problems of the city and set forth new urban policies and urban science that will be offer useful guidelines to the world's cities. At present we are continuing to do research that embodies that basic direction and basic rationale of the university.

In 2006 we were designated as a Global Center of Excellence by the Ministry of Education and Science, and we are now well into our fourth year pursuing "Reinventing the City for Cultural Creativity and Social Inclusion", and intend to continue advancing our research with a total staff of about 130 which includes many younger researchers.

One of our goals in this international symposium is to discuss together with all of you some of those results. Osaka International House Foundation, which operates this hall, on many different occasions has held many symposia on various themes related to Osaka City or the major cities of Japan. They have also held on ten occasions now a symposium titled "The New Urban Generation" which was begun by the renowned cultural anthropologist Tadao Umesao, who recently passed away. I myself have been honored to coordinate three of those, but I must say Osaka International House Foundation has done outstanding work.

We have three objectives in holding this symposium. The first is to open up a new dimension in urban research. Already, as has been said, we have had neo-liberalist globalization centered around the financial economy which began in the latter half of the 1980s. This absorbed the world in a money game that stirred up competition between global cities, and in the midst of a competitive struggle for existence between winners and losers, worked to wider social and regional disparities. On the other hand, however, the world plunged into the greatest recession since 1929, which has given people an opportunity for reflection, and it seems to have begun making people recognize the need to break away from market-driven ideologies and distance themselves from globalization that is centered around finance.

In these circumstances, the global society is being pulled towards a transition away from the existing socio-economic system, and this calls for a rethinking of existing theory in the social sciences as well. In urban theory too, the ideas of global cities, creative cities, and sustainable cities which emerged at the beginning of the 21st century have become contentious issues. In the midst of the current worldwide depression, the creative city has taken center stage in urban theory in place of the global city.

Against the background of these times in which the Fordist-style city based on the manufacturing industry has declined, and in the midst of the transition to the age of a knowledge and information-based economy, the creative city has been conceptualized based on the successful examples of cities that have been revitalized through the creativity of culture, and terms like creative industries, the creative economy, and the creative class have spread to related fields, and variations on them have suddenly become popular around the world.

In particular, in America they have given impetus to competition between cities in attracting the creative class. However, a creative city does not necessarily come about just by attracting the creative class. In order for the creative industries, which are the economic engine of growth for creative cities, to develop, it is necessary to utilize the indigenous value of the city's cultural capital, and without the formation of networks and creative clusters based on the spontaneity of creators and artists, one cannot look forward to a sustainable development of the city's economy. Also, if the concerns of urban policy are directed solely towards attracting the creative class, one can expect that social frictions will increase.

The new concept of the creative city comes first of all from the experiences of the European Cultural Cities that have been promoted by the European Union. This is an experiment in which cultural creativity has proved useful in creating new industries and jobs and solving social exclusion and environmental problems, bringing about not only economic, but social and cultural revival to the city as well. Rather than socially excluding old people, the homeless, or the handicapped in the midst of living difficulties brought on by the current worldwide recession, the issue of social inclusion, conquering the disparities that thrive in the knowledge and information economy, and solving the problem of refugees created by rapid globalization, stands in the face of creative city theory. Based on our awareness of this issue, we gave this symposium the title, "Urban Regeneration through Cultural Creativity and Social Inclusion."

Our second objective is to expand our research network around the world. If we are to plan a transition of the social system in the direction of fundamentally escaping from the current worldwide recession, I believe there are four important issues. The first is a transition away from market-driven globalization centered on finance towards a harmonious globalization that encourages cultural diversity. The second is a struggle between Fordism and post-Fordist cultural production, and the development of cultural industries. At present, the creative economy is a concept that seems to hold great promise.

Third is the reenfranchisement of creative work that highlights the value of things themselves which are backed up by cultural values, and the appearance of cultural lifestyle-creating firms that transcend the false boom in consumption and create their own living culture.

Fourth is systematic design of an inclusive society in which everyone participates and each and every citizen can exercise their creativity, while scrapping the current welfare payments system for one in which a basic income is guaranteed for each person. I think these are issues that need broad consideration.

In creating a new social system beyond the great recession, for looking forward theoretically to new urban models that are appearing in this age of systemic transition, and objectively analyzing both theory and practice, as a place to bring forth a myriad of valuable experience and information, we have begun publication of the new international journal, *City, Culture and Society*. At this time, with the cooperation of the frontline researchers who have come here from around the world, together with *CCS* we would like to open up a new horizon in urban research and build a worldwide network. This is the second objective of the symposium.

Germinated at the Urban Research Plaza, and published with the collaboration of researchers around the world, *City, Culture and Society* is a academic journal that deals with central themes of leading-edge urban management and governance under the banner of cultural creativity and social inclusion. Its main goals are not only to promote groundbreaking research on cities, but also in relation to not yet experienced issues, to present a vision of a new kind of creative town building, and offer and contribute a variety of solutions to actually occurring problems that are besetting Osaka's and other cities' governments.

This afternoon's Session 2 and tomorrow morning's Session 3 have been set aside for debate and research presentations for that purpose. Also, *City, Culture and Society* will emphasize dealing with the radically developing and changing Asia-Pacific Region. Centered around the seven overseas Sub-Centers that the Urban Research Plaza has established around this region, we will sum up empirical surveys we have undertaken in collaboration with local researchers, and the results of a variety of social experiments. This is also an ambitious attempt to develop new urban theory from the Asia-Pacific Region. Tomorrow afternoon's Session 4 is set aside for networking the research activities of these overseas Sub-Centers and charting the course that lies ahead.

The third objective of this symposium, in order to continue providing a venue for the new urban research that is discussed here, is that we would like to set up a new scholarly association, the Association for Urban Creativity. On the third and last day, at the final session, Session 6, we would like to carry out intensive discussions for that purpose. These three days that I have outlined make up a long schedule, but we as the organizers hope that all of you who are gathered here today will participate with deep interest and involvement until the end.

Session 1
10:30-15:20 December 15th, 2010

Keynote Addresses

Urban Regeneration through Cultural Creativity and Social Inclusion

There has been some truth to the idea that the engines of a city's growth are flourishing economic activity and economic promotion by the city government. At the same time, a social safety net that is abundantly provided by the city government and the community has kept building cities that are livable.

Entering the 21st century, there is no prospect for further economic growth and it has become obvious that the safety net is dysfunctional. This can be most starkly seen in Osaka. In the opening session that adorns the beginning of this symposium, using Osaka, which has encountered the age of difficult urban management the fastest, as a stage, we would like to introduce a new proposal for creative city-building and urban regeneration in the cases of New York, Singapore, and Tokyo.

The creative industry, which does not necessarily demonstrate economic effects nor have a solid foundation based on regular full-time employment, appeared spontaneously in New York. In Singapore it fell outside the planning of the city government. Under the tradition of strong government leadership in city building in Singapore, it is necessary to respond flexibly to creative management or to back it up in the manner of a prompter on the stage. For that reason as well, there must be a tolerant, relaxed, and open activity space incorporated somewhere into the city, and an inclusive space has to be provided somewhere, as is shown in the case of Tokyo. Such an experiment is not impossible in Osaka, and would it not be a contribution to new urban values?

Sharon Zukin Professor, City University of New York

One of the world leaders in urban theory who always has a fresh perspective, Prof. Zukin is concerned with consumer society and consumer culture, especially shopping culture, urban change and class development among prosumers, the arts and economic development, and ethnic diversity.

Lily Kong Vice-President and Professor, National University of Singapore.

Prof. Kong has published widely on cultural policy and cultural economy, and actively contributed to policy making as well. She has focused her research on Singapore, and other East Asian cities of Hong Kong, Taipei, Shanghai and Beijing.

Takashi Machimura Professor, Hitotsubashi University

Prof. Machimura is working on formulating theories of urban social structure and change since the period of high economic growth, blending together the three perspectives of mobilization and integration, polarization and conflict, and networks and alliances.

Facilitator: **Toshio Mizuuchi** Vice-Director and Professor, Urban Research Plaza, Osaka City University

Prof. Mizuuchi has done extensive groundbreaking work emphasizing research in contemporary locally-embedded grassroots activism related to urban social problems and housing from a political- and social-geographic perspective.

Toshio Mizuuchi

Current academic position
Vice-Director, Urban Research Plaza,
Professor, Department of Geography,
Osaka City University

Academic experience
2000- Dr. Geography, Osaka City University
1984- M.Phil., Kyoto University
1980- B.A., Kyoto University

2006- Professor, Urban Research Plaza, Osaka City University
2003- Professor, Department of Geography, Osaka City University
1995-03 Associate Professor, Department of Geography, Osaka City University
1990-95 Associate Professor, Department of Geography, Toyama University
1988-90 Senior Lecturer, Department of Geography, Toyama University
1985-88 Research Associate, Department of Geography, Kyushu University

Research interests
Historical and Geographical analysis of urban development and planning, Studies of urban inadequate housing, and homeless issue in East Asian Cities, Advisory activity to urban rejuvenation projects

Major articles and papers
Current Status of Assistance Policies for the Homeless in Seoul, Hong Kong, and Taipei (editor, Osaka, Japan: Osaka City University, 2006, 81p.)

The new mode of urban renewal for the former outcaste minority people and areas in Japan, with Jeon Hong Gyu, *Cities*, 27, Supplement 1, pp.525-534, Elsevier, June 2010

1-0. Opening Remarks

We will now begin the main part of Session 1, and I would like at this time to introduce the three keynote speakers. I would like to briefly describe what it is we will be studying and what new things we would like to learn during Session 1.

This spot where Osaka International House stands is called the Uemachi Upland and it rises about 20 or 30 meters above the surrounding land. Actually, this location has the oldest urban history of anywhere in Japan. When I am teaching classes at the university I am always bringing up this Uemachi Upland. There is virtually nowhere else that has as long an urban history, and it is the oldest in Japan. Beginning probably with the Palace of Naniwa at the seventh century, then the envoys to Sui and Tang China, or the Shitennoji Temple which is the oldest Buddhist temple in Japan. There is also of course the Sumiyoshi Grand Shrine, and the Uemachi Upland stretches to its southernmost point at the tomb of the Emperor Nintoku as one of the world largest tomb. It is the core location where much of Japan's history has been created. It is a place with more than a thousand years, as much as 1500 years, of history. The city of Osaka of course grew enormously in the 16th and 17th centuries, and spread to land that was artificially created in the low marshlands to the west of the Uemachi Upland. The low-lying marshlands were developed under extremely difficult geographical conditions. However, based on its economic power and various cultural activities, the City of Osaka has really spread its shoulders, so to speak, and I feel it is a city that has really been built while overcoming geographical disadvantages.

The City of Osaka reached approximately its current boundaries in 1925. I believe that Osaka in some senses reached a kind of peak from before the war to roughly 1940, under Mayor Hajime Seki who was just mentioned by Director Sasaki. In other words, I think it is correct to think of Osaka as one of the most typical of 20th century-type cities. Currently, there is a widespread debate over what form the city of Osaka should take. The background context of this is that originally Osaka reached a peak in the 1930s. It is the city most in question when we ask what kind of city should it become in the 21st century, and how do we make a smooth transition from a 20th century-type city?

The locomotive of growth for the city has up until now been economic activity and industrial activity. While these have been supplemented by the twin axes of welfare and education, it is economic and industrial activity which have made the society the way it is, and I think this is the typical pattern of a 20th century-type city.

However, as all of you know, Osaka's economic activity is in rather dire straits. The choice of substantially changing the city in the future through economic promotion puts Osaka in a very severe situation. At the same time, with respect to welfare-related problems, as you know Osaka is confronted with the difficult phenomena of having the highest number of welfare payments, and the highest number of homeless people in Japan.

In that sense, when asked what direction we should take, we cannot expect much in the way of economic growth from now on. And, with a rather dysfunctional safety net, what kind of new form for the city are we thinking about? This is where we now, for one thing, bring up the words cultural creativity and social inclusion. It is necessary to realize that this may not necessarily generate money or create jobs, and in that case we do not have the option of pouring out money to build facilities and make economic activity flourish as we have done up till now. So, trying to think about what we should do is our current theme. It may be that just thinking about Japan or Osaka by itself may not bring forth any good ideas. At any rate, once it comes to a question of money, Japanese have a habit of not being able to go beyond that, but in the sense of a transition in our thinking and imagination, from these three people might we not learn something about new ways of building the city?

First, we will have Sharon Zukin, then Lily Kong, and after that Takashi Machimura. The extremely interesting points which they will introduce to us will be unique ways of building the city, proposals for devising means towards that, and things they are doing now. To put it simply, Professor Zukin will talk about New York, and it may be part of today's presentation, but the New York City government does not simply say, "Do this," or "Do that." People who have various kinds of know-how, people with various talents, come together and build a so-called 'creative district.' If one wonders what will happen to it, it may change into something quite different. But, seen as a whole, it creates an atmosphere where people with a range of ideas come together and discuss things. That is one kind of status for the city, it raises the city's standing, and it lends a certain attractiveness to the city. She will describe such a case in New York. By the way, In the Professor Zukin's title, the word "found" is written in brackets. It is important that it is in brackets, and she will explain activities characterized by things being secretly "found."

Our second keynote speaker is Professor Lily Kong. Because her subject is Singapore, in some sense it is a lifestyle that somewhat resembles Japan, somewhat resembles Osaka. What that resemblance is, is 'planning.' Managing the city according to planning, this has ostensibly been done in Japan as well. Is it possible to create a new creative economy in Singapore that was not necessarily intended by the economic plannings, or was not even considered in the economic plannings? I suspect this way of thinking is very close to the themes of Osaka City. A creative economy that puts out ideas a bit different from whatever the city government is trying to create, and does not conform to its plans, is something very insecure and it may be frail, but might not dealing with it, on the contrary, lead to a kind of energizing and renewal of the city? I wonder if she will not be making such a proposal.

Then, finally, we have Professor Machimura from Tokyo. In his summary, he uses the extremely interesting term, to me at least, of 'slowness' and introduces this concept. In the feverish running around of Japanese society, opening things up, moving slowly and transparently, and slowing down the pace a little of thinking, accepting everything, and running about. What kind of a city would result from being based on this kind of 'slowness' I wonder? How this concept can be adapted to Osaka is, I believe, another important issue for urban management in the future.

The introductions have been a bit long, but for all of you who have come here from Osaka, from the Keihanshin Region, or from here and there, I hope we can share together a new alternative to what Japanese up until now have thought of as urban development or urban management.

Sharon Zukin

Current academic position
Professor of Sociology, Brooklyn College and Graduate Center, City University of New York

Academic experience
1986- Professor, Ph.D. Program in Sociology, City University of New York Graduate School
1985- Professor, Department of Sociology, Brooklyn College
1979-84 Associate Professor, Department of Sociology, Brooklyn College
1973-78 Assistant Professor, Department of Sociology, Brooklyn College
1972-73 Lecturer, Department of Sociology, Columbia University

Research interests
Cities, Culture, Economy

Recent articles and papers
Naked City: The Death and Life of Authentic Urban Places (New York: Oxford University Press, 2010)
"Changing Landscapes of Power: Opulence and the Crisis of Authenticity," *International Journal of Urban and Regional Research* 33, 2 (June 2009): 543-53
"Consuming Authenticity: From Outposts of Difference to Means of Exclusion," *Cultural Studies* 22, 5 (September 2008): 724-48
Point of Purchase: How Shopping Changed American Culture (New York and London: Routledge, 2004)

1-1. Public Art: Tracing the Life Cycle of New York's Creative Districts

Summary

In contrast to other cities of the world, New York's creative districts do not reflect explicit governmental strategies either to aid artists or to encourage cultural production. To some extent they do respond to macroeconomic conditions and policies, but more important, they are "naturally occurring" creative districts that respond to the ebb and flow of private capital investment in manufacturing and real estate. What appears to be a spontaneous or even an anarchic process, however, reveals repeated regularities: an absence of capital investment and state intervention, a groundswell of innovative art and positive attention by the media, and a commercial mobilization of deviant aesthetic tastes. These conditions have shaped the successive development of New York's creative districts from Greenwich Village, in Lower Manhattan, in the late 1800s to SoHo (in the 1970s), the East Village (1980s), Williamsburg (1990s), and Bushwick today.

The path from derelict or undervalued district with working class, and often "ethnic" residents, features low-rent industrial spaces, gritty streets, and an intangible "character" that artists integrate into their own aesthetic practices. Along the way, however, cultural producers change this local character by establishing new retail businesses (cafés, restaurants, stores) that cater to their aesthetic practices and the social networks that develop around them. The result, as shown by the successive migrations from SoHo to Bushwick, is to signal that each area is "ripe" for investment. Promoted by the media and unprotected by public policies, New York's creative districts set a well-known pattern of gentrification which, paradoxically, makes it difficult to sustain the area's creativity.

The presentation concludes with a consideration of the ambiguous benefits of indirect though official "regularization" of New York's creative districts by the Loft Laws of 1982 and 2010.

Good morning. I am honored to be invited to speak this morning by the Urban Research Plaza of Osaka City University. I thank Professor Masayuki Sasaki for organizing this event to bring us together, and I congratulate him and wish him good luck in his multidimensional efforts to establish a network of research on creativity, culture, and cities, and also to establish a journal that will make an important contribution to this discussion. I am glad that the program says I have a fresh voice in this field of study because I will bring a somewhat critical approach based on the experience of New York City. In a way, New York represents a prototype free-market experiment in creating cultural districts and encouraging with very little financial support the efforts of creative artists. Together with my research assistant Laura Braslow, who is here at the conference with me, I took a camera to walk around my neighborhood, Greenwich Village, a historic creative district in Manhattan. Laura took a camera to walk around her neighborhood, Bushwick, a new creative district in Brooklyn, and we will use these images of public art that we found, as Professor Toshio Mizuuchi says, we found on the streets of our two neighborhoods to make a contrast between the birth and death of creative districts in New York City. So I will present the social, economic, and cultural conditions that shape the lifecycle of creative districts in New York City. These conditions are not like the conditions in Osaka today, but perhaps they may be similar to conditions in the future.

Two sides of cultural policy

The conference theme makes us aware that there are two sides of cultural policy. On the one hand there is the good side of cultural policy as the best aspirations of humanity. Cultural policy can confirm human rights, particularly the rights of every individual to develop his or her creative potential and the right of every creator to criticize this society, to criticize the state, to criticize other human beings and to criticize other creators. Another part of the aspirations of cultural policy is to establish social equality by acknowledging, by recognizing that every social group has the right to develop its own culture. And third, of course, is the policy of social inclusion as Professor Mizuuchi described it, to try and compensate for the financial and social inequalities of different groups by permitting them, by encouraging them, by giving them the tools to express themselves in cultural ways. But there is another side of cultural policy, where cultural policy has become in the past 20 years another sort of industrial policy. Number one, cultural policy has become a means of stimulating post-industrial growth when factory production has moved to low wage countries and the cities that grew in the 19th and 20th centuries on the basis of factory work now have to develop new kinds of economic activities and new means of employment. Cultural policy is also a tool, perhaps not so much in New York City, but it is a tool to develop intellectual property in the form of software, films, design and brands of consumer products that then become monopolies for the companies that are located in different countries of the world. Cultural policy is also a tool to establish the status of individual cities, whether they aim to be global cities or they aim to be larger, more important cities. And finally, cultural policy is a tool to build art museums, art galleries and performance spaces for the consumption of local elites who are highly educated, who are affluent and who are cosmopolitan in their cultural tastes.

How to make a cultural space?

In cities though, we face a spatial problem: "How do we make a cultural space?" We may have a cultural policy but how do we make a cultural space? Number one, cultural policy is supposed to make a new kind of industrial district where artists and other kinds of creative people produce new culture. Second, a space must be created socially. In English we might call this a "social scene" for cultural producers to speak, to meet, to exchange ideas and even to enjoy themselves in the nighttime which then will lead to further creative innovation. But the social scene of creative producers often becomes a cultural scene for consumers who go to the bars, the cafes, the galleries, the lofts to see new fashions; new fashion in clothing, new fashion in speaking, new fashion in presenting the identities for cultural consumers. However, from an economic point of view, the land that is necessary to create new scenes is a commodity and in cities like New York, London and Hong Kong, cultural policy conflicts with the policy of producing new land for new urban construction. So on the one hand we have cultural producers who try to claim land of low economic value for their creative uses. On the other hand, we have property developers who claim the same land for their redevelopment and new construction. In New York then, we do not have the state giving land or giving buildings or subsidizing space for artists.

"Naturally occurring creative districts"

When we have creative districts emerging such as Greenwich Village in the distant past, Soho in the recent past, and Williamsburg and Bushwick in the past few years, these creative districts develop spontaneously, and we call these "naturally occurring creative districts." Of course, nothing is natural in cities, everything is socially and economically created but in contrast to the deliberate efforts of government policy, we call these creative districts "natural occurrences." And the first factor in their birth, is the supply of unused or relatively unused low-rent industrial space. This low-rent industrial space has been made possible by the decline of competitive manufacturing in older cities. Factor number two is demand, this is a very traditional economic relationship between supply and demand, but often the demand comes before the supply is ready. The demand for creative districts comes on the part of a larger group of professionals, artists, and also business services that hire graphic artists, software producers, video makers and idea creators, the so-called creative class. This is not the complete creative class that Richard Florida writes about because he includes bankers and accountants and other sorts of financial professionals in his definition, but I am speaking mainly of people who create and buy creative products. But the 2nd factor in demand is something that is not so widely known in Asian cities, and that is individual choice, individual mobility where young people when they graduate from art school or graduate from university, separate from their family and parents and they look to rent their own apartments. They often choose an area to live in the city on the basis of price because they are just starting their careers, they cannot afford to pay high rents. But another reason for their choice of neighborhoods to live in is lifestyle choices. They look for neighborhoods that are edgy, cool, hip, that look a certain way, that present visible signs of cultural difference from mainstream culture. And these are the factors that create a naturally occurring creative district.

Definition of "creative district"

So what do we mean by a creative district? We mean both a production and a consumption space. Primarily a creative district must be where artists both live and work. Richard Lloyd, an American sociologist, uses the phrase "Neobohemia" a new bohemia, to describe these kinds of production and consumption spaces. But we emphasize that these spaces also develop a reputation, because of their aesthetic characteristics, because of the way they look, because of the consumption opportunities that they offer to have a different sort of lifestyle. What we mean by production space is typically the studio where an artist works. The streets of the creative district where these artists work are often gritty as we say in English, they are dirty, they are shabby, they look abandoned. But behind these doors you will find artists' studios and these are the true spaces of cultural production, at least in New York. But they are also spaces of new kinds of consumption. This is an old factory building in Brooklyn which during the 1990s became a space where artists held parties and created new unions, new combinations between internet technology, electronics and using the body as a source of performance art. That building has since been torn down and rebuilt as new condominium apartments. But that kind of space is then advertised on the basis of the artist's reputation. So we have words unlike anything that was known before: chic, well-educated, avant-garde, diversity, cutting-edge, trendy, city life and traditional life, distinction, and people even make references to bring a new creative district like Williamsburg in the early 2000s together with Soho and Tribeca, which developed as artists' districts, again naturally, in the 1970s. And the meat-packing district in Manhattan which became a more expensive and trendy restaurant area in the early 2000s.

Life cycle of a creative district

But you can see that all these aesthetic factors lead to the promotion of stores and the profits of property developers. So the lifecycle of a creative district begins when artists move into a space, because of work the artists see, and they meet each other. They begin to form an artists' community by cooperating to establish events and spaces like cooperative art galleries. And the artists become entrepreneurs in a business sense. They become social entrepreneurs because they establish a community where none existed before, and they also become cultural entrepreneurs by developing a very new, visible style of life. This attracts journalists who must write about new things everyday and so the journalists create a buzz, a noise about the new districts and their art galleries and cafes and restaurants and this leads property developers to invest capital in the area, which then leads to higher rents, which then displaces the artists who must go to another area of the city and begin again to shape a creative district.

Production of urban space

So that like other urban spaces, creative districts are shaped by capital, by the state that may take action or not take action at all, but whether the state takes action or does not take action, usually that helps the property developers. The third factor is media images and the fourth factor is consumer taste on the part of consumers who are attracted to the archetypal spaces that are created by artists. In New York the archetypal consumption space created by artists in the 1970s was lofts for loft-living and there is a little bit of a parallel with artists who restore machiya in Japanese cities. So that in Soho in 1971 we saw artists moving in, taking factory spaces and also restaurants like this Latino restaurant where factory workers ate, and developing their own restaurants, their own art galleries and their own studios in this neighborhood. This eventually developed forty years later into luxury retail stores where art galleries once stood. The machiya looks different of course and they are much smaller but you can see the restoration, the polishing, the grown sophistication of these spaces to become a lifestyle model of their own. And this is an example of how the economic value of these buildings, these spaces changes. Here is a very normal, formerly low rent factory space in Williamsburg in Brooklyn which by this time is on sale for US$ 5,000,000. That is very expensive, even in New York or in Tokyo. And this is obviously a value, an economic value which reflects something more than factory use. This is the advertisement for this building and I have highlighted the important words: creative, unique, savvy (meaning knowledgeable and sophisticated), developer, loft, a keyword, live-work spaces, artist studios, office or commercial space. We see here the process of revalorization of an old factory space in new aesthetic terms. And so inside the old factory space looks quite elegant, modern, sophisticated, polished and it appeals to people with creative and cosmopolitan tastes. But not necessarily to artists who do not have the money to rent this space.

A New York City geography lesson: Migration of Creative Districts

This causes the migration of creative districts from one area of New York City to another following the rents. And the migration begins with perhaps the first creative district in New York City, Greenwich Village in lower Manhattan, in an earlier time period, the late 19th, early 20th century and then after WWII. By the 1950s and early 1960s, when the urbanist Jane Jacobs lived in the west part of Greenwich Village, the rents were already much higher than in the rest of Manhattan. And so in the 1960s and 1970s, young artists migrated to other areas of lower Manhattan. The artist Yoko Ono came from Japan and moved to a loft in this area of Manhattan during the 1960s. Of course, after she married John Lennon, she moved uptown. The next neighborhood that developed when Soho became very expensive was the East Village in the 1980s by a group called the "East Village Artists", who became very well-known in the media. But a result of their prominence is that the East Village became very expensive and artists could no longer afford to live there. So the next district that became popular among the graduates of art schools and universities was Williamsburg in Brooklyn, which was another manufacturing district. The population of residents was African-American and Latino. Many of them were immigrants, also Polish I should say. Many of them were immigrants and it was a low-rent industrial and working class neighborhood. When Williamsburg became expensive in the early 2000s, artists began to concentrate in Bushwick and East Williamsburg (Figure 1).

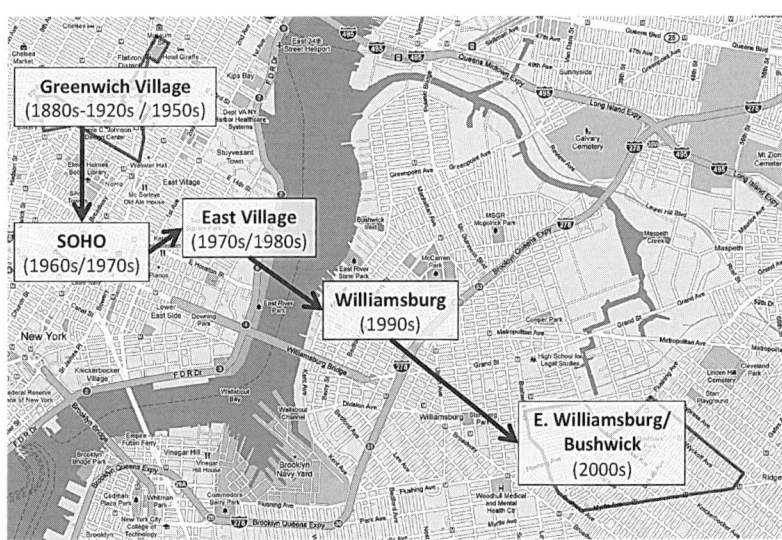

Figure 1: Migration of Selected "Centers of Artistic Production"

So Laura, my research assistant, and I, thought it would be interesting to make a comparison of my neighborhood where I live and her neighborhood where she lives, to show the death and birth of a creative district in New York. There is a cartoon that was published as early as 1978 in a magazine in New York which shows the process of migration of artists from district to district. The wife of the artist says to the artist, the artist happens to be the man of this couple, often both the man and the woman are artists, but in this case the woman is leaving the man and she says: "I've had enough! I have migrated with you from Greenwich Village to the East Village, to Soho, to another village North of Soho, to Belowho", which is a made up name, "to Hoboken," which is in New Jersey, "but I'm not going to move to New Jersey now, I've migrated enough from place to place because you as an artist cannot pay high rent and I'm finished, I've had it with you" and I guess she is going to get a divorce. But this is a funny way of looking at the migration of creative districts from place to place because of the rents.

Found Public Art: Aesthetics of the Street

So again, Laura and I took a camera and we went into the streets to see what we thought would be public art or the visible aesthetics of creative districts at two periods in the lifecycle. Greenwich Village is my neighborhood and I walked around here in one 24-hr. period and Bushwick is her neighborhood and she walked there in another 24-hr. period. We did not consult with each other in advance to define public art. That would be the subject of another discussion but we took pictures of more or less the same types of art work. And we found together three types of public art: monuments built by the state, expressions of individuals' feelings, and commercial displays to persuade people to buy products.

Monumental Art

Let us take a quick look at the monuments that we found to show the difference between the beginning of a creative district and the end of a creative district. This is my neighborhood Greenwich Village and we see the true monuments of the state. This is a statue of George Washington, the first president of the United States, the leader of the army of the colonists against Britain in the 18th Century and in the American Revolutionary War. And you can see in this picture here he is quite a military leader. He is riding his horse and he points his finger, very much a decisive leader of the state (Figure 2). This is a statue of the man who was Secretary of State when Abraham Lincoln was the president and he was the person responsible for the United States buying Alaska from Russia in the 1860s. And this is another example of monumental public art, this is my neighborhood post office. Usually we do not think when we walk in and out of the door to look up but because I had a camera in my hand I looked up and I found this official symbol of the United States, the eagle spreading its wings, but all these three are very official, large monuments. In Laura's neighborhood Bushwick, the public monuments are much smaller, more modest. This is her neighborhood's post office. We can see it is very modest compared to the architecture of my post office. Here we see a mosaic seal set into the ground of a public park in contrast to the statues of leaders of the American State that I showed you. And here is a much more modest statue underneath the elevated subway tracks in Bushwick. Again, showing that in the beginning a creative district is poor. It is

Figure 2: Park in Greenwich Village

not well financed, even in terms of the state-financed art that you would find in the district. This is another kind of monumental art that we find, this so-called "Astro-cube," which is deliberately balanced like this. You can interpret it in many ways. One way to interpret this monumental piece of art is that it was sponsored by a non-governmental organization, a sort of non-profit cultural organization. One way to interpret it is to show that this tilt symbolizes the history of the creative district. I prefer to think of the monument as showing the neighborhood balanced between a real creative district and an upscale expensive creative district that is sort of teetering on the edge here and might fall one way or the other. This is another kind of monumental public art in my neighborhood. These are mosaic pieces that were made as decorations by a former soldier in the US Army who became homeless and was living in the streets of the East Village with his dog for about twenty years and he took it upon himself as his mission to decorate these public spaces and to make a set of mosaics to commemorate, in this case, the fire department of New York and whatever he wanted to make as monuments as an individual. In Laura's neighborhood though, the individual public art is not sponsored by big cultural organizations. It is much more modest. Like the monumental public art, it refers to the images of the factories of the neighborhood and in this case a local artist was commissioned to design a protection for a tree. But the tree is quite small and the tree guard is quite small also, again demonstrating that at the beginning a creative district is small, modest and does not have much money. By the same token these are expressions of creativity and the financing does support the work of cultural producers.

Expressive Art

Let us move to the second type of public art, the expression of individual feelings. In my neighborhood we have graffiti, painted on the wall of apartment houses and on the construction wall around the wall of a site of a future hotel. In Laura's neighborhood the graffiti is painted on the sides of factory buildings and this is definitely not the site of a future hotel. We do not know exactly what it is for the moment. It is an unused demolished site that was a factory. In my neighborhood we have the individual paintings made by schoolchildren after 9/11, the attack on the World Trade Center, and these little pictures have remained in place for almost 10 years. In Laura's neighborhood we have a different sort of memorial. This is a mural painted in sympathy with the victims and the families of attacks by street gangs. In my neighborhood we have the well-financed installation of sculpture designed by a well-known British artist, Antony Gormley. And in fact the group that financed the installation of his sculpture, this is one of the group of sculptures that he was commissioned to build for this neighborhood in New York. That was all financed by a Business Improvement District which manages a public park in this area. But in Laura's neighborhood, the public art is not commissioned, it is put up on the wall by a kind of guerilla artist who criticizes the free market system with his ironic slogans: "No demand, all supply, all demand, no supply."

Commercial Art

The third type of public art, commercial art, is imported into all urban neighborhoods because all cities thrive on local shopping streets. But in my neighborhood we see the aesthetic design of wine bottles in a local restaurant window. In Laura's neighborhood we see the same sort of aesthetic design made up by bottles of laundry detergent and household cleaning supplies. In my neighborhood we see this sort of cute image that advertises a café selling a mocha coffee, a special coffee. But in Laura's neighborhood we see the promotion of a café that looks like graffiti and it looks much rougher, much less cute. We can call this kawaii and the other anti-kawaii. In my neighborhood we see a very sophisticated representation of an audio equipment store. In Laura's neighborhood we see a very different sort of window display for a food store.

Industry and Ethnicity in street aesthetics

So you see by looking at the public art that in an old creative district there is no reference to the industrial, the ethnic or the working class history. But in a new creative district, at least in New York City, industry and ethnicity shape the look of a space. These aesthetics even shape the artwork of new cultural producers who live in the neighborhood. Their murals, their graffiti, their designs. The Latino immigrant residents of Bushwick are well aware of what might happen to their neighborhood, and they have painted this mural referring to people who have come from Latin America in the past 20 years, reading a newspaper which dramatizes the gentrification of their neighborhood with higher rents and the development of new condo's, new condominium apartments that are offered for sale, not for rent and the prices are generally much higher than what the immigrants can afford to pay. We also see a mural painted not by immigrants but by artists, but the mural refers to, I guess all of these murals refer to, this kind of art done by the other residents, the earlier residents. We also see a commercial display for Latino owned stores that is quite artistic. And we see the façade of a new, probably upscale store that uses the design aesthetics of industries, in this case rusty steel, to refer to the factories of the area. So there is, what we want to say is that in looking at public art in the new creative district, we see a fusion and an exchange between the immigrant residents, the industry, and the new cultural producers who live and work in that space. What happens again in a creative district in New York, and I believe also in London and Hong Kong, is that the representation of industry, of immigration, of ethnicity, and of criticism, the representation then gains a reputation for avant-garde, creative, hip, cool culture.

Public Art is a Visible Sign of Capital Investment

And the public art that initially looks so critical becomes a visible sign of capital investment. What looks like the product of a guerilla artist, looks to the developer's eye as a sign of aesthetic interest which will bring a higher social class to live in this area. And indeed in my neighborhood, we do move from one kind of public art to another kind of public art, where an artist becomes a street vendor selling his paintings on the street. In Bushwick we see developers renovating old buildings, turning them into new apartments and then advertising retooled condominiums. This advertising indicates a completely new use of an old building that no longer has a productive use (Figure 3). And we see that the advertising very cleverly appeals to young people who look different. These do not look like salary men and salary women. These look like people who consider themselves the rebellious. The man wears an earring. He has a little beard. People have different visible ethnicities, so that there is a suggestion that Bushwick should be a multi-cultural young place for people who want to shape their own creative identities around the identity of a district as a sort of creative lifestyle. And the slogan indeed speaks to individual production of identity: "Are you Bushwick"? The identification is made by the person and the space, but the advertisement makes this very explicit again in words. The advertisement pretends to be a dictionary definition of the name Bushwick, a vibrant neighborhood. It is cultural, it is nightlife, meaning it is bars and restaurants, and an artful scene referring to the kind of social and cultural scene of artists and artful consumers. A place for people with a soulful character, again people who think about the higher purpose of life, not money. And yet, it is all about money because the property developers are trying to sell the land and the buildings and sell the apartments to people who are attracted by this kind of image of themselves. In my neighborhood though, by the end of the process, artists have painted a mural to say when the promotion of that kind of lifestyle succeeds, the cultural district dies. And this is actually not a permanent mural. It was a mural for a few weeks on a bar but it certainly expresses the point that our presentation tries to make. The end of the lifecycle of a creative district is reached when the district becomes popular among consumers. And that is the lesson that I bring from New York. It is not a lesson that Osaka will take at this moment, but it should serve as a warning to other cities when they begin to walk down the road of cultural policy. So, thank you.

Figure 3: Shops in Bushwick

Toshio Mizuuchi: Thank you very much, Professor Zukin. In the talk we just heard about New York, I think she talked about how do you all observe the various movements in the city from the surroundings in which you live, and how do you attach a broader meaning to them? Well, I suppose Osaka and New York may be different, but what we need to learn now are, I think, the words 'art' and 'city building.' As for art, it will best be covered in tomorrow's session by our own Professor Shin Nakagawa, it is said to be the energy for living. It expresses how one is to go on living. Another way of saying it is, I think, how should a community be built? In this case study from New York, I think that there may also be bound up in it in the form of some kind of artist, but that is really included, and the district becomes creative, and money is invested. However, in a cyclically changing form, the arts clearly draw people to the neighborhood and draw in money in a construct that I think has occurred particularly in the cities of Europe and North America. I think that Professor Zukin and her colleagues in particular have talked about this using the English word 'gentrification.' But the meaning that the word 'gentrification' has now can be a matter of life or death, so 'gentrification' does not necessarily hold the key to success in renewing the city.

Thinking about the case of Osaka, there is the direction towards an ordinary city, and the direction towards a diversified city. Osaka is not particularly waving flags saying "I'm from Amerika-mura" or "Senba" or "Minami-Senba," but wouldn't it lead to a kind of upgrading in the status of the city if there were some kind of appeal, whether using words in English or Japanese, from Osaka saying, "…many different people gather here, and the town is built, it's that kind of town building." But, even saying that, I think we know, we have to know, that such a city has rises and falls.

Last year a big event was held in Osaka called "Water City 2009" and that was the first time artists emerged in relation to building the city. The mayor also participated, but what he said there was after all that artists are poor. Because they are poor, they go to live in poor districts. When they pursue their expression there, next money gets spent, and the value of the neighborhood increases. Then, the artists become poor again, and move to another place. These are tough circumstances, but that kind of town building, if we think about Japan somewhere in there, maybe one of the things we learned is that it is all right to deal with it diversely and autonomously.

Lily Kong

Current academic position
Vice-President(University and Global Relations)
Professor, Department of Geography,
National University of Singapore

Academic experience
Ph.D., University College, London.
M.A., National University of Singapore
B.A. (First Class, Direct Honours), National University of Singapore

Research interests
Geographies of religion
Cultural economy and cultural policy
Constructions of 'nation' and national identity
Constructions of 'nature' and environment

Major articles and papers
Kong, L. and O'Connor (2010) (eds) *Creative Economies, Creative Cities: Asian-European Perspectives*, Dordrecht: Springer.

Kong, L. (2009) Making sustainable creative/cultural space in Shanghai and Singapore, *Geographical Review*,Vol. 91, No. 1, pp 1-22.

Kong, L. (2007) "Cultural icons and urban development in Asia: economic imperative, national identity and global city status", *Political Geography*, 26, 383-404.

Gibson, C. and Kong, L. (2005) "Cultural economies: a critical review", *Progress in Human Geography*, 29, 5, 541-61.

Kong, L. (2000) "Cultural policy in Singapore: negotiating economic and socio-cultural agendas", *Geoforum*, 31, 409-24.

1-2. "Precariousness" in the Creative Economy: Implications for Economic Planning in Singapore

Summary

The growth of the creative economy in developed economies has seen an acknowledgement of the important place of the oftentimes "hidden" independent worker, or freelancer. These creative workers do not belong to the traditional employment set-up organized around firms, but instead, move from portfolio to portfolio, assignment to assignment, interspersing jobs with corporations with periods of self employment. Their work offers freedom, independence and creative space, but has also been characterized as precarious, because the securities of old working patterns no longer hold. While governments in many countries and cities have become attracted to the potential of the creative economy, those that have a strong tradition of economic planning, such as Singapore, will also have to come to grips with a new creative economy in which there exists a great deal more amorphousness and a hidden ecology. This paper will examine how the growth of "precarious labor" entails three shifts that the Singapore government is attempting to make in the face of a more "precarious economy": new methods in mapping and measurement, new directions in education and training; and new experiments in social and economic organization.

Introduction and aims

Good afternoon everyone. I would like to begin by thanking Professor Sasaki for inviting me. It is a real honor and privilege to be here and I look forward to learning from everyone. I apologize that I just recovered from a cough so my voice is going to come and go, so I probably sound better than I usually do but my apologies if my voice fades away a little bit.

So I realize that in the program my title is a little bit different than what you see here but essentially speaks to the same thing which is about a very different situation from that described by Sharon Zukin this morning, where in New York a great deal happens spontaneously, organically, naturally, whereas in Singapore, the situation is very different.

There is a great deal of planning that usually takes place, and what I would like to speak about this afternoon, with the task of keeping you awake after lunch, is to talk about how, in a society and economy for which there is a great deal of planning, does a very different kind of economy which does not necessarily lend itself entirely to planning, how do those two situations work together? So will I begin with a short introduction about the growth of the creative economy or certainly the creative economy discourse, and I would to share a little bit about the aims of what I am trying to do in this paper. I will then move on to talk about precarity in the creative economy and what it has generally meant in conventional wisdom. I move on then to talk about Singapore and to paint in the background, the backdrop of Singapore as a hyper-planned economy in some ways, and then I move on to talk about three dimensions of how the Singapore government attempts to introduce a method, an approach to management and governance of what I might call a precarious economy.

The three ways are as follows: first, an attempt to understand what the creative worker is and who the creative worker is, and to identify exactly who these protagonists are in such an economy. And the effort of finding new methods and measurements of who these people are. Second, an attempt to try to develop a new workforce, a creative workforce that speaks to the needs of the new economy and in this, the efforts at rethinking education and training, would be where a lot of the efforts from the Singapore government have been directed in recent years. And third, assuming that we have a workforce that is prepared for such an economy, assuming we can identify who they are, how then do we help to make the work of this group of people doable? How is the precarity of this particular group of creative workers to be managed and to be improved through the introduction and the invention of new mediating institutions?

And then I draw some conclusions about whether or not it is in fact a new creative economy that is precarious in some ways and how does a government well-known for its efforts of planning and management, how does such a government try to introduce new forms of management and governance?

Precarity in the Creative Economy

So let me begin by saying that the growth of the creative economy is something that has been heralded to a very large extent in many cities, and some in my earlier work, I tried to trace the spread of the creative economy discourse to our part of the world here, particularly form the UK and the US. With this growth in the creative economy discourse and policy and direction, I also recognized that there has been a tremendous growth in creative economy literature.

And my interests here are in one particular dimension of that creative economy literature, focused on the creative workers themselves, and the kind of portfolio careers that they hold when many of them perform different work roles simultaneously, often for different clients at the same time. Because they are so fluid, because they move from portfolio to portfolio, assignment to assignment, what happens is that they replace of a job for life with one particular cooperation with frequent changes of employment over periods of self-employment. So working lives for this particular group are organized very much around projects, rather than careers and firms, which have up till now represented the core bodies of industrial civilization. So many independents work on assignments from project to project, but they also work formally in other sectors of the economy, and they could also be unemployed at various points in time. So what happens is that during the conduct of formal employment surveys, very often they can escape tracking, and it is very difficult to identify who they are, where they are, how many of them there are, and what are the conditions under which they work. So this group in effect represents a hidden and an amorphous ecology. Hidden because they often escape conventional statistics on employment and on investment, and amorphous because they join projects, leave them, join with another group of some assignment, and then they regroup again with others for yet other assignments. So this particular group of creative workers have portfolio careers and hidden ecologies and are difficult to track and monitor and manage and govern in a sense.

While this literature is well-established and there is a great deal that has been done to study their conditions and their contributions, what I would like to do in this paper is to turn from analyzing precarious labor as such to understanding how that precarity is translated into the economy itself for the particular city-state of Singapore, and how the notion of a precarious economy is one that encourages its government to seek ways of management and governance. And it is these ways of governance and management that I try to research and understand in this particular paper.

So precarity in the creative economy first really is about precarious labor rather than the precarious economy in the first instance. And these creative workers are wellknown for particular characteristics. Andy Pratt, who is here with us, describes their careers as bulimic careers because sometimes they have very many projects and other times they have no projects at all. And they have unstable incomes, there is uncertainty over where the next project is going to come from, and that is probably why people take on multiple projects at any point of time, in case the next project doesn't come along. There is stolen intellectual property in the sense that sometimes these creative workers will come up with ideas, present them to a potential client, find that they are not hired, but their idea may be taken or adapted and their contributions are not recognized as such. Very often they are not paid on time and they do not have the regular benefits of regular workers in a firm economy. So, for example, there are no medical or health benefits for them. There is a lack of mediating institutions and by that I am referring, for example, to the lack of a union that is there to speak up for the rights of the creative worker, for example, because they don't belong to any particular firm. And the combined effect of all that is very often a certain lack of clarity about where the career development path leads. While these are kinds of well-studied characteristics of precarious labor, one consequence of this is the study of the ways in which these sorts of risks might be managed, might be mitigated.

And here there are at least three ways that are well acknowledged in the literature. First of all, the fact that the next job for the creative worker, the freelancer in particular, generally doesn't come from a formal human resource channel. You don't go for a job interview and get a job for example, but your work comes through networking to the extent therefore that social relationships become a form a social capital. You are able to find your next job because a friend has made an introduction, or somebody you formerly worked with is making an introduction for you. In order to also mitigate some of the risks of this form of work, it also means that very often the creative worker who is an independent or freelancer tries to assure that he or she is on top of new skills, new technology, new methods of doing things, so that continuous upgrading, continuous up-skilling is necessary. But as I will talk about later, this often poses a challenge. And third, as I have mentioned already, the risks can be mitigated if there is a system of bargaining and representation system to support the freelancers so that if they do not get paid on time, if there is a mediating institution to help give such workers recourse to resolution. So with that sort of background of the rise of the creative economy, the fact is that this creative economy is very often sustained through the work of individuals in the freelancing context.

Singapore: a hyperplanned economy?

Let me now turn to talk a little bit about the Singapore background. And here I am going to spend a little bit less time to talk about the creative industry strategies as I am going to talk about the Singapore economy and the approach to the Singapore economy in general. And here there is a question about whether the Singapore economy is a laissez-faire one or whether it is a highly regulated state one.

The fact that Singapore, except for one first development plan in the 1960s, has had no development planned, unlike many other developing countries, has meant that some scholars have argued that Singapore's economy is a very open laissez-faire sort of economy. On the other hand, the lack of development plans does not necessarily mean that there is no state intervention and regulation. And I would suggest that there is in fact a relatively high degree of state involvement in regulating and intervening in the economy. And I say this because I point to various evidence of such government planning and intervention.

First, through government agencies that are very much involved in stimulating the economy, developing the economy in different ways. EDB is the Economic Development Board, which plays a very large role in developing different sectors of the economy, and in the last several years for example, it has been very involved in trying to stimulate and develop a biomedical science industry. IE is the International Enterprise, which tries to develop trade. Its former nomenclature was the Trade Development Board and PSB, which is the Productivity and Standards Board, GLC would be the Government Linked Companies, and in fact a lot of locally owned companies somewhat linked back to 3 major holding companies that our government owned. But it is not just through agencies, it is also through incentives that are used by government, whether it is in the form of, for example tax breaks, or more recently during the financial crisis, the government introduced what was known as the jobs credit schemes and it really intervened very directly by offering direct subsidies to companies that chose to keep their workers rather than to retrench them. So it was a form of subsidy to try and keep people employed as such. Incentives, and infrastructure… as far as business and industrial infrastructures are concerned, the government is pretty much the sole supplier.

In regulating industrial relations, the government has a very big role and this is made possible by legislation such as the Employment Act, the Industrial Relations Act, the Trade Union Act, and so forth. And also by not so much managing the demand but the supply of the labor market through close monitoring through a council for professional and technical education, CPTE for short. And what happens here is that this council looks at the demand for different kinds of professions and workers in the economy. How many accountants do you need, how many engineers do you need, how many lawyers do you need, how many doctors and nurses do you need? It then fits together with universities and polytechnics to try and shape the intake into the universities and polytechnics so that the right numbers of supply into the labor market can be managed to match the demand.

However, it doesn't work quite so neatly. But what I intent to show here is that, whether it is through agencies and centers and infrastructure, industrial relations or labor markets, really there is a great deal of government planning and intervention and regulation of the economy, and to that extent I would suggest that it is a very highly planned economy. So the question that I am most interested in this paper is this: When you have an economy that is planned to such a large extent in so many different ways, through so many different instruments, when you are faced with a new economy, in which it is difficult to track who the workers are, and what their needs are, what kinds of education and training might be needed, and what kinds of support can be lent to this group of new creative industries' creative economy workers? How much does the government try to insert itself, and how does the government try to intervene in terms of introducing ways of management and governance in this new arena?

Developing the precarious economy

Developing the precarious economy is what I would like to turn to now. And here I would say that there are three ways, three measures which the government has attempted, or three large baskets of approaches as such.

The first is really about methodologies and measurements in trying to identify who the creative workers are and particularly the freelance workers, who from many reports from different parts of the world, it would seem are a very big part of the creative economy. How does the state in Singapore try to go about understanding who they are, and identifying who they are, and measuring the size of this group and what they do? Who constitutes creative workers and how are they to be identified? The second area, and by far the most major of effort on the part of the government would be to try and rethink education and training in order to nurture creative workers. And that is something that I will spend a little time talking about. The third is in an attempt to try and introduce new mediating institutions to cater to the needs of the freelance creative workers.

So for example in a country where the tripartite relationship between government, employer and employee is actually very tightly arranged, how does this work when you have a new freelance population? What are the mediating platforms? And what are the mediating platforms between employer and employees and members of the creative class, the creative workers? How do they organize themselves, and what are the mediating institutions there?

Identifying the protagonists of the creative economy: new methodologies and measurements

Let me take each one of these in turn, and first of all is new methodology and measurement. As I said before this is a hidden and amorphous ecology. It is hidden because very often this group escapes conventional statistics on employment. It is difficult through the formal means of data collection to identify who they are and where they are. At the same time, they are amorphous because they are constantly changing jobs and portfolios and projects and it is very difficult to track them. So the reality of it, not just in Singapore but in many places, is that when there are existing reports on the creative workers of the freelance complexion, the reports very often lack details, quantitative details about how large this group is, and if there are efforts to share the measurement, there is a lack of detail about methods.

I would also say that there is very often a great deal of contradiction in the data available, even for the same place, because of different methodologies and the difficulty of identifying of who they are. So it is very often data that is not collected through the formal channels, through the government, but through surveys that are done with freelancers, but how successful it is, how accurate it is, is very often dependent on the willingness of freelancers to participate in these surveys. And very often there is overreporting, but there is also under-reporting of self-employment for various reasons. I might not report how much work I am doing for tax purposes but I might also be overreporting because I am doing multiple projects at the same time, and it looks like it is more than one person but actually just one person doing that work. So there is overreporting and there is also under-reporting of self-employment and very often in the official statistics, freelancers are not treated as a separate category. They are treated together with all other employees. And all this is true, and all these challenges are true, in the context of Singapore as well. I have been involved with one of our government departments, the Ministry of Information, Communication and the Arts, which has primary responsibility for the creative industries. They have been on my back to say "can you help us to try and come up with a methodology to track who these people are and so forth?" And it is difficult.

In working through some of these methodologies, I have discovered some of the specific challenges facing Singapore. For example, there is no standard definition of freelancing. In all existing data-collecting bodies, the only definitions are of fulltime workers and part-time workers. But of course freelancers can be working fulltime but they could also be part-time workers. And so that lack of definition of freelancing has meant a great difficulty in pinning down what each agency means when it talks about freelancing. There is no clear categorization of creative industries either in existing data-collection bodies. So for example, publishing and printing are in one category. Where does creative work end and where does technical work begin? And I make cross-references to Andy's work again where he talks about the creative industry production system and how it is that when you are talking about the production of a cultural product, one needs to look at the entire production system. So if you are looking at performing arts, it is not enough to look at actors and actresses. One needs to look at the technical people doing the lighting and the sound and everything else down the line as well. But the question then is where does the creative end in this particular conception? There are also issues to do with the technicality of data collection, as for example with the accounting and the corporate regulatory authority in Singapore, which is the authority where you register yourself if you want to set up a sole proprietorship and that is where a lot of freelancers have to register themselves. It is all self-identification. I discovered many cases where I called companies to interview them because I thought they were in the interior design business. But what I found was a contractor, sort of building private residences, and all sort of things like that, so that selfidentification lends itself to all kinds of blurring of boundaries as to what work a sole proprietorship for example is actually doing.

So all of this is to say that this is an area that the Singapore government has found great difficulties grappling with. And the standard records have looked at statistics coming out of institutions of higher learning about whether the graduates are getting employed, whether degree holders are diploma holders, and the general sort of sentiment is that people are not getting employed. But that is because the people who let us say come out of an arts institution, are possibly for the most part going into freelance work. They are not tracked, they cannot be identified and therefore they are thought to be unemployed. So this whole area of identifying who the creative workers are is fraught with difficulties and it is an area of this new creative economy that the Singapore government is having great difficulties grappling with.

Developing a new workforce: rethinking education and training

A second area of attempting to manage and to cultivate is in the area of education and training, and here there have been a whole lot more efforts with a lot more sense of direction, although it is not entirely clear that the outcomes are necessarily what are desired as yet. Singapore views education as pivotal to developing a creative workforce. In contrast to a place like New York where there is very little by way of actual formal policy, in Singapore a great number of initiatives have been undertaken by the government to try to reshape education so that the new worker, the new creative worker or the new economy worker, is better prepared for that new economy.

Some of these key initiatives are follows: first of all, a revamping of the approach to teaching and education in schools with much greater emphasis on art and music in the curriculum compared to almost a total lack of it in the past. The creation and the support of specialized institutions catering to creative art education, the attraction of top foreign art schools to Singapore, and emphasis placed on continuing education for upgrading of skills for those who are already in the workforce. I will speak about each of these in turn and provide some evaluative comments on their relative success or failure.

First of all, in relation to the revamping of teaching in schools. I think the question that the government asked itself was this whole question of whether Singapore's education system, which by many accounts is said to be very successful, is in fact really all that successful, and whether it is a talent meritocracy or an examination meritocracy. And one key member of the parliament, the former minister of education, who from many accounts is thought to be quite forward-thinking and progressive, has characterized Singapore as much more of an exam meritocracy than a talent meritocracy, by which he means that the students are extremely well trained, and I use the word very deliberately, very well trained to take exams but not necessarily terribly creative nor critical in theoretical approach to understanding knowledge and to producing new knowledge. So, in an effort to shift from that exam meritocracy to a talent meritocracy, the efforts to try and revamp teaching in the schools have been very apparent in the last several years. One of these key initiatives is a "thinking school/learning nation" initiative in which there were several sub initiatives. For example, there is an explicit attempt to teach creative and critical thinking skills in the classroom. I am not sure of how that is actually done but it exists. The reduction of subject content, so that people are not so hung up and focused on learning content, the revision of assessment methods, a greater emphasis on processes instead of outcomes when appraising schools. The prime minister himself, the new prime minister at his first rally speech addressing the nation, talked about teaching less and therefore learning more.

Other initiatives such as introducing innovation and enterprise teaching in the school system, not so much for developing business entrepreneurs but to help to let students think more innovatively and as much as possible about that. And a new knowledge and inquiry initiative which derives from the International Baccalaureate system, a subject that is absent currently in the GCE curriculum which is primarily what Singapore relies on. So all these sorts of initiatives have come on board at a very rapid pace in the last several years in an effort to revamp teaching in the schools and therefore to create the now creative workers. And despite these efforts, among a number of the creative practitioners who I have spoken to as part of my interview process, despite the recognition that this shift is a positive one, there are many skeptical views about whether it has been successful or whether it is perhaps too early to say. For example, the key challenge remains of being able to go beyond examination results, to encouraging a culture of learning that is willing to challenge conventional wisdom, even if it means challenging authority. And critics of the approach in Singapore and the culture and system in Singapore argue that Asian values, in so much as there is such a thing as Asian values, do not endorse the right to question and to challenge, and therefore it will be very difficult to make this shift that the Singapore government says it wants to make, and this culture of openness, if it is not present, it is going to be very difficult to make this particular shift.

The second sort of direction that I have mentioned in rethinking education is to emphasize much more the arts in the school curriculum. Art and music were for the longest time peripheral subjects taught by teachers who had spare time and did not have a full work load, and so despite the fact that they had absolutely no inclination or expertise in art and music, they could teach those subjects. That is changing and there is an effort to bring more experts into the school system, and there is an effort to bring practitioners into the schools as well. The writers-in-residence scheme and other kinds of schemes enable students to interact with the practitioners themselves, whether they are performing visual artists, or writers, etc. But the challenge remains that whole generations, my generation, and the generation before me who are now at the stage where we could be teachers in the schools, have had very little education in the creative arts. For example, it is difficult to find from among this generation teachers who are able to go back into the school system and do well by that system. The lack highly qualified teachers is a very real challenge.

The third direction in education and training is not just to focus on the specialized, on the mainstream schools, but to create specialized institutions catering to creative art and creative art education. And so specialized art schools have been developed at the secondary level, so Singapore has had its first dedicated art school at high school level in the last five years. It has had new diploma programs and new degree programs have been introduced especially for the creative arts. And private local schools are also getting into the act. The real problem here is at the degree and postgraduate level, there has not been sufficient attention. But at the same time employers that I interviewed have said that sometimes it is not the education you have had in schools, the theoretical education which you had in schools, but the practical education which you need to have along with that more academic education that is very starkly lacking. And so the constant exhortation that there should be internship opportunities incorporated into the school system is an area which has just not been given any attention.

A fourth area, and this is very typical of Singapore, is to attract foreign art schools, to have foreign experts to come into the country, to help jump-start something or to develop an initiative. And here in higher education, the Economic Development Board which I spoke about earlier has in the last ten years woken up to the fact that education could be, God forbid, an industry. And in seeing the industrial potential of education, has come up with what it has called the 'global schoolhouse initiative' in Singapore where it has tried to bring in well-known schools to set up campuses in Singapore and through that to make Singapore an education hub bringing students from around the world, and particularly Asia, to Singapore. In the arena of the creative industries and creative arts, two such examples of New York's Fifth Avenue School of the Arts and Milan's Arts Academy. And they have done quite well in terms of being able to attract students not just from Singapore but from the region and establishing a sense that Singapore is serious about developing education in these directions. This has not been however without its detractors and its critiques. For example, local practitioners in the creative industries have criticized this as a missed opportunity for Singapore to try to develop its own stellar world-class sort of institution, that instead of focusing on the Western institutions that can bring their expertise, we are missing an opportunity in Singapore to develop an institution that emphasizes Asian and intercultural art forms and idioms.

Finally by way of education and training I will just say that the recognition that continuing education is very important for the workforce is one that is recognized by the government as a way of managing and developing this particular workforce and here there have been efforts to put in place a framework for skilled qualifications and skilled developments through an agency called the Work Development Agency, working with a consultant from the UK, and an education and training framework for professionals in art and culture, design, media, and education has been established to try and make sure that there are continuing education opportunities for workers in the creative industry. But what the creative workers themselves are saying is that very often what is needed is not so much occupation-specific or industry-specific skills. In other words not skills in technical lighting or animations and design, but much more generic skills development in areas such as management, financial accounting, legal contracts and advertising, because these are the skills that they need to work really effectively as sole proprietors who have no protection and who need to have an understanding of these sorts of areas in order to not be cheated.

Inventing new mediating institutions

I have spoken of two areas so far that the government has tried to examine to try and introduce means of management and governance. A third, very much about management and governance, has to do with inventing new mediating institutions. The challenges facing the freelancers and the creative economy I have spoken about already, and it has prompted the development of new processes in the entry to the labor market, has prompted new modes of labor organization in the form of collectives, and has prompted new modes of labor organization in the rethinking of the role of unions and the forms they take. Let me take each of these in turn. Because as I said earlier, entry into the labor market by freelancers is very much about social networking, through informal mechanisms rather than about formal mechanisms.

The government agencies that attempt to speak to this particular characteristic have responded by developing matchmaking platforms. So for example, the government has introduced a creative industries fair, where employers and potential employees on a freelance basis can meet and showcase the employers' needs and the talent of the workers. The government has also teamed up with a sort of creative cluster enterprise to come up with something called '6degrees.asia' which is an e-platform for doing that matchmaking role as well. And so that helps to mediate between employers and potential employees. Between creative workers themselves, new institutions have also developed. While the idea of the collective is quite commonplace in some other cities and countries, in Singapore it hasn't been very prominent at all, but in the last several years this has gained some traction and design collectives in which independent workers team up have become more prominent. And with the idea that they can achieve more collectively than as individuals, they work together under a shared brand name and yet they can maintain their individual distinctiveness and creative styles as such.

And it also offers transnational opportunities because these collectives cut across natural boundaries and there are many examples of collectives that are based in Singapore but which have creative workers from other countries as well, which then opens up the opportunity for those creative workers in Singapore to also have their work taken to other countries. And finally the role of unions as another mediating institution. There is a need for traditional unions to evolve to incorporate freelancers because traditional unions are used to working with the workers in the traditional, usual setup of the firm. But when you have creative workers or freelancers, how do the unions speak specifically to their needs, indeed, how should unions be organized and what role should unions play? And here there is opportunity for other kinds of roles for unions. For example, in establishing a central directory for employers and employees, in coming up with systems of accreditation and certification for freelancers, that can be useful for employers but also for freelancers themselves. I have eight minutes left, so I am not going to elaborate a great deal more except to say that these new institutions are developing, evolving, often with the help of the state which sees a need to try and intervene and facilitate. So these have all arisen with the rise of the creative economy as such in Singapore.

Can precarious economies be planned?

So let me now turn very quickly to some concluding statements. And so the question I ask is, can precarious economies be planned and can the forms of amorphous, hidden ecologies be managed and governed in a way that the Singapore government would like it to be in the pattern that it is very much used to? Let me just say that in the first decade of the 21st century, much more attention has been given in Singapore to the potential of the creative industries in not only contributing directly to the economy, but in catalyzing growth and tourism, retail, manufacturing and education. In 2004, Singapore's creative industries contributed 3.6% of the GDP and this was a rise of 8% over the previous year. Jobs in the creative sector grew by 5.5% per annum from 1995 to 2003. And this is compared with 2.3% for the entire economy. From 2003 to 2008, Singapore's creative industries averaged about 6% value-added growth yearly. And annual employment growth averaged about 4% during the same period.

All of this is very encouraging, especially given the fact that if you compare it to another new industry that the government has been trying to develop and support, the biomedical sciences industries, far less money has been pumped into this industry than into the biomedical sciences. And if you compare the relative performance, the creative industries have been much more encouraging in their results and outcomes. So that is very positive but if you compare it for example to the traditional manufacturing that Singapore has been doing, and which we sometimes think is no longer going to be as important, that is not true because the manufacturing industries continue to do very well and much better than either of the new industries, accounting for a steady 25% of Singapore's GDP for a good 20 years.

So the question is, if the creative industries are to progressively contribute more significantly to the economy as the government would like them to, whether it is in terms of GDP or terms of employment, the question needs to be asked whether that progress is to be achieved in laissez-faire manner, or is it in fact possible for the Singapore do to what it is used to, to plan ever more? The answer might lie somewhere in between. In order to know how the creative economy is contributing to employment, for example, one of the most fundamental things that it needs to do is to grapple with those new measurements and methodologies that I was talking about earlier.

And it is not making any headway. Does this mean that this industry is not contributing to the economy? No, it doesn't, it simply means that the government is unable to track the contributions to employment for example.

Second, with regard to preparing potential future creative workers for this new economy, a great deal of planning has already gone into educational reform and training programs in Singapore and I have described in some detail all the efforts in this direction. The plans here are only as good as their implementation. Deeply-rooted cultural practices and values cannot be planned away. The approach to teaching and learning, the privileging of what I might call 'pragmatic' disciplines that lead to well-established careers, and the attitudes toward artistic and related endeavors are all underpinned by value systems that need time to be modified. What is needed is consistent, patient and wide-spread action for effective change across the system, and despite all the efforts that already have been introduced, I would say that we are not even at the tip of the iceberg yet insofar as achieving some results. As for the well-being of a class of workers, whose very existence is characterized by precarity, thoughtful plans and careful management can offer them some assistance, and provide a measure of relief from that precarity.

Here, Singapore's first steps at developing platforms for matchmaking and for sharing experiences and advice among the freelancer class itself, have been welcomed and well-received. And in these sorts of ways, some of the precarity of this particular part of the workforce can be managed and moderated somewhat. To the extent that careful planning and management can moderate the state of precarity for creative workers, the economy need not be a precarious one. The lives of the creative workers may be, but the economy need not be a precarious one. Indeed, the creative economy can thrive if its key resource, creative individuals, have room to thrive with a nurturing education system, a willingness and ability to recognize who they are and a concerted effort to develop mediating institutions to moderate their precarity. If not, it would never be possible to eliminate the precarity, but to moderate and mediate that precarity.

Those are things that can be helpful. But as we have seen from the previous talk, the creative economy can thrive and does thrive in conditions where there is no planning whatsoever, no intervention by the government.

Is that something that can be done in a situation, an economy, like Singapore, that is very much built on planning? I don't know the answer to that but I do know the answer to another question which is: Will the Singapore government let this creative economy, this part of the new economy, evolve on its own without intervention and efforts, not necessarily at regulation, but certainly at facilitation?

I think the answer to that is no because coming from a certain trajectory, a certain direction historically of always getting involved, it is very inconceivable that the government wouldn't get involved. That involvement can be a positive thing if managed in particular ways, so the management of the creative economy and the governance of the creative economy can be helpful, can facilitate, but only if done in certain ways with perhaps a light touch. And the jury is out on that in Singapore. It has come some way but whether it is going to make that next growth through the creative economies is very uncertain. The latest effort at policy making and strategic intervention, this new committee that is called the Art and Culture Strategy Review Steering Committee, is now talking not about the art and culture, design, and so forth as an industry and part of the economy, but talking about it for its purely social and cultural ends. Whether that comes to pass, whether those recommendations are accepted by the government or not remains to be seen, but here again the possibility for a change in the wind appears to be on the horizon. Thank you.

Takashi Machimura

Current academic position
Professor, Graduate School of Social Sciences, Hitotsubashi University

Academic experience
1982- M.A., The University of Tokyo
1979- B.A., The University of Tokyo

2001- Professor, Graduate School of Social Sciences, Hitotsubashi University
1999-01 Professor, Faculty of Social Sciences, Hitotsubashi University
1991-99 Associate Professor, Faculty of Social Sciences, Hitotsubashi University
1988-91 Lecturer, Faculty of Social Sciences, Tsukuba University
1984-88 Research Assistant, Faculty of Letters, The University of Tokyo

Research interests
Impacts of globalization and neoliberalism on urban structures
Urban social movements and new forms of state intervention (evaluative state)
Historical sociology of developmetalism: its structure, mentality, and media image

Major articles and papers
Narrating a 'Global City' for 'New Tokyoites': Economic Crisis and Urban Boosterism in Tokyo, in H. Dobson and G. D. Hook, eds., *Japan and Britain in the Contemporary World*, London: RoutledgeCurzon, pp.196-212, 2003.

Living in a Transnational Community within a Multi-Ethnic City: Making of Localized 'Japan' in Los Angeles, in R. Goodman et al., eds., *Global Japan: The Experience of Japan's New Immigrants and Overseas Communities*, London: RoutledgeCurzon, pp.147-156, 2003.

1-3. Power and Openness:
Appropriating City Space for Re-creating "the Urban"

Summary

When urbanization was viewed as a form of modernization, city space was considered unique because it represented a tangible manifestation of modernity. However, as the basis of economic competitiveness in the city has shifted from how much (physical) "space" people own to how fast they communicate each other, that is, "speed," a symbolic meaning that the city seems to have changed drastically. The city space is now beginning to represent not swiftness but inertia in people's attitude toward change, compared with the developments in cyberspace. Yet, from my point of view, such materiality or physical nature contains an important clue for understanding the current state of urban reality, particularly, the significance of the city itself. How is it possible to keep such slow or inert cities open to diversified actors and changing events? In order to answer this question, this paper investigates the historical developments of open spaces in urban settings, by studying the case of Yoyogi Park in central Tokyo. Attempts to protect open urban spaces are always accompanied by conflicts among actors who have different ideas for using such spaces. However, from such experiences, the city can learn how to keep its space livable and, therefore, creative.

First, let me to thank you for inviting me here to speak today. I am grateful for the efforts exerted by Professor Sasaki, Professor Mizuuchi, and everyone else. And I would like to apologize to the international guests here today from many different countries. Many of the people in the audience are Japanese, so I will be speaking in Japanese, but the Power Point slides in my presentation are basically in English, so you should be able to understand the contents of my lecture.

Introduction

Today we are talking about cities, and in particular I would like to talk about a very specific, very distinctive place in Tokyo, which is Yoyogi Park. The premise of this talk is that at present urban society is in the midst of great change. For a long time urbanization or the city was thought to be at the very forefront of modernization, the place that was changing the most rapidly. And this was thought to be the attraction of the city. However, at present we are in a situation where the meaning of the city is gradually changing. It doesn't need to be said that at present in the midst of many changes brought on by information, globalization, etc., rather than being a world that is pursuing speed, it has become a world that is being overtaken by speed. The basis of economic competition in today's world is no longer how much space one possesses, but rather the situation has arisen in which things depend on how fast we can communicate and get ideas across, in other words on speed. In the midst of this, the symbolic meaning that the city holds is also changing.

At present, the nature of the city is still that of a place that represents speed and rapidity, but at the same time it has aspects of a space that has come to mean not that but rather an appearance that changes slowly or not at all, a space of tranquility. I think one can say this is characteristic of the city particularly in comparison with cyberspace and the world of the Internet. This materiality of urban space or its physical character has nowadays gradually taken on importance in understanding the reality of the city, and I believe it is the key to understanding the shape the city should take on in the future. Actually, each and every one of we human beings has a physical body that we inhabit. This body makes it necessary to always have an actual, concrete place. Inasmuch as our physical bodies cannot yet simply inhabit the world of the Internet, as long as we have physical bodies, we are saddled with the fate of always having to occupy a place. Since that is our nature, on one hand when we think about cities (this is now up on the screen), we are in a situation where fear, and the fears surrounding our bodies, will always become issues.

Safety and security in the city are seen as being ever more important. The more that is the case, the more the feeling of wanting to control the space will arise, and so as a means of controlling space, for example, video cameras, surveillance cameras, private police forces, security guards, and physical structure like gated communities have rapidly increased. At present, the mechanisms that are used to control space have taken on a multiple variety of forms, and while the politics surrounding these fears and anxieties try to create reasons that justify banishing all sorts of things, the objects of these attempts at exclusion are not real, actually existing risks, but rather we are in a situation that gives rise to the feeling of wanting to eliminate everything that smacks of uncertainty or 'otherness.'

Taking these circumstances into account, what I would like to consider here today is the significance of what I would like to call 'openness.' In the city I have just described, the slowly changing or unchanging city, how can it be made 'open' to a variety of people or to a variety of cultural forms? I think that the themes of the city's creativity or the city's inclusiveness must begin from this theme of 'openness.' Today, instead of directly trying to answer this larger question, I would like to consider the question by taking up a very specific place, a rather large place, which as I said before is Yoyogi Park, and talk about the historical development of this place and its present circumstances.

Thinking about this opened up space will, I think, be an important route to considering the relationships between power, or authority, and openness, which is today's topic. I would like to think about the openness that I am now talking about not as a result but as a socially created process. Consequently, the question I am asking is, how and when is an open space actually open or free? Or, looking at it another way, openness as I said before gives disputes and tensions in all kinds of forms. On the other hand, openness gives rise to all kinds of creativity in the city, and I think that it is necessary to think about under what conditions that comes about. And then, in order to make it so that this space is open or free, what kinds of things are necessary, what things are truly essential? I think that is something we need to consider.

The Making of Yoyogi Park : Power loves open space

So, now I would like to move on to the specific case of Yoyogi Park. Here is a map of central Tokyo showing Yoyogi Park (Figure 1). Specifically, Yoyogi Park is the area enclosed by the red circle. Here is the Imperial Palace. And next, here is its position in relation to Shinjuku and Shibuya. Yoyogi Park has the largest area of any public park in central Tokyo. It is a municipal park, administered by the Tokyo Metropolitan Government. As I just described, this park is situated in between Shinjuku and Shibuya, the most representative commercial centers of Tokyo, and it is in a place with extremely good transportation linkages. Look at this map on the left. On the left side are signs, in the middle are mainly trees, a forest. And then there is a space covered by a grassy lawn. Here what you see are maps of four different cities, the central core area of the four cities. Starting at the upper left, here is New

Figure 1: Map of Yoyogi Park

York, and this area is Central Park. Next on this side is the downtown area of Singapore. Next, here is Osaka. This area around here is Umeda, and this area is Osaka Castle. So, we are at present located about here. Next, here is Tokyo. Yoyogi Park corresponds to this area enclosed by the red boundary. The immediately adjoining area to the north that is green represents Meiji Shrine. As you can realize by looking at these, Yoyogi Park is a very large park for Tokyo. The scale of each of these four maps is the same for comparison, and compared to Central Park, for example, Yoyogi Park is not quite so large. However, in Tokyo, aside from Yoyogi Park there are also the gardens at the Meiji Shrine and the Shinjuku Imperial Garden, and a number of other green spaces besides, so if they are all lumped together the amount of green space rivals Central Park, making Tokyo a city with a surprisingly large area of green.

Turning to the history of Yoyogi Park, during the Edo Period a number of estates and residential compounds of samurai families were located here. This location, at the time of the Meiji Restoration, excuse me, this should be 1868, not 1968, after the Meiji Restoration for a while the area was used for agricultural purposes, largely vegetable fields. Then, with the beginning of the 20th century we are entering the era of modern Tokyo, and modern Tokyo was called the capital of the Empire of Japan. The words 'Imperial Capital' were actually used at that time, and during the era of the imperial capital, the era of today's Yoyogi Park began with its conversion to use as a military training ground. Consequently, the army carried out all kinds of military exercises and parades in this location. Additionally, immediately to the north of this area is the place where, after the death of the Meiji Emperor, the Meiji Shrine was newly constructed in 1920. This was for 'remembering the Meiji Emperor's legacy of ancestral virtue' which was the language used at the time, in other words, the Meiji Shrine was built as a memorial to commemorate the Meiji Emperor.

Going back to Yoyogi Park, as I said before, in the days before the Second World War it was an exercise ground for the army, but after Japan was defeated in the war, the area was absorbed by the American military, in actuality the army of occupation, and it was converted into a residential housing district for the families of American soldiers. This is the area that today is Yoyogi Park, and as you can see, it was a place with rows of single family houses. The black area at the upper left is the Meiji Shrine. A total of 827 houses were built here, and in addition facilities for supporting an American residential lifestyle were built in the same location. For example, an ice cream factory was built here, and garden fields for producing a variety of vegetables. Next we come to 1960. This was an extremely important year for Japan politically. In 1960, the Japan-U.S. Security Treaty came up for renewal, and citizens' and social movements opposed to the treaty erupted on a large scale. The Japan-U.S. Security Treaty itself ended up being renewed despite these movements, but in the midst of the very strong tensions that arose between the United States and Japan, out of consideration for the position of the Japanese government, made the decision to return to Japanese control this piece of land, which was known as Washington Heights, and which was in the middle of Tokyo and as I have related was used for residences for the American military.

At the time of the staging of the Tokyo Olympic Games in 1964, this spot was used as an athletes' village for those competing in the Olympics. So, the history of this place is that it was rebuilt from a village for the American military into an Olympic Athletes' Village, and after the Olympics it was rebuilt again, opening to the public as the new Yoyogi Park in 1967. So, next I would like to consider who it was that discovered and made use of this newly made Yoyogi Park.

Who discovered open space in the city? : Public park as a contested place

Basically, the people who used the park were young people, and newly formed young families. Especially, since this was the period of rapid economic growth, many of the young people living in Tokyo were people who came from other regions outside of Tokyo, and I myself was one of these people. These young people had no money, an a park that they could go to for free and enter for free was an ideal recreation spot, and that form of use was the main utilization of the park. However, aside from that, it has also come to be used for divergent purposes. I will talk about three of those.

The first is the use of Yoyogi Park as a place for social movements and the raising of political voices. Here once again is a map of Tokyo, this time from the decade of the 1960s. Just at the end of the 60s or the beginning of the 1970s was an era in which student movements and peace movements erupted around the world, and Japan was certainly no exception. During the decade of the 1960s, there were a number of social movements that erupted in Japan as well. The goal for demonstrations at that time that consisted of thousands of people, at times tens of thousands of people, was the Diet building (here) or the complex of national government buildings (here). Well, this is after all the center of Tokyo. The problem was, where could such huge crowds of people come together, and it was natural that finding a place for people to assemble was a big issue. In such cases, it is roughly five kilometers from Yoyogi Park to the Diet building, and it was discovered by the various movements that Yoyogi Park was a very expansive place where many people could assemble, and so it actually came to be used in that way. What you are seeing here is a photograph taken of a demonstration by a student movement or peace movement group from the late 1960s. Here is an international anti-war demonstration from 1969. At that time 41,000 people gathered in Yoyogi Park, the following year, 1970, on May Day 210,000 people started a march from Yoyogi Park. These kinds of events were carried out. In some sense it is ironic that this place was remade in such a short time from being

Washington Heights, a place for American soldiers, into being a place that was symbolic of the anti-Vietnam War and anti-security treaty movements.

Thereafter, the history of this place as a place for movements underwent a change, from being a place for so-called leftist movements into one for movements to protect the environment, the kind of movements espousing green and ecological themes. However, the history of this place as one for the broadcast of political messages is still being preserved. In this photograph that you are now looking at, you can see that at present this is a spot with a lot of what in Japan are called 'flea markets' (or 'free markets'), abbreviated as 'furima.' In 1980, NGOs in the ecology movement began holding these outdoor flea markets. With this spot being one of the origins, Yoyogi Park was used as a place for interaction between people promoting ecological and recycling movements of this kind. It is one of the places where this began and this history is engraved in the spot. Today in 2010 if you go to Yoyogi Park you can see these flea markets still being operated at present, usually on weekends, Saturdays and Sundays. This is what is called one 'shop,' and this shop is one block among the 400 to 600 blocks there are each time the market is held in this space. Many young people come here, and they can be seen selling things to be recycled. I should also probably add that an Earth Day celebration is held every year in Yoyogi Park.

In regards to the history of park users, the second type is a word that may be very familiar to many Japanese, the word 'zoku.' It is hard to translate into English, but the literal translation is 'tribe.' Every weekend, young people belonging to various subcultures that have their own distinctive fashions or dances gather together here, perform music or dance. This kind of scene has developed, and these groups are called 'tribes.' Some have been given names like the 'bamboo shoot tribe' or the 'rock'n'roll tribe,' but these are the groups I am talking about. In this area around Yoyogi Park, as I described before, American military families used to live, and so there were also stores there for helping to realize an American lifestyle, toy stores, shops selling food, and also shops selling used American clothing. And consequently young Japanese came here as well in order to consume parts of an American lifestyle. That is the kind of place this used to be. Having that as its background is the district around Yoyogi Park. This has become the area called Harajuku, and Harajuku since that time and up to the present has become the center of the fashion industry in Japan. One can even call it an industry cluster. Additionally, in 1977, the roads in the area around Yoyogi Park, over which normally automobile traffic ran, were made into a 'pedestrian paradise' on weekends. The Japanese expression 'tengoku' is difficult translate into English, but what it meant was that every weekend vehicles were blocked off and not allowed to enter, the roads were changed into open spaces that people could use freely just. These temporary, weekend-only events were called 'pedestrian paradise' or hokosha tengoku. This started in 1977. The result, as you can see in this photo which is in the middle of the road, is that young people came onto the roads and as I said before every weekend put on dances or staged performances. Here is a picture from 1993 that shows a scene with the rora-zoku or rock'n'roll tribe. The history of this tribe continued through the 1990s, and this road became a temporary stage on which many young people displayed their performances and large crowds gathered to watch them. That was the kind of stage that was created.

However, beginning in the 1990s, many people in the fashion industries that I talked about before had gathered in the Harajuku District, and such shop owners were at the center of voices that were raised in opposition to the weekend pedestrian paradise. During the 1990s, the number of stores selling French and other European brand goods rapidly increased in Harajuku. As that happened, they needed to appeal to customers who had a lot of money, and such customers tended to travel by private car. So, if the roads were blocked off on weekends so that cars couldn't enter, it would be very inconvenient for the kinds of customers they wanted. For this, and some other reasons as well, there were demands from the locals to do away with the pedestrian paradise, and in 1996, after a lengthy debate, the pedestrian paradise began to be abolished in gradual stages. The result has been to bring about the disappearance of the weekend stages.

And now for the history of the third type of park user. In the decade of the 1980s, under the influence of globalization, Japan entered the era of the Bubble Economy. During the 1980s, economic boom times continued in Japan, and the domestic labor force became insufficient. Japan did not officially open up its labor market or acknowledge that it was letting laborers especially in the heavy industries enter the country, but nonetheless the number of people coming from other countries to work in Japan in various ways increased during the latter 1980s. The graph that you are seeing now shows the number of people entering Japan from Iran in the years 1989, 1990, 1991, and 1992. The time of the greatest number, which was probably October of 1991, at this time during one month approximately 7,000 Iranians were admitted into Japan. They came on tourist visas, and while they were staying here their visas would expire, and they continued living in Japan even though their visas had expired. The number of these Iranians living in Japan in April 1992 had reached the level of approximately 40,000 people. It was in the midst of these circumstances that Yoyogi Park was discovered by the Iranians.

Here is a photo taken in 1992 of the entrance to Yoyogi Park. In the crowd that can be seen here, almost all the people are Iranians. At the beginning of the 1990s, every weekend, mainly on Sundays, several thousand Iranians would come to gather here, talk among themselves, do their shopping, and exchange information. On the biggest days, something like seven or eight thousand Iranians would be gathered near the gate to Yoyogi Park. In front of this gate to Yoyogi Park a bazaar area where people sold things, and a gathering area where people talked together emerged spontaneously as a temporary space, and such things as this videotape here or Persian language magazines were sold. As an example, the magazine that you see here is called Javanan, and this a magazine that was published by Iranians living in Los Angeles, but very quickly it found a market for itself in Yoyogi Park in Tokyo, and every week it was shipped by airplane to be sold here. Most of the other merchandise as well was not made in Japan but rather in Europe, Turkey, or America. The fact that these kinds of merchandise, much of which had been made by Iranians living in exile, were transported to Yoyogi Park meant that Yoyogi Park had been incorporated as part of the Iranian diaspora.

This is part of the park's history. However, as so many Iranians gathered in the park, as you have just seen, a variety of tensions arose. This went on until after the collapse of the Bubble Economy in Japan, and so the economic circumstances of the Iranians gradually worsened. Also, as rumors of criminality circulated, the Tokyo Metropolitan Government became concerned and started wanting to control or regulate this so-called loitering spot. Because public parks are places where anyone can gather, they couldn't say that people can't gather there just because they are foreigners, so the reasons they gave in the beginning were for a welfare survey, or for the sake of hygiene. Next they talked about park beautification, the 'parks beautiful' program. And then, for reasons of crime and security the authorities intervened at this loitering spot, and then finally in 1993 they encircled this area here, the bazaar area, with a fence. They said that it was to protect the trees, but with that objective they shut down this loitering spot, and the previous gathering place disappeared. These have been the various uses of the park from the period of rapid economic growth onward through the bubble period.

"Culture" in tension : Public space in a "declining" global city

At present, Japan is confronting a long economic recession that has lasted since the 1990s. In particular, this has included globalization and the cutting of government programs by neo-liberalist reforms, and in the midst of this people's economic circumstances have worsened and a situation has arisen that is shaking the foundation of social unity. These new circumstances have set the basic tone in Japan up until the present day. In the midst of this, I think that one can point to a new type of park utilization that is gradually taking shape.

In the case of Yoyogi Park for example, there was a period when people didn't much go there, and that is true for me as well, but recently I started going back to take a look, and many times I have been surprised to see how many people are there. I felt that people are coming back to this park. There are probably a number of reasons, but one is that the park is free. In the midst of the economic uncertainty that I described before, people's disposable income has declined and that may be one of the reasons. And then, another important factor is that Yoyogi Park is in the central core of Tokyo, and in the area around it many high rise condominiums and apartment buildings have been built. A part of these can be called gentrification, which was talked about before, but the fact is that residents are coming back to the inner city. As seen by these residents living in the inner city, mention Yoyogi Park and it is the park nearby to their homes, the park they can walk to, and including these new users, there are new encounters with users in the park, and new uses of the park are being created.

For example, while this is a case of park use brought on by economic uncertainties, one new use is that by homeless people or rough sleepers who live in or utilize the park. Yoyogi Park itself has a long history as an important place to live for homeless people (Figure 2). As this graph shows, the numbers of homeless people living in the center of Tokyo, according to figures from research by the Tokyo Metropolitan government, from the end of the 1990s dramatically increased, doubling from about 3,000 to around 6,000.

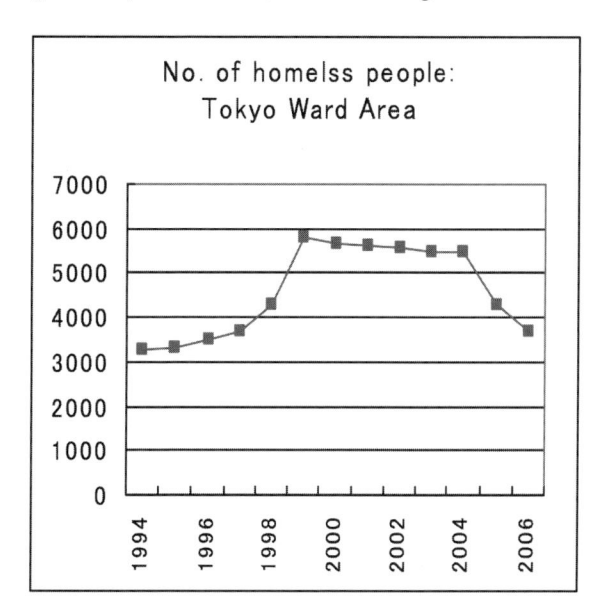

Figure 2: No. of homeless people: Tokyo Ward Area

And among those, the number living in Yoyogi Park was conspicuously high, along with Shinjuku and Shibuya. In 2002, a new law was passed in Japan, the Homeless Support Act. This was probably the first law to help the homeless. In accordance with the law, the Tokyo Metropolitan Government initiated housing policy measures for the homeless. The substance of these measures for helping the homeless should be seen positively, but seen from the park's perspective they brought about a rather ironic result. There were about 600 or 700 people living in the park according to one report, and of these about 250 or so moved into apartments or temporary shelters. After that, this space here that is outlined in black, which is where a lot of the homeless people had been living, this space was rebuilt into a so-called 'open space,' and it has been preserved up until now as a space that no can enter, with a rope stretched around it and a signboard. This was done with the object of making it so that homeless people could not enter, which you can easily see by looking. Also, here next to the park is the JR station which is an important gateway to the park, and there were a lot of homeless people living here in a spot that was in the public eye. They were banished to the innermost area of the park where even today the tent dwellings of homeless people can be seen. And here is an entrance that is comparatively close to the gateway, this is a scene from 2004, when after the new housing measures the area was rebuilt into this formal space to create an environment where it would be difficult to pitch a tent.

This situation has a connection to the theme of 'culture' as well, and it exerts a variety of influences on the aspect of culture. The sign that you see here has a list of the rules for the park. It says that selling goods, making public announcements, or playing music are prohibited. However, in actuality sometimes these rules are enforced and sometimes they are not. The people of the 'tribes' that we saw before have come back to the park. However, the people in these tribes now are already in their 40s and 50s. On weekends this turns into a place where people entering middle age come back once again as a rock'n'roll tribe. This spot, as it was before, is still today great spot for the tourists. I don't know if you can see it here well or not, but recently on the day I went there, there were a lot of foreign visitors who had come from overseas to watch the scene. This scene is on the one hand nostalgia for the former days of the tribes, but as an object for consumption it's possible that it could be misunderstood as a symbol of the new Japan. I think this could be said to be a kind of cultural scene.

Park authorities also come here regularly. This photo shows some of the staff trying to enforce the rules. These people look as if they were standing there for a period of hours, and at regular intervals they go over to where people are dancing and warn them, and after quite a bit of talking, they withdraw again without doing anything. So they are not stopping the dancing or banishing the dancers. One could say that this place has come into being through a delicate balance. As I said before, this is a place where playing music, especially loud music, is supposed to be restricted. This is written in Japanese on the signboard, although what it says is that loud music should not be played. However, in actuality in the middle of the park or outside bands are playing, there are percussion groups, even people playing trash buckets. Performances are going on that are really loud with everybody stomping their feet. It is certainly not quiet. Here again, on the one hand it is forbidden, and while that rule is being enforced a fair bit, at the same time it is being broken, and this delicate balance is the scene that jumps into one's vision there.

Or, yet another cultural example are the street performances (for which there is a word in Japanese, daidogei). At the beginning of the 2000s, the Tokyo Metropolitan Government started a new program the 'heaven artists' (they are also called 'heaven artists' in Japanese). This is one part of the cultural policy in which street performers are auditioned, and if the results of their auditions meet a certain standard, they can get certified as street performers, and with that credential they are allowed to show off their talents in parks or a variety of other public spaces. In this picture on the right is a scene of one of these 'heaven artists' who has obtained certification performing in the middle of Yoyogi Park. He is performing with balloons... I guess this is a genre that could be called 'balloon art.' However, at the same time at this spot one can see aside from the heaven artists scenes of street performers who do not have this so-called 'certification' performing in the park... this is an important stage for avante garde street performances. There is additionally the example of graffiti or street painting (we just heard about the situation in New York). This park as well was originally a thriving stage for street painting. The Tokyo Metropolitan Government carried out a street painting project in 2007, and after an open competition, the artists who were selected were allowed to paint pictures on concrete walls and made pictures like this. However, just across from this same pillar, on a facing wall, this painting was made. However one looks at it, rather than the one that was sanctioned by the Tokyo Metropolitan Government, this painting looks like a street painting in the true sense of the word. In this way, in this park we can see a situation where cultural activities that are sanctioned officially as part of cultural policies or cultural projects co-exist with independent activities that have no such sanction, as in the case of street performances or street painting.

Conclusion

As a final conclusion, although it's not much of a conclusion, let me look back briefly on what I have related. One thing is about openness and its relationship to power. Tokyo is Japan's capital city. I think it can be said that unlike Osaka, it's a city where authority is very strong and space is very strongly regulated, including for example the fact that the number of regularly manned police boxes (koban) is very high. Because it is that kind of space, it is very difficult to just leave that space open and free. Buried in the midst of the long history of Yoyogi Park, its openness has been preserved, at times utilized by feudal lords and samurai, at times used by the Imperial military, and at times by the American military, and the other space nearby has been used by various forms of the emperor system. In actuality it has a history in which its openness was always preserved by power. Without that, the space probably could not have been preserved. There is a high probability that place like this would have been divided up into a variety of markets and buildings would have been erected above them. Consequently, in some sense, openness requires power. However, the fact that openness cannot be preserved with power alone is a matter that goes without saying, and it is necessary to always ask the questions, who has the power, and who has a right to the space?

And then, space is always on the move, always changing. At times it falls under strong control and becomes unfree, but that situation as we have just seen can change, or just because there are strict regulations doesn't mean that all usage is restricted, or in the midst of total chaos, ways of utilization can arise spontaneously. The history of this park proves all of these things. As place where we can carry out experiments of this kind in how to create rules and regulations for a civil code of space, a code for its social usage, is an important role of open space, and open spaces that can fill that role, movements and experiments in creating a civil code of space, are probably not limited only to parks. I think we can apply this to the city as an entirety. Finally, our three lectures today began with New York, and I would like to return to New York once again. One of the great works of urban theory is Jane Jacobs' Life and Death of Great American Cities, which was also mentioned in the earlier lecture. In it, Jacobs says that, "Parks are very volatile things." She may have been mainly referring to New York, but she points out that parks either become popular places with lots of people, or else very lonely, empty places where no one goes. Such empty spaces with no one there Jacobs calls vacuums. Japan has many parks, but regrettably many of them, even though they are extensive and could be used for all kinds of purposes, many of them have become cold spaces with no people in them. Many of them have become this kind of vacuum. On the other hand, as we have seen today, while Yoyogi Park is a very broad space, at each point in time it has been utilized by people in various ways, utilized by people in spite of various problems and frictions, and has become a very vibrantly active and livable space.

Consequently, in thinking about what is called cultural creativity, I think the most important point, is how can we make a place into an open and vibrant space rather than turning it into a vacuum? I will say this for the conclusion of my report in place of a conclusion. Thank you very much.

Toshio Mizuuchi: Thank you very much. Once again, thinking about this in the context of Osaka, Osaka's Tennoji Park was the first western-style city park in Japan. Sumiyoshi Park is Japan's oldest park, and Nakanoshima Park is valued for being the third or fourth oldest western-style park in Japan. I think parks may be places that express the condition of the human body. In that sense, while now the words 'cultural policy' have been talked about, the homeless problem, especially as related to parks, including Osaka Castle Park, has been debated a great deal in the city of Osaka. In that sense, what kinds of things emanate from parks and public spaces, or in what way they are used, can be used as one kind of barometer to measure the richness of a city. That's what this talk made me feel. Thank you very much, Professor Machimura.

Session 2 *15:40-17:40 December 15th, 2010*

Plenary Speeches

Perspectives from the New Journal *'City, Culture and Society'*

While taking up the problems and issues that appear in contemporary urban research and talking about what the experiences and concerns of each discussant are, we will debate what kinds of scientific practical work communication we need in order to achieve mutual understanding and interpenetration between 'researchers' and 'practitioners' who are engaged in actual work. Also, while digging deeply into what kind of mission is desired for the international journal *'City, Culture and Society'*, we would like to discuss the mission and organization of the International Network Organization (AUC) that we are trying to set up centered around the Urban Research Plaza and based on *CCS*, and more broadly, discuss what research themes and research methods are necessary.

Ritsuko Miki Representative Director of Elsevier Japan K.K.

A career professional in education and/or research organizations for nearly 25 years. She is currently a director of Elsevier Japan K.K.

François Colbert Professor, HEC Montréal

A pioneer in culture and art marketing, he is editor-in-chief of the related journal IJAM, and founder of the International Association of Arts and Culture Management (AIMAC).

Andy C Pratt Professor, King's College, University of London

Recognized around the world for his research on culture, creative industries, and policy, he is a leading theoretician in the world academic community.

Hyun Bang Shin Lecturer, The London School of Economics and Political Scinece

Recently, while doing geographic research on urban problems related to urban regeneration, gentrification and mega-event hosting in East Asia, he is very active in London's urban research network building.

Jung Duk Lim Emeritus professor, Pusan National University

Some Thoughts on Urban Studies Towards the Century of Cities

Coordinator: **Hiroshi Okano** Vice-Director and Professor, Urban Research Plaza, Osaka City University

Prof. Okano does research on strategic management of social and organizational practice in enterprises and cities. He has served as president of the Academy of Accounting Historians and is managing editor of *CCS*.

Hiroshi Okano

Current academic position
Vice-Director, Urban Research Plaza,
Professor, Graduate School of Business,
Osaka City University

Academic experience
1998- Dr. Business Administration, Osaka City University
1985- M.Phil., Osaka City University

2010- Professor, Urban Research Plaza, Osaka City University
1998- Professor, Graduate School of Business, Osaka City University
1992-98 Associate Professor, Graduate School of Business, Osaka City University
1989-92 Lecturer, Graduate School of Business, Osaka City University
1988-89 Research Assistant, Graduate School of Business, Osaka City University

Research interests
Strategic city management, Social, institutional and cultural analysis for urban studies, Cultural branding, Strategic Cost management, Accounting history

Major articles and papers
Strategic Global Accounting: Comparing Cost Managementof Product Development, Yuhikaku, 2003.
"A History of Management Accounting in Japan," *Handbook of Management Accounting Research*, Elsevier, 2007.
"Cultural urban branding and creative cities: A theoretical framework for promoting creativity in the public spaces", *Cities,* Volume 27, Supplement 1, June 2010.

2-0. Opening Remarks

Welcome to the session 2. My name is Hiroshi Okano. Vice-Director of Urban Research Plaza, and as a same time, professor of the business school. Session2 title is a Perspective from the New Journal 'City, Culture and Society'. 'City, Culture and Society' is we just launch the first issue March 2010, June issue and September issue. So we are still waiting for the December issue. We will publish four issues annually. This session tried focus on the sum how to make 'City, Culture and Society' succeed and talk about how to make good journals for the everyone not only academics but also professional people like a international organizations UNESCO or UNDP or some other peoples.

So a first presentator is Ritsuko Miki. She is Representative Director of Elsevier Japan. So please Ritsuko.

Ritsuko Miki

Current business position
Representative Director, Elsevier Japan K.K.

Academic experience
M.B.A., University of Washington (Seattle, Washington, USA)
B.A., American Studies, Tsuda College (Tokyo, Japan)
B.A., American History, Lake Erie College (Ohio, USA)

Business experience
2005- Representative Director of Elsevier Japan K.K.
2000- Associate Sales Director of Elsevier Japan K.K.
1998-99 Marketing Manager for Education Industry Asia Pacific, IBM Asia Pacific Service Corporation (dispatched from IBM Japan)
1989-97 Senior Client Representative for Higher Education (Sales Department), IBM Japan K.K.
1986-89 Opinion Leaders Programs, Communication Department, IBM Japan K.K.
1977-84 Para-legal Researcher, Anderson, Mori & Rabinowitz (an international law firm)

Research interests
Support for researchers in Japan to better meet research requirements from accelerating science by providing with innovative and advanced open platforms for academic information. Also interested in cross-cultural communications personally.

2-1. Elsevier - Open to Accelerate Science

Hello. My name is Ritsuko Miki and I am the Representative Director of Elsevier Japan K.K. On behalf of the Social Science Publishing Group of Elsevier, I am greatly honored to be here on the podium today for celebrating the inaugural publication of *CCS* and being a part of this international symposium. The time I have today is limited, but I would like to talk about the academic information environments that Elsevier thinks about providing and moving ahead into the future of the academic information environments we would like to provide you with.

Elsevier has a long history of scientific publishing

First, a brief description of Elsevier's history. It first began when Lowys Elsevier started a university publishing organization at the University of Leiden in Holland in 1580. After that, it started functioning as an enterprise in its current form in the year 1880. Thus, it has a long history, and it has published the papers of such historically outstanding authors as Galileo, Erasmus, Descartes, and Alexander Fleming among others.

Talking about Elsevier today, it receives about 800,000 article submissions every year. From among those, about 300,000 articles are published by Elsevier each year. There are about 500,000 referees who are involved in that process. Since we publish approximately 300,000 articles out of 800,000 submitted, the acceptance rate averages 37%. Monitoring the acceptance rate level closely, we believe this is related to quality, and so we think this is a very important number as it offers good indication of quality.

Size of Elsevier Operations in Journal Publishing Cycle

Also, there are about 7,000 editors, and they each have editorial boards consisting of about ten members, so there are about 70,000 editorial board members.

Talking about the use of the contents published and their users, we have about 12 million researchers around the world who are accessing Elsevier articles on a daily basis, and this service is provided to more than 4,500 organizations in more than 180 countries.

Last year, in 2009, article downloads from ScienceDirect have exceeded 500 million in 2009 and 600 million in 2010 per year respectively. ScienceDirect is Elsevier's electronic journal collection. ScienceDirect is a database of over 10 million articles that is increasing every year and every day.

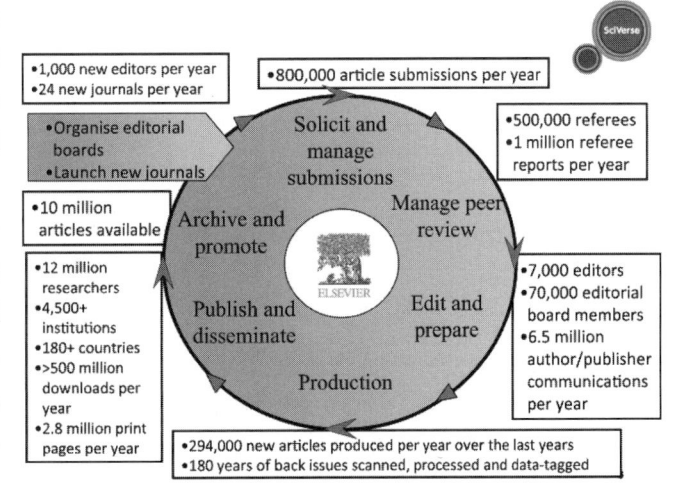

Figure 1: Size of Elsevier Operations in Journal Publishing Cycle

Article Share

We publish new journals every year. Elsevier is among the major commercial publishers such as Wiley-Blackwell, Springer, Taylor&Francis, and Wolters Kluwer. Of course the academic societies in eg US and UK shown here play a very important role as well. In the category of 'others' there are about 2,000 (some says as many as 4,000 or 5,000) publishers. Elsevier academic publications cover Life Sciences, Health Sciences, Materials Science, Engineering, Chemistry, Physics, Math and Computer Science, and the Social Sciences are all important, and in recent years the rapid growth in numbers of articles in Environmental Science has been quite remarkable.

Journal Coverage of Two Major Elsevier Products

Next, looking at Elsevier's two major products, one is the electronic journal collection, ScienceDirect which has the full-text articles. ScienceDirect includes only the articles that are published by Elsevier.

And then there is SCOPUS, which is a secondary information database providing abstracts of world literature as a whole but extensively covering all peer-reviewed articles that are published by other publishers than Elsevier. These two 64 products, ScienceDirect and SCOPUS, at present share a single platform, and this platform is called SciVerse.

SciVerse ScienceDirect - Continuously Expanding Contents & Usage

The contents and usage of SciVerse Science Direct show an upward trend, you can see that all three graphs show an upward trend, and the one on the left shows the number of articles each year published by Elsevier, which as I said before has reached just about 300,000. The middle graph shows the number of articles cumulatively uploaded on SciVerse Science Direct. This has exceeded 10 million articles to date. The graph all the way to the right shows usage, the number of downloads.

Roughly 600 million, that is 600 million articles a year that are being downloaded around the world, which means, calculating simply, that more than 18 articles are being downloaded every second somewhere in the world from the SciVerse ScienceDirect.

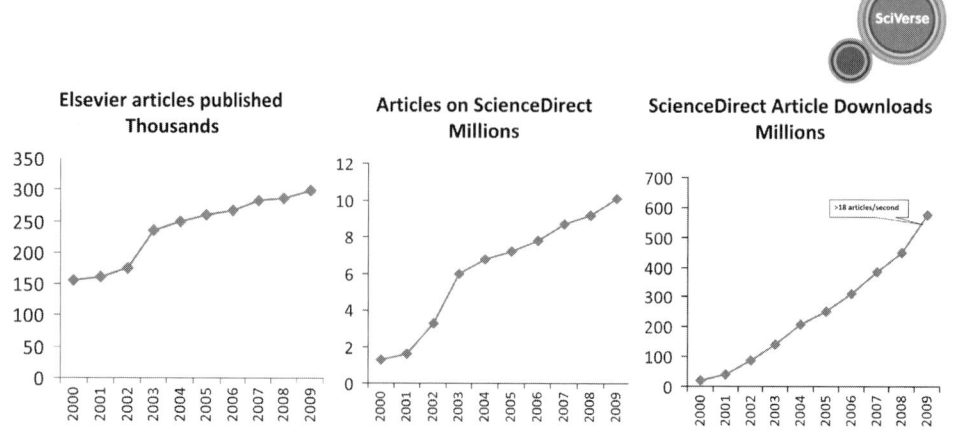

Figure 2: SciVerse ScienceDirect - Continuously Expanding Contents & Usage

SciVerse Scopus-The World Biggest Abstract & Reference DB

In SciVerse Scopus, which does not include the main text bodies, there are 43 million records. This covers the contents of 18,000 different journals. Many different disciplines are covered, Medicine, Chemistry, Physics, Engineering, Life Sciences, and of course Social Science, in which 5,300 journals are covered. Recently the contents of journals in the Humanities are also being posted, and SciVerse SCOPUS is planning to move further in that direction. However, the necessary requirement is that the journals be peer reviewed.

Research more exciting but more challenging

Here are the results of a question asked of 6,300 knowledge workers: what takes up more of your time, information gathering or information analysis? The reply was that they spend an average of 6.5 hours per week on information gathering, and 5.8 hours on analysis. In other words, more time is spent in gathering information than in analysing and using it.

Changing Face of Contents By Article of the Future & Enjoying More Benefits of Online Dissemination

In order to change this situation and to provide a scholarly information environment where people can spend more time on analysis, we at Elsevier have initiated innovations in a range of products. I would like to describe a few of these innovations:

One is in the formatting of our electronic journal material on SciVerse Science Direct. Up until now, when you use SciVerse ScienceDirect, the interface of the contents has not been different from that of the paper version, but in an experimental project we are now carrying out, first of all we are using a tab structure. We are creating tabs for the parts of an article such as the Abstract, Introduction, Result, Discussion, etc., so that without scrolling up and down on the pages, by clicking the tab you can jump to the part of the article you want to read. We are making this kind of structure.

Another innovation, one that has been applied to *CCS*, is Article Highlights. In addition to the existing abstracts, we have added an additional part where we have the highlights written out in several bullet points to aid on-line retrieval.

And then another innovation, which is also being applied to *CCS* (and this is rapidly being used more and more), is multimedia such as the on-line presentation of video materials. At the same time as that, up until now the article one searched for was the end destination of the information.

We are now planning to attach links to the articles so that you can jump to new relevant information from them. For example, here is information on the author, and by clicking on the author, more information about the author comes up, such as how many documents, references and 65 citations this author has. In case of this author, there are 77 documents, 1,775 references, 2001 citations… such information allows the reader to quickly know how far an author has accomplished and accumulated research. Also you can find a place here and there in a searched article to be linked to relevant information via keywords selected.

Another Example for Online Benefits – Most Prolific Authors

Another thing is "Most Prolific Authors". By using the application of "Most Prolific Authors", you will immediately see a ranking list of authors who have written most articles including the keywords selected by you, which helps you to know whose articles you may be interested in reading next regarding keywords selected by you.

Elsevier's High-Profile Journals & SciVal Spotlight

Finally, I would like to talk about social science publications. Elsevier has a number of high profile journals, such as *CITIES, HABITAT INTERNATIONAL, WORLD DEVELOPMENT, LANDSCAPE AND URBAN PLANNING*, etc.

And in the meantime, we have a new product called SciVal Spotlight. SciVal Spotlight is a tool that visualizes the performance of the research activities of a particular organization or a particular country. SciVal Spotlight tells you where your organization or country is strong based upon articles published for a particular year; the information includes where the organization or country has competencies also in multi-disciplinary areas. As shown in the pie chart of distribution of strengths by subject areas of Japan as compared to US and UK, the yellow color representing the subject area of the Social Sciences is smaller than in the other two countries.

As a Japanese who works for Elsevier Japan, I am hoping that you will enlarge this Social Sciences section more. From these charts apparently, we can see that UK is strong in the Social Sciences. Consequently, we are hoping that *CCS* will act as a pioneer in expanding publication of Social Sci-

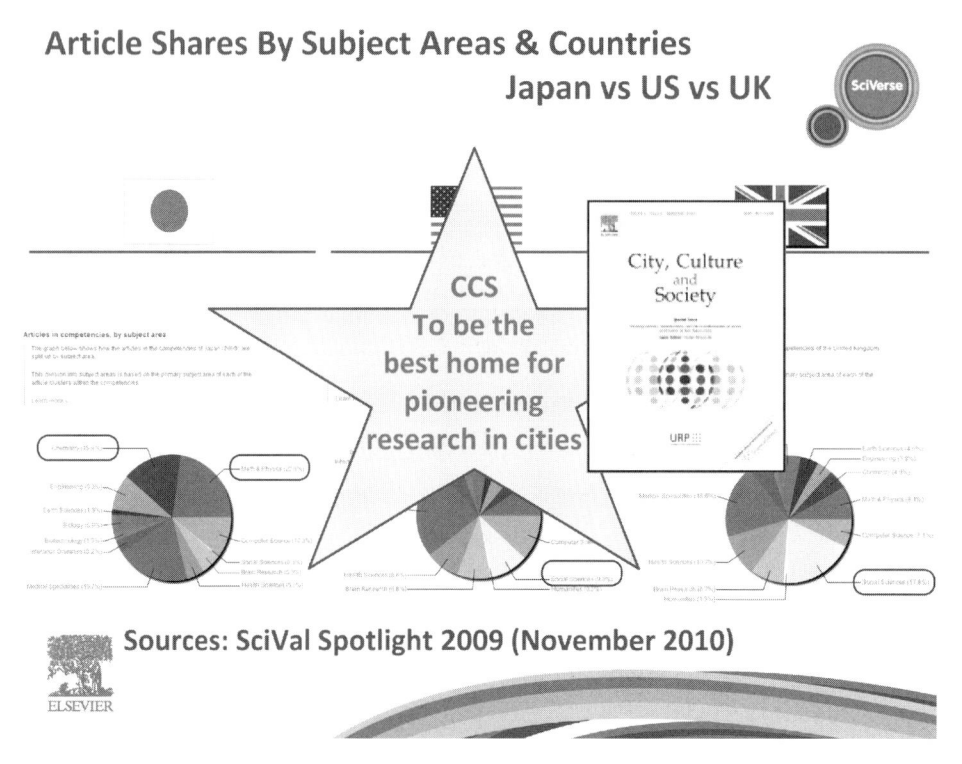

Figure 3: Article Shares By Subject Areas & Countries : Japan vs US vs UK

ences publication in Japan. Of course, *CCS* is an international journal, and not just about Japan, but I hope that it will also play a role in stimulating the Social Sciences in Japan.

Now I sincerely look forward to Osaka City University continuously working to make *CCS* a 'rising-star' journal that will contribute to bigger visibility of Social Science and enhance the reputation of Elsevier publications for quality. The fact that you at Osaka City University are successfully holding this symposium now is promising, which is and will be effective in advancing the disseminating power of *CCS* and directly contributing to the world of research, and we at Elsevier are very pleased to continue to assist Osaka City University in every way in their challenges. Thank you very much.

Hiroshi Okano: Thank you very much. When I see this kind of ranking, it becomes very clear what the social sciences will have to do to raise the ranking of the university, but in this session today, rather than talking about where a particular university may rank and so forth, I think what we need to talk more about is how can *CCS* increase the various benefits it will provide to people who are actually engaged in the practical work, and what we at the Urban Research Plaza need to do to help that happen, so I hope you will discuss this a bit more from that perspective.

François Colbert

Current academic position
Full Professor, Marketing and Chair in Arts Management Carmelle and Rémi-Marcoux,
HEC Montréal

Academic experience
1998- Founding Editor, International Journal of Arts Management, HEC Montréal
1991- Full Professor, HEC Montréal
1991- Chair in Arts Management Carmelle and Rémi-Marcoux, HEC Montréal
1991-96 Vice-rector Faculty Affairs, HEC Montréal
1985-91 Chair of the Marketing Department, HEC Montréal
1983- Associate professor, HEC Montréal
1976- Assistant professor, HEC Montréal
1973- Senior Lecturer, HEC Montréal

Research interests
Marketing Culture and the Arts

Major articles and papers
Beyond Branding: Contemporary Marketing Challenges for Arts Organizations, *International Journal of Arts Management*, vol.12 no 1, 2009, p.14-20.

Product-Country Images in the Arts: A Multi-Country Study, A. d'Astous, Z. Giraud Voss, F. Colbert, A. Carù, M. Caldwell et F. Courvoisier, *International Marketing Review*, vol. 25, no 4, 2008, p. 379-403.

The Effectiveness of Art Venues Sponsorship: An Attribution Perspective, F.A. Carrillat, A. d'Astous, F. Colbert, *Journal of Sponsorship*, Vol. 1, no 3, 2008, p.274–285.

Consumers' Receptivity to Brand Extension and Co-Branded Products in Arts Organizations, A. d'Astous, F. Colbert, M. Fournier, *Journal of Service Marketing Research*, Vol.21, no 4, 2007, p. 231-240.

Marketing Culture and the Arts, 3rd Edition, F. Colbert and al., HEC Press, 2007, (currently in 10 languages and two in translation).

2-2. Academic Research in Arts Management

Summary

The cultural sector is recognized as important by societies and by international bodies such as UNESCO. Its importance is primarily about the work of arts of course, but it also is about social cohesion and economic contribution to a given society. While market surveys were conducted since the sixties, academic research is a relative new field when compared to older discipline like economics, mathematics or philosophy.

Before 1980, very few works were published by academics in management or marketing of the arts and culture. This being said, economists already had their research Conference in the late seventies and there were economists that tried to understand the market dynamics of the fine arts (painting, sculpture).

The first articles published by academics in marketing or management appeared only in the eighties though. Since then, a research Conference is held every second year since 1991 (AIMAC), this Conference was founded by professor François Colbert from HEC Montréal as well as the 'International Journal of Arts Management', the major publication in the sector of arts management. Now the field is growing fast, more and more papers are published. This is a healthy sign since the arts and culture sector faces an oversupply of works of art, oversupply that is challenging public bodies that are trying to help artists. On the positive side though, this proliferation of works of art is presenting to the consumer more that he or she could attend or buy in any given year, giving them a vast choice of outings.

The management and marketing principles and the knowledge that it brings is of utmost importance to help cultural organizations to survive and more, to do well for the benefit of the artist who is at the center of any strategy of commercialization in the cultural field.

Thank you very much for letting me talk about whatever I like here. So, my presentation… I will talk about *CCS*, but of course from the standpoint of our experience with the International Journal of Arts Management, so I will start by defining what we mean by arts management, and then the place arts management can have in *CCS*, and then maybe positioning *CCS* within other journals in arts management, and maybe also talk about what we do at the HEC very briefly.

Arts Management: a new field

Arts management is about the management of arts organizations. It is about the production and dissemination of works of art. According to my own definition of the sector I can divide the sector in three in parts.

1. Arts

First, I consider the art itself, high art if you wish, which is the production and conservation of prototypes. In the performing arts, in the heritage sector, we work with prototypes, every new show is a prototype and not reproduce.

2. Cultural Industries

The cultural industries are those which are reproducing prototypes : films, publishing novels, or recording an artist.

3. Medias

Lastly, we have to include also the media because the medias are producing and disseminating at the same time. They disseminate films, they disseminate music, they disseminate all kinds of cultural products.

At this point, I would like to make a distinction. I use the word "art." A lot of you probably use the word "culture." In fact, culture has two meanings. It can be defined as the equivalent of art, but it also has an anthropological meaning, the language we speak, how we consider the world, how we define ourselves, and so on. So in this presentation, I am talking about art, not about culture in its anthropological sense. The arts organizations tend to concentrate in large cities and tend to regroup in certain districts. In Montréal for example, there is a district called the "Quartier des spectacles" where you will find most of the theaters, the museums and the galleries. Large cities attract artists.

When we are talking about art, we can use different perspectives. Let's name three. We can consider art as a religion or a substitute for religion. In the artistic discourse, one can perceive that people talk about art as if it was a religious encounter. Often, if you replace art with religion and artists by priests, you will see that it works. It can also be defined as education, as a complement of formal education, like museums for example (which is probably the best example). Lastly, it can simply be entertainment, leisure activities based on consumer tastes and preferences.

So in arts management, if we are talking about the management of arts organizations where we are talking about the different disciplines that are used in managing a museum, or a film production, or a movie theater; it is then about marketing, it is about strategic management, about project management, human resources management. The other distinction I would like to make is between what we could call an elite art, and a popular art. If we consider the perspective of religion or education, usually it is considered or defined in an elite perspective (high art), it is usually the kind of art that interests the elite of a society, meaning people who are well-educated. On the contrary, popular art attracts everybody in the society. Popular art, in terms of transmitting social norms or the culture of a people, is important. That's why UNESCO for example has a mandate to protect the different cultures. Protecting them against what is considered as the mass production of an American entertainment machine.

If we are referring to the theme of this symposium, we may ask the question "can the arts organizations that are dealing with works of art, can they have a role to play in a city for inclusion of people or for urban regeneration?" This constitute a new perspective even if it is not the essential role of artists and arts organizations in a city, but of course they have a role, even if it is only as the vehicle of what the culture of a society is.

Arts Management and CCS

The "culture" part of the title of CCS could refer to the management of the arts, that is the way I will consider it with this part of my presentation.

One thing we need to know about the arts field is that it is a field that is oversupplied. It is a field where everybody can call itself an artist and form a new company. We can easily say that the supply surpasses the demand by 10, 20, or 30 times depending on which art form we are talking about. So it is a really crowded market. Defenders of the arts have adopted either the 'creative nation' or the 'creative city' in trying to make the case for more public support. It doesn't mean that they cannot contribute to the efforts of making a creative city, but it is not their main task. The cultural sector or the arts sector is a network of institutions both private and public. And of course they make an impact, they produce economic movements if you like. The traditional view of using arts organizations and arts production as a case for cities started with the tourism dimension. Of course, tourists are interested in cities mostly for the culture or the arts they can find in them. The arts and culture can also be used for branding a city. And we see more cities that are trying to brand themselves around art and culture. Cities are in competition with each other for tourism. Using art and culture can served as a good positioning statement to get an edge over competing cities.

Using art in a city for the development of a this city is another way of going. Let's use the example of Bogota. The mayor of the city decided to build public libraries in poorer parts of the city and considered using them as multi-cultural centers, actually as a meeting point. Those public libraries are doing a lot for the fabric of the neighbourhoods. So yes, it is possible to look at arts as a way of integrating people.

CCS, International Journal of Arts Management (IJAM), Other Journals

Any journal to succeed has to find a niche, has to find a clear focus so that it will do something that is different than any other Journal. The analysis that I did before launching the International Journal of Arts Management what was about competition; in this field of arts management there are several refereed journals. The Journal of Arts Economics, which deals with the economic aspects, pure economics, and the other one is Cultural Policy, another aspect of the cultural sector. There was nothing on the market addressing the management of arts organizations per se. It is exactly the niche that we decided to target. It is a success because there is a community of researchers interested by this specific field. We also have built the journal around a scientific Conference called the "International Conference of Arts and Cultural Management" that I started in 1991; the journal was launched in 1998. Both are working together, and articles are coming from the community, the researchers in arts management. The next conference is next July in Belgium, and we have received almost 300 abstracts of which we will choose 150. So as we can see, it is about a niche, about finding a niche and about being different from any other products in a way.

It is true that artists and arts organizations are located in cities around a meeting point which usually is downtown. Discussions of the place of the arts and art organizations in the city don't fit with the mandate of IJAM as such but I think it fits in the kind of journal that *CCS* is.

The International Cluster for the Management of Arts and Culture at HEC Montréal

The *International Journal of Arts Management* fits in a larger portfolio of products that HEC Montréal currently offering. We are involved in research and teaching of arts management. Among the Faculty, there are 20 of us researching and teaching arts management. We are running programs a master's programs in arts management and a PhD program with a structured field in *Arts, Cultural Industries and Media Management*. The Cluster is also comprised of a Book Series in Arts Management, on line seminars and short term intensive seminars for Arts Managers.

To conclude, arts and culture is an essential component in a city. It has always been like this for centuries. Artists have always gathered in cities on which they have had a profound impact. Arts management is about good management, and the marketing of the organizations that are trying to disseminate as much as possible the work of artists in a crowded, oversupplied market. *CCS* can certainly play a role in disseminating research about the place of the arts and culture in the city, and the role they can play in those cities. Thank you.

Hiroshi Okano: Thank you very much François. In your slide, 60% is from the academic area and 33% for company people who write some papers, and 7% is from the government. Maybe later we will talk about that. I think that balance is very good. What did you do? What kind of the activities did you do with company people, maybe museums or the cirque de soleil, that is a well-known circus, or the local government or some international government, I would like to ask you later.

Andy C Pratt

Current academic position
Professor, Culture, Media and Economy,
Head, Department of Culture, Media and Creative Industries,
King's College London

Academic experience
1989- Ph.D., Department of Geography, University of Exeter
1981- B.Sc., (Hons) Geography, Huddersfield Polytechnic

2009- Professor, Media, Culture and Economy, King's College London
2006-2009 Reader, Urban Cultural Economy, London School of Economics and Political Science
1998-05 Senior Lecturer, Human Geography, London School of Economics and Political Science
1992-97 Lecturer, Human Geography, London School of Economics and Political Science
1991-92 Lecturer, Bartlett School of Planning, University College London
1990-91 Senior Lecturer, Local Economic Development and Planning, Department of planning, Coventry University
1988-90 Lecturer, Planning, Department of Planning, Coventry University
1987-88 Lecturer, Department of Geography, North Staffordshire University
1986-87 Lecturer, Department of Planning, Coventry University
1982-83 Research Assistant, Department of Geography, University of Leicester

Research interests
Cultural and creative industries
Cultural industries; space and place
Urbanisation and culture
Globalisation and global cities
Organisation of work in the cultural economy
Cultural Policy; Urban Policy; Cultural Industries Policies
'Creative' Cities

Major articles and papers
2009 *Creativity, innovation and the cultural economy*. Routledge, London (with Jeffcutt. P)
2001 *The secret life of cities: social reproduction and everyday life,* Prentice Hall, London (with H. Jarvis, and P.C-C. Wu)
2009 Urban regeneration: from the arts 'feel good' factor to the cultural economy. A case study of Hoxton, London. *Urban Studies* 44.6: pp1041-61

2-3. Journals in the Age of Limited Attention Span

Summary

My intervention will reflect upon the role and potential of the academic journal in today's knowledge environment in general, and in relation to *'City, Culture and Society'* in particular.

I have had several conversations about what I was going to say: I am glad that it is following on very well from what the two presenters here before me have said and what I was recommended to have a look at, which is looking at the research horizons in a way that this all fits together.

I want to talk about what directions and what the focus is and suggest some potential areas to generate new articles and new directions for the research for *CCS* might be. I think it is interesting to reflect upon the development of this journal and the precise moment that it has happened. I would see it conceptually as the intersection of a number of bodies of study. I think each of these bodies of study have undergone changes in recent years. It seems to me that this is a great opportunity for a new journal to capitalize on a number of emerging trends.

City, Culture and Society: the field

I think that in urban studies, it is fair to say that there have been a number of years where urban studies has fallen out of favor to a certain extent. It is not as popular as it was in the 1960s and 1970s for example, when it really came into its own. It has been a period where there has been a decline in interest. Certainly one of the things that I was doing at the London School of Economics, when I taught there, was setting up a master's program called 'Cities, Space and Society' which is almost the same as this journal. One of the things that we had identified as an opportunity and a need was a newly emerging intersection of interest between the economic and the social and the cultural, as they came together, as was exemplified by cities. I think urban studies has been changing, and what we are now witnessing is a reinvigoration of this field.

Cultural analysis has been through a period when it itself has become dominant in much of the social sciences and across the arts in the humanities as well. There has been a huge interest in the culture of everything. Cultural analysis, etc. In particular, the latest shift over the last 10 years or so is the 'spatial turn': the spatial inflection of cultural analysis. So again, this is a really good opportunity for this journal to capitalize on that. But I think also, and particularly what François mentioned, the policy and management issues are also now engaging very strongly with culture. So cultural analysis has been expanded quite dramatically, not only to include the broader range of public policy but also issues about governance and management, management of culture, and also the culture of management as well. This is another area that is growing and developing.

Social and economic analyses are also undergoing huge changes. I mean, of course, traditional economic analysis that has been the bedrock of this area. There are some really interesting changes that are happening in economic analysis at the moment that are leading to the questioning of the traditional borders and concepts. Whether the borders of what is economic and what is not economic have been conceptually too firm in the past. I think the most interesting areas are those at the boundaries, and I think culture, lying between the economic and the non-economic, the formal and informal, is one of those areas. So we have three fields that are coming together which offer very interesting intersections that aren't really dealt with by other journals. This is a great opportunity for the journal and its development.

Conceptual Challenges

What I want to say are two broad things. The first is that there are a number of particular challenges, eight at least, and I will talk about those in a moment. But first I want to point to a number of conceptual challenges. This is an area of study, because it is to an extent a synthesis or coming together of a number of areas, that generates problems in terms of epistemology and ontology, in terms of concepts and theories. But in this field it is not a self reflecting abstract theoretical debate, but one that is engaged with both empirical and theoretical domains.

Over half the world lives in cities, more than half of that –the growing part – lives in non-western/Northern cities.

An example is an empirical fact but also a profound epistemological and ontological one. As we have heard this morning, of course a well-known fact is that populations are moving to cities. However, and this is the key point, the fact is that half of the world is living in cities, more than half of those are living in cities of the Global South, not the Global North. And much of urban theory is theory generated in and about the Global North. Therefore, we have a problem in explaining the actually existing cities we have now and in the future, and I don't think that we will be well-prepared for that using the existing theoretical framework. There is a challenge to those norms because they were developed and refined in the particular historical circumstances and economic circumstances that pertained in Europe and North America.

Theory is dominated by an Anglo-American lens/historical perspective and hegemony. There are a number of challenges there; for publishers this works well, because there is an international audience rather than the traditional Anglo-American audience. So this domination by the Anglo-Americans lens is an historical perspective which I think is changing, it opens up new opportunities.

The default urban narrative is of the winners. The default narrative, the way that stories, whether they are scientific or not, are told of cities, have tended to be of those that have won, those that have been successful. Increasingly we are getting alternative stories, stories that are both of the losers but also stories that are more complicated and cut across these traditional boundaries. There are four points here:

1. Neglect of the informal and the not for profit. I think one of the most interesting boundaries that we have already mentioned is the boundary of the formal and informal, the for-profit and non-profit, and this is precisely the field of the global south and cities in the global south. If you don't understand the informal and the not-for-profit, you are

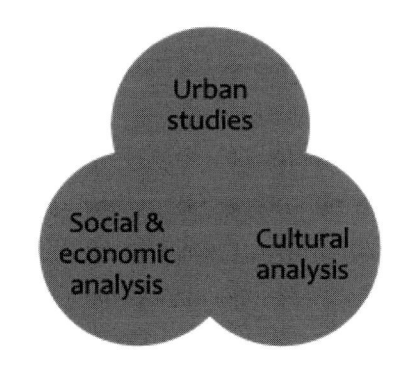

Figure 1: *City, Culture and Society:* the field

not going to understand those cities and the sort of interaction in those cities.

2. Focus on pre-defined cities, not flows, nor 'making up' cities. Second, there is the focus on predefining cities, and traditionally in Europe and America, ideas of what cities are and what they are not. Academics spend a lot of time talking about these issues. One of the things that has opened up, has been about issues of flows across boundaries and across cities. And here we have flows that are not just across cities but across the world. Those issues about flows, whether they deal with migration, ideas, or knowledge, have got to be the new locus of analysis rather than just on the static things.

3. Obsession with Quantities, not qualities. Traditionally in the past we have had an obsession with quantities. This goes for social science as a whole, and I think this is now the age of qualities. This is what we need to understand in the new emerging cities and the transformation of cities. So we need quantities but we need qualities even more.

4. Limitations of the neo-classical economic field. And I think we have a number of limitations that have been set by particular paradigms of neoclassical economics that need challenging, only in part of what one might say, because of the categories that that field of study is based upon, the firm, and this narrow definition of the economic certainly are not the best tools when faced with a world that is based upon the non-economic or the informal and the boundaries of these activities.

Eight future challenges

This leads me to talk about a number of future challenges, and for that purpose I have just divided them into eight. I am sure that we can all come up with more, but the new research and the new topics that are likely to find a space in this journal, and those that the editors ought to chase after to find space for within the pages of this journal, will lie in a number of areas; my list this is as follows:

1. Global cities. I think the first is global cities, because global cities have been a hugely successful paradigm for research, very, very successful. However I think it is time for a refreshing, renewing in many senses, and of course not only for the reason that the global cities paradigm was based upon cities dominated by financial services, and that industry has had a few problems in recent years, so I think there is a questioning of exactly whether that is the only show in town. And clearly, if I just look to places that I'm working on at the moment in London, the 3rd most important economic sector of the city of London, which on all rankings is one of the top global cities, is the cultural sector. And this has been a sector generally not regarded as being of economic importance. So, financial services, yes, but the cultural sector is a player here, if that were the only reason, but then there are lots of other reasons one might want to consider it. And I think the work on global cities again has focused on global cities in the north and actually the largest cities in the world we all know are actually in the global south, so again there is a need for reinvigoration of these approaches as the right framework.

2. Economies. I have already mentioned about the economic. We do need to talk about economies, varieties of economies, how economies are constituted, to look at different ways in which they are practiced in different places in the world, and how that gives rise to quite different formulations of urban economies.

3. Work-Life. The third area which I want to point out is the changing nature of work. We have already had Lily Kong giving us a very good presentation on some of the changing dimensions of pre-

carity, but I think more generally, one of the things which is most striking is the changing relationship between, if you like, work and non-work. While non-work might be informal, it might be absolutely the thing that supports work. You cannot separate them out, but also the increasing intersection of work life and non-work life and in the way that it spills over into all sorts of activities. These things have changed, and these are reflected in how we organize our life in cities in terms of transportation systems, in terms of interconnection. So work life also has a manifestation in terms of the built form we create to accommodate this new work life bounds.

4. Built form. As we know, most cities have been developed on the model of Fordist division of work life, which is not the one we are living in, let alone the one that Lily was talking about. Built form has to respond in some way to that as well.

5. Making places. And all of this comes together in terms of the fact that we are engaged in making cities, and remaking cities, in quite different ways in a quite different environment. The agenda which people are talking about, the trans-local captures this quite well, of new forms of interaction that aren't necessarily international, that aren't based on nation states but are based on the multiplicity of locals and the interaction between those local spaces.

6. Post financial cities. Very briefly, I have already mentioned that we have the challenge here of the postfinancial-services- dominated city. What is that city going to look like? What role for the cultural economy is there? Some people are hoping for very much, but what will that new configuration be?

7. Governance. Very briefly, there are issues also about how cities are to be governed. One of the challenges is about more open cities, about more intersected cities, the cities of flows that are no longer contiguous, that are no longer bounded by the administrative lines on the map. This presents huge problems for governance. There are also huge problems because many of the organizations that constitute the cultural sector don't look like those formal hierarchical organizations that could be governed by a city government or an Asian state, just the problems such as Lily was talking about.

8. Social exclusion. New forms of governance are required, and that is a real challenge for interacting with a policy community and why the policy community needs to know about the current research in this area, because those are going to be future challenges.

All of this comes together in terms of how we engage with issues of social exclusion as well, and in the post-Washington Consensus Era, hopefully, of post neo-liberalism era, then what form will the cities take? How about those that are not included in the vision of the successful? How will they manage, because they are also part of the city, and if we look at the cultural sphere, we see that there are vital parts that keep the legitimate cultural sphere going. These are all topics that should find a home within the pages of *CCS*.

There are a number of other issues that we could point to. That is just eight topics for discussion, but I think they are at the cutting edge of research, and all point in a positive direction for the content generation of this new journal at this point in time. Thank you.

Hiroshi Okano: Thank you, Andy. You have pointed out the theories dominated by an Anglo-American lens and historical perspective. So, maybe this point is very important for looking at some other areas for instance.

Hyun Bang Shin

Current academic position
Lecturer, Department of Geography and Environment, The London School of Economics and Political Science

Academic experience
2006- Ph.D., Social Policy (Urban and Housing Studies), The London School of Economics and Political Science
2000- M.Sc., The London School of Economics and Political Science
1994- B.Sc., Seoul National University

2008- Lecturer, Department of Geography and Environment, The London School of Economics and Political Science
2007-08 Postdoctoral Research Fellow, White Rose East Asia Centre, University of Leeds

Research interests
Urban renewal and gentrification processes
Urban governance and community participation
Housing and social change
Urban heritage conservation
Mega-events

Major articles and papers
Urban Conservation and Revalorisation of Dilapidated Historic Quarters: the case of Nanluoguxiang in Beijing, *Cities*, 27, Supplement 1, pp.S43-S54, 2010
Residential Redevelopment and Entrepreneurial Local State: The implications of Beijing's shifting emphasis on urban redevelopment policies, *Urban Studies*, 46, 13, pp.2815-2839, 2009
Property-based Redevelopment and Gentrification: The case of Seoul, South Korea, *Geoforum*, 40, 5, pp.906-917, 2009

2-4. The Rise of China Inc. and Challenges for the Next Generation of Urban Scholars

Summary

During the last ten years or so, the number of academic papers on China's urban transformation has been exponentially growing. About twenty years ago, what goes on in mainland China hardly contributed to academic debates on cities, and now the China factor is becoming increasingly influential in urban studies. Nevertheless, debates on the nature and direction of changes in urban China tend to be confined within 'China studies' without making connection with what goes on outside China. The speed of urban change also posits challenges to urban researchers who struggle with 'fact-finding' missions. In this regard, the paper revisits the current status of urban studies in relation to contemporary urban agenda for the next generation of urban scholars with interests in mainland China as well as East Asia as a whole. In particular, the paper addresses three key aspects: (1) the narrow focus of on-going research in China studies: (2) the high entry barrier of conducting field research in China for overseas scholars, (3) the absence of comparative studies as well as comparative perspectives.

Neoliberalism and China

Well I would like to start by thanking Professor Masayuki Sasaki and the journal *CCS* and all the colleagues of Osaka City University for inviting me here today. It is quite an honor and a pleasure to participate in this symposium. My title has also changed slightly, but I would like to address the issue of the trends for the next generation of urban scholars by linking the discussion with neoliberal urbanization.

Today I would like to discuss this from the viewpoint of what China studies can contribute to urban studies and what needs to be done in order to broaden and deepen our understanding.

I will look at my own thought by referring to my own areas of recent research, the issue of neoliberal urbanization in the Chinese context.

In recent years, it is interesting to see the emerging amount of literature on neoliberal practices in Mainland China and to me this is quite intriguing given the fact that neoliberalism has been inherent in capitalist strategies to avoid its crises, especially since the demise of the general welfare state and the Fordist accumulation within it.

However the emerging literature on neoliberalism in China does not so much engage with investigating the neoliberalisation of China, but with the identification of neoliberal elements in China. In short, the discussions do not directly address the fundamental question that was once raised by an American anthropologist, Donald Nonini, who was asking the question, "Is China becoming neoliberal?" In many instances the emerging body of literature on neoliberalism in China tends to bypass this question and simply assume that neoliberalsm is only present in the contemporary globalizing world with the hegemony of the American economy order led by the US, and that assumption leads to the conclusion that China, as a rapidly globalizing country, must also be neoliberal. The essence of the discussion about how and in what process neoliberalsm has come to dominate Chinese cities is quite damaging. And this academic shortcoming will plant a serious methodological error that can be seen in other economic debates where advocates' specific theories are important from one context to another.

Neoliberalisation as an analytical framework

Well, if you will allow me, let me first make a brief comment about what neoliberalist urbanization or neoliberalisation means as an analytical framework. It should be quickly noted that neoliberal urbanization does not suggest that neoliberalism is an external force or extra-local project imposed upon a territorial space at various geographical scales.

Neoliberalsim is an ideology aiming at the principles of free market principles and state retrenchment, private appropriated institutions, and self-interest and the reserved interests of reasonable individuals. But neoliberal urbanisation in practice is a path-dependent project, built on an existing inherent institutional landscape and regulatory frameworks. So therefore, the analytical view is opposed to an over-generalized account of a monolithic and omnipresent neoliberalism while at the same time, avoiding excessive concrete and contingent analysis of local neoliberal strategies.

The tricky issue that has sometimes tainted urban studies of the Global South in particular, however, stems from this very statement. That is, the notion of neoliberalism as an omnipresent being, that neoliberalism has penetrated all the nation states, is still influencing researchers' thoughts. Jamie Peck and his colleagues in 2009 conclude that cities have become strategic sites of unfolding neoliberal urbanism. This, however, does not necessarily suggest that all cities on the globe experience neoliberalisation. While the global integration of exploitative transnational capitalism makes it difficult for any individual city to stay out of its influence, it needs care not to treat the process of local neoliberalisation as a homogenizing, universal process.

But, neoliberal urbanisation thesis takes…

But neoliberal urbanization in the understanding of Jamie Peck and his colleagues occurs in the context of the post Keynesian and post Fordist world of Western cities.

Have the political neoliberalization principles of a particular type of government restructuring, regulatory frameworks and institutions of configuration, been substantially different from those experienced in cities in the global south? From the works of insightful critiques that we now have come to know, we have come to understand that urbanization and urbanism in the global south in particular play out in very innovative ways different from the urbanism dominated by post industrial cities.

Well, a neoliberal urbanization thesis also takes the post-industrial transformation of Western cities at the centre of its discussion. Well, it is also evident that not all cities in the Global South and the Global North have been positioned in the same manner. They are essentially exposed to differentiated challenges and uneven global development. It is therefore essential to discuss the extent to which cities in the Global South are going through a similar process and if they have become indeed neoliberal.

David Harvey: A brief history of neoliberalism

So let us now shift our attention back to China. When David Harvey's renowned book on this trend towards very fast-paced neoliberalism was first published in 2005, his claim that China is part of the global neoliberal order was received with much controversy, and this was created by the lack of argument in his book as to why China is neoliberal.

As Nonini pointed out in 2008, Harvey's notion of neoliberalism with Chinese characteristics has been proposed without hard evidence, and at best he mentioned that the post Mao reforms since the early 1980s, and I quote, "just happened to coincide with the turn to neoliberal solutions in Britain and United States." Similar quotes about the study of neoliberalism in China tend to dominate the recent literature, and one example can be seen in the work of George Lin who is a professor of the University of Hong Kong, writing in 2007 stating that, "the urban population size has expanded dramatically since the 1980s as the neoliberal state abandoned the Maoist approach of urban containment." But he doesn't really go into this deeply as to how this neoliberal state came about. And here is another example which is an article about the gated communities in Shanghai, which takes the view that, "the emergence of gated communities as the new middle-class landscapes of Shanghai reflects the spatial manifestation of neoliberal agendas." And from the author's point of view, the neoliberal agenda refers to the articulation of the politics of exclusion. But the author doesn't really go into the detail to elaborate how it is that China can exhibit neoliberal characteristics. And even though the paper goes on to note that the Chinese leadership has never experienced neoliberalism as an official ideology, all the author says, as with Harvey's claim, is that China has experienced a neoliberal turn.

Party-state in neoliberal Chinese cities?

So we have to be careful not to simplify the influence of global investment capital and transnational institutions in China's global economic integration.

We also have to pay attention to China's local conditions that interact with the external conditions. Neoliberalism as a regulatory reform project requires researchers to pay attention to the way in which the role of the state in China has been reshaped and how the state economy and state-society relations have changed in the reform process.

In order to delve more deeply, there are four aspects that I would like to touch upon. Given the time constraint, I will probably focus on the first two points: the nature of the party-state at any point of time in neoliberalism, and with the competition issue and the state monopoly.

For the first issue about the party-state, it will be necessary from my point of view, to discuss how neoliberalism fused with the authoritarian Chinese state, the state's party socialism as the governing ideology. There has been no academic consensus as to whether the Chinese state has become a capitalist state, and only a few critics will report that China is a capitalist state or only drawn to capitalism.

Given the fact that neoliberalism always made a political regulatory project with its ideological roots in classical liberal economics in order to address the expansion of Anglo-American economic models in the contemporary world, it is quite important to discuss the extent to which China has become neoliberal when its party-state has not committed fully to the neoliberal ideologies. Then there is a shift in urban governance and the role of the Communist Party of China.

In liberal democratic societies, where elections take place, and political elites get replaced once in a while, there is an oscillation between policies that accelerate or slow down neoliberal urbanisation. This of course depends largely on state-society and state-economy relations, and the stronger the social resistance is to neoliberal policies, the greater the chance that such policies are slowed down, are modified, or even are aborted. To this extent, the history of neoliberal urbanisation in postindustrial cities could be explained as the history of the neoliberal state, constantly engaging with the civil society and market participants to suppress and attain various movements that make change in the neoliberal order.

There is a limit that this line of argument can be applied to urban China, where civil society development is still at its infancy, the participation of the various specific civic organizations that exist in Mainland China occurs in invited political space and the country also displays a powerful presence of the Communist Party in every social, economic and political sphere. The argument can be made that there is a persistent fusion between the state and the economy with the communist polity acting as an intermediary of this fusion.

Competition versus state monopoly

For the second issue, competition and state monopolies, competition is at the heart of liberalism and capitalist accumulation.

And in China, it is doubtful that full-scale liberalization from all forms of necessary interventions is what the Chinese state is willing to concede. While the neoliberal goals are stated in the clear intention to give more power to the market and private sector, state intervention in China has been biased in favor of the state sector's interest.

Competitiveness seems to be treated as equal to the competiveness of China's state enterprises and the nation itself in the global economy, which is pretty much different from what we see in the global north. State monopolies still dominate various key sectors, and competition is a luxury for most private companies when they face state enterprises. And this has become evident now with the history of economic reforms in place over three decades in China since the 1970s, the importance of the state sector economy has not diminished, contrary to what critics used to prophesize in the 80s or 90s.

Conclusion

So if I may move now to the conclusion of the talk today, my talk today is based on the understanding of the emerging literature of the practices of neoliberalism in China's urbanization process, which has yet to fully engage with some substantial issues that we may have to closely examine. I would address the changing nature of the state economy and state-society relations, and it would be premature to argue that Chinese cities are neoliberal or neoliberalizing. The historic similarities of what has happened in China, at least on the surface, may lead some researchers to conclude they can mechanically apply the framework of neoliberal urbanization in the analysis of China's urban transformation.

And I would like to emphasize that this should be approached with great care. And as I have discussed today, there are few signs of the state losing its grip over businesses, rather, state control and the importance of the state sector in the economy continue to be prevalent. Any diversity of state – business relations would usually involve diversity within the state sector, and that is the situation I see happening in China.

It may be more appropriate to hypothesise

And in fact, and if I may propose so, it would be more appropriate to hypothesize that the global integration of the Chinese economy has meant a more statist developmental post-Maoist state cooperating with neoliberal capitalist states that hold the global hegemonic position in the world economy. The nature, characteristics, and degree of power practiced by the nation-state and some major actors will determine how global actors and institutions tend to influence the local environment.

And hence to my second hypothesis, it may be possible that neoliberalism has been received as a multi-scale experience, and a more statist developmental state at regional and national scales may coexist with more localized practices of neoliberalism in selective special economic zones, such as local cities like Shenzhen or Dongguan or Dalian in China. This may explain the emerging amount of academic literature that examines the signs of neoliberal changes in the state – societal relations in these cities.

The recent incidents of laborrelated unrest which you may have come across recently, and in South China where the Foxconn factories that used to make a lot of parts and products for Apple for instance, labor disputes in these factories are largely the result of neoliberal governing strategies that went too far in these areas. And these disputes have occurred mostly in selectively designated economic regions such as Shenzhen, and the way these disputes and strikes have been contained within foreign-invested companies demonstrated that China is trying to tame the neoliberal forces in order to promote gigantic capitalist accumulation based on the paternalistic and developmental state. This does not necessarily have to be neoliberal, as was the case with worker oppression in times of rapid urbanisation and economic growth under the South Korean developmental state.

Challenges for China urbanists

My last point here, which is also related to the future of *CCS* is that, what I would like to discuss here makes up the core of the challenges that lies in front of the next generation of urban China researchers as far as I am concerned and from my viewpoint. And with the rise of China within the world economy, the volume of research concerned with urban China has also exponentially increased, but with few exceptions, however, most of the research concepts have focused on empirical findings and their interpretations through the lenses of analytical frameworks that have developed out of the experiences of Western cities. And the lack of discussion of how neoliberalism has been domesticated within China's context, in urban study disciplines, is owing to the lack of critical reflection on the evolutionary trajectories of these analytical frameworks. For instead of taking theoretical assumptions in the existing China studies for granted, it may be the time to raise questions at the very foundation of Chinese urban studies and ask more fundamental questions about what is often assumed without verification. It is in this regard that I really welcome the launch of *CCS* for the URP at Osaka City University, and I hope the journal will be an excellent place for critical academic reflection on theorizing the urbanization experiences of Chinese cities as well as cities in the global south, which often lie outside the mainstream of urban studies.

As my concluding point is that out of 3.4 billion urban residents in the world, and that figure is from 2009, about 73% or 2.5 billion urban residents are living in less developed regions. And it is the lives of these urbanites, from my viewpoint, in the less developed regions, the lives of these residents in this area that we really know little about. Thank you very much for your attention.

Jung Duk Lim

Current academic position
Professor emeritus,
Pusan National University

Academic experience
Professor, Pusan National University
President, Pusan Development Institute
Professor, Wingate College (NC, USA)
Fellow, Population Institute, East-West Center (HI, USA)

Research interests
Industrial Organization
Urban studies
Creative economies, Creative industries
Cross-border regional cooperation

Major articles and papers
"The Causes of Social Capital in a Neighborhood Community Context," International Journal of Urban Sciences, 1-11, 6(1), (2002/01)

"The Restructuring of Pusan's Economy under The Current Economic Crisis," Asia Geography, PP.107-117, 19(1-2), (2000/01)

"Restructuring of Footwear Industry and Industrial Adjustment of Pusan," Environment and Planning A, Vol 26, (1994/05)

"Urban Growth and Industrial Restructuring : The Case of Pusan," Environment and Planning A, Vol 25, (1993/01)

2-5. Some Thoughts on Urban Studies Towards the Century of Cities

Thank you very much for inviting me to this important symposium on a very short notice. Today I would like to say some thoughts on urban studies, especially for the *CCS* or other works on creative economies, creative cities and creative industries.

Five questions on urban studies related to the Journal

Let me ask some questions on urban studies associated with creative city. I would like to raise these questions to all participants including those of you who are prominent scholars and specialists.

Firstly, the position (hierarchy) of a city. As far as I have observed, there have been no national or macroeconomic factors reflected in the analysis of creative cities. We know cities are important and cities are growing in terms of governance or status compared with the national economy. What I think is that a city is still subject to the national economy or to a national performance. Is a city able to surpass the nation, especially in the long run? In the short run, I think, a city is able to surpass the state or is superior to the national performance. However the question is on the availability in the long run. It may be an extreme question but could we imagine a declining nation with a growing city? Could it be possible? What I would like to emphasize is that we need to put the macro economy as a proposition in our analysis. Repeatedly we can hardly imagine a growing city in a shaky country economically as well as socially.

The second point is that we tend to forget about resource allocation in our analysis. What I mean is the ignorance on national, regional, and local resource allocation. That could be similar to the opportunity cost concept. As we put more resources into a specific field, the opportunity cost increases too. That is a very fundamental principle in the prism of economics. Let me take an example. I am absolutely in favor of social inclusion. The concept of social inclusion is very important to be a creative city in most cities in the world. My question is how could we distinguish it from a welfare state or welfare city? A welfare city is a terminology I made up, of course. What is the borderline between a creative city and a welfare city? I am for the social inclusion and we need to study more and move toward social inclusion in order to be a successful city. The question still remains. In addition, could we adopt the criterion of John Rawls of Harvard University? How can we reconcile his welfare concept in our creative city studies?

The third point is on the consideration of city size in the creative city analysis. Imagine urban policies for the creative city of Shanghai or creative city Osaka versus the creative city Salzburg, Austria. They are completely different in terms of structure, size and environment. In my opinion the size matters in creative city analysis. Hong Kong and Singapore may be an exceptional case. In the case of the City of Busan, as an example, she is preparing to apply for the UNESCO Creative City Network as film related city. I think the possibility of acceptance would be high because of the Busan International Film Festival and many related activities and favorable environment. However would that make Busan of 3.5 million a creative city? The size of city is apparently to be considered along with governance system and financial situation.

A more fundamental question is on the possibility of a creative city as a regional development model. Let me take a Korean case again. I worked for the Presidential Committee for Regional Development of Korean Government as a committee member, and I chaired the Special Committee for

Creative Region in the PCRD. Korean government (at least the PCRD) considers the creative region concept as a future regional development model. In this case region means local area or administration. The question is "Does a creative region (city) model suffice necessary and sufficient conditions for regional development?" Personally and as a member of PCRD I tried hard to encourage local government to adopt the creative model for more than two years. It has not been successful so far because of negligence of regional and local government employees and less financial incentives from central government. All of us need to answer to this question again "Is the creative city a new and advanced regional (local) development model or only a supplement to existing regional development models and an auxiliary function of current policies and strategies." The UNCTAD report of 2008 suggested the creative economy model should be a new development method for developing countries. What about the creative city models then?

A related point is the attitude to the existing industries. Busan has been an industrial city like many other Korean cities. If we decide to transform the urban structure with existing industries to creative cities what shall be the urban policies to the present industries?. This could be another question. Lily Kong previously mentioned about existing industries and Andy Pratt partially expressed his opinion on the existing industries, but we need to think about more on policies toward existing industries in order to generate more employment, added value and relation effect within a city.

Three Key Points in Creative City Formation

Lastly, let me just briefly present three key points in the creative city formation as I have observed. Firstly, network is a main factor for a creative city formation. That means we must turn away from territorialism or compartmentalization. Secondly, soft power. The way of approach may be different: one is cultural and the second environmental. Scholars may have different stances in two approaches but the theme is the same, I think. Thirdly, governance. All of us recognize the importance of governance and it is a time to come up with an exemplary model of proper urban governance system.

2-6. Discussion

Hiroshi Okano: With the advice of Director Sasaki, we would like to hear some more comments not only from the panelists but from the floor as well, so if you have any, there is a proposal for that, and I'd like to proceed in that manner.

But before that, first I would like some brief comments from each of the 5 panelists. First, for Ms. Miki of Elsevier Japan. As you showed in your slides, the Elsevier company publishes a large variety and number of international journals, and especially in relation to cities, the journal *CITIES* which appeared in your slides. *CITIES* is one of the top journals, and actually Professor Andrew Kirby, who served for a long time as editor in chief, was supposed to be here today, but he had a family emergency and was unable to attend. He says that by all means he hopes to come to Osaka City University sometime early next year, but it was this Professor Andrew Kirby who agreed to publish a special issue of *CCS* in *CITIES* in June of 2010 as the first promotion for *CCS*. This was something that we at *CCS* were extremely grateful for, but for example the UN Habitat Program also publishes such an international journal, *UN HABITAT*, and besides that there are many other journals being published related to cities and to urban research. For the next step in the promotion of *CCS*, aren't there any more such possibilities? If there are any such proposals out there, I would certainly like to hear them.

Also, the younger researchers, beginning with the graduate students, have a lot of interest, and I think the earlier presentation had a big impact on the younger researchers, and I think their own research will be included in global research, should be included in it. I feel that for Japan, first of all, research in the future will most likely enter the arena of worldwide competition. There are so far few in Japan in the social sciences and the humanities who are competing in English, but sooner or later that is what it will come to. I think we got a lot of hints about what we should do now so that we can manage when that time comes. If you have any messages for the younger researchers, please let us hear them. Could you respond to those two points?

Ritsuko Miki: For us at Elsevier, as a publishing group, there are three things that are important. First, when a journal is published, is to increase the number of submissions, and then to increase the number of subscriptions. After it becomes an electronic journal, then there is usage. However, while of course it is the publisher's goal to increase submissions, there has to be a balance with quality, so the number of citations is also important. In the first year of publication, it's pretty hard to get many citations, but publishers usually oversee about from 10 to 20 journals, and among those they try to keep a balance between those two numbers. Of course, things vary a bit depending on the particular publisher, but if submissions are increased, then citations should increase by 1% of that, the goal can be set so that both the volume increases and the quality also increases, but I myself work in the Tokyo office, the Japan office, and unfortunately we have no function in publishing. We are only involved in management, and do not do this work directly, but what we are always hearing from our colleagues in Amsterdam or Oxford is, I have my numbers, everywhere the numbers are a problem… but getting these three things up, and then citations after the second year… we hear that one has to keep a balance of those things.

At Elsevier, as for marketing support, we have experience with a lot of journals, so in the matter of how to foster a journal, I think we can give a lot of assistance in marketing support, of the kind, for example, where if you were to do this, here's a case of what happened… Among the people in the publishing company, we exchange information across disciplines, and in that way accumulate the wisdom of many predecessors and we have the value of experience, such that we can say, "In that kind of situation, if you do this, it will be effective." And I think it would be useful to utilize that to the fullest extent.

Hiroshi Okano: Well then, as managing editor, there's one more thing I'd like to ask about. One of the conditions of the contract we have with Elsevier is that we are supposed to maintain *CCS*'s 'impact factor,' the rate of citations, at 0.5 for three years. In other words, this impact factor level of 0.5 is the same as for *CITIES*, which is one of the leading journals, and its impact factor has declined quite a bit recently. So we are being told to match the same impact factor as *CITIES*. What about that? While some editors might say, "It's OK to do that," there are other editors who will say, "For such a new journal? 0.5 is impossible." What about that?

Ritsuko Miki: For a publishing group at Elsevier, there are three things that are important. First, when a journal is published, is to increase the number of submissions, and then to increase the number of subscriptions. After it becomes an electronic journal, then there is usage. However, while of course it is the publisher's goal to increase submissions, there has to be a balance with quality, so the number of citations is also important. In the first year of publication, it's pretty hard to get many citations, but publishers usually oversee about from 10 to 20 journals, and among those they try to keep a balance between those two numbers. Of course, things vary a bit depending on the particular publisher, but if submissions are increased, then all efforts should be focused on increasing citations more than the submission increase. Thus, the goal can be set so that both the volume may increase and the quality also may improve.

I myself work in the Tokyo office, the Japan office, and unfortunately we have no function in publishing but we are a sales organization. In fact, I am here to present on behalf of the Publishing Director, our colleagues in Amsterdam or Oxford. Aiming at getting these three things up, and then citations after the second year… we hear that it is always important for an Elsevier publisher to keep a balance of those things.

At Elsevier, as for marketing support, we have experiences with a lot of journals, so in the matter of how to foster a journal, I think we can give a lot of assistance in marketing support, of the kind, for example, where if you were to do this, here's a case of what happened… Among the people in the publishing company, we exchange information across disciplines, and in that way accumulate the wisdom of many publishers internally and Elsevier publishers are ready to use the internally proven valuable experiences for our customer support, such that we can say, "In that kind of situation, we suggest that you may wish to do this, because we know it will be effective according to our experiences." And I think it would be useful to utilize that to the fullest extent.

Hiroshi Okano: Also, Elsevier may have been thinking this also for *CCS*, that if we don't raise the impact factor, then it won't become one of the top journals listed in the premiere index level in the Social Science Citation Index. So it may be a kind of 'tough love,' telling us that we have to make it a high quality journal with high quality papers and essays as soon as possible.

Ritsuko Miki: The debut of *CCS* was very smooth, of course I talked with the supervising publisher before coming here, but for the debut you have got manuscript submissions from really top class authors, and they hope by all means that you will continue at this level.

Hiroshi Okano: Thank you very much. François, I would like to talk about, you said that "60% of the papers are academic papers, and 33% are from company people, and 7% are from government people." Is that the same situation as in the early period, or is it changing, and changing because you did a lot coordination or some sort of the activities? Please let me know the balance of the academics and companies and government in terms of the *CCS*.

François Colbert: Well, we consider our journal to be what we call a scholarly professional journal. So we won't do the transfer between what the academics are finding and the practitioners. So it is a matter yet of making the academic be of interest to the public in the journal. It has to be of high quality scientifically. But if we want the practitioners, well a certain level of practitioners, those who won't relate to speculate on another level, it has to be understandable by the practitioners. So, it is within what we tell the authors how to package the article that we succeed in doing this.

Now the other thing also is that we also, right at first, we decided to accept some articles by high level practitioners. That is why we have a section devoted to that. And also, to give another perspective to the journal, we always have what we call a "company profile," which is a case study of good practices from a major or smaller art organization somewhere in the world, and the picture on the cover page is a picture from the company that is in the company profile. Now, the balance changes from time to time. Of course the practitioners for example, when times are rough, in a recession for example, we immediately feel the recession because they cut some subscriptions and they cut our journal. But I hope we will be able to be interesting to practitioners as well.

Hiroshi Okano: Well, so far the scientists are doing the judging of whether the articles are good ones or not. So the scientists themselves are judging, they are doing the peer review. But this role of judgment, should not be given only to the scientists, but also to people in general like the citizens. So, the role of the judge should also be performed by the citizens. So if there is one proposal, and then there are the pros and cons, and as for the background, the practitioners or the citizens in general can be divided into an opposing group as well as a supporting group. So, so far this has been done by the scientists or the researchers, but as for city planning, the practitioners are also asking to judge the articles, and these should also be judged by these people. So the way of understanding in publishing has changed. And Director Sasaki, editor in chief, can I ask your opinion regarding the future direction of *CCS*? The balancing between the academics and also the professional people, how do you foresee the balance of these two criteria?

Masayuki Sasaki: Well, I am planning to give my comment, just an overall comment, afterwards. So I will wait for a while.

Hiroshi Okano: Next, this is a question for Professor Pratt. The three areas, urban studies and social and economic analysis, and cultural analysis. That is the same concept as the *CCS*. So what do you think about that? How can we make some new research area for the mixture of the three circles?

Andy Pratt: I don't necessarily think that it is a new research area. I think it is the future direction of research to look at the intersections of those. I think there are established journals that look at the source areas, but there must be a space to look at the intersections of those as well.

I think that that is always the challenge, either existing journals expand, or you find a new and emerging space, and certainly for those that are wanting to follow these debates and the intersections of the debates, then it is useful to have a dedicated journal in those areas.

And I think, the publication of a journal is a sign of the vibrancy of research in a particular area. So I think all these are useful indications. I think it is also interesting that we have a perspective of the, if you like, the economics of publishing, which is important too. We need reflections on the nature of content as well, the writing. And we have talked about the writing in very abstract academic terms of the topics, but there is an intersection when people write articles they submit to journals. Which one do they submit it to? Clearly issues like impact factors are very important for the continuity of people's careers, because they may be disciplined within their department if they don't publish in particular journals, etc. So this is a real challenge, and I guess we can be reflective about this.

Publishing is a cultural creative industry. We analyze cultural creative industries. Let us analyze what we do here in terms of organization and change. It is interesting if you look at the way when you increase the citations of articles, etc, and that is about collective citation. I mean, in the sciences, people make whole careers out of this. They create workgroups and people cite, co-cite papers and this increases the citations and increases the impact factor. So there are a number of rather instrumental things one can do if you want to understand how these things work. And I think somehow we have to engage with the reality of the way that the publishing industry works, the way that universities now need to validate their position in the world. I mean if you look at the top, the ranking of universities, one of the components of those is publications and citations. Now this is a big business now, of big importance for all the players.

So what I think we need to understand is a little bit more in detail how new journals play a role in this, but there is a real danger for new journals because they don't have the same impact factor as the more established ones, and therefore younger faculty will be advised by the heads of their department not to publish in that journal. Because it will damage their career, their chances for promotion, etc. And this is wrong, but it is the reality. So I think we need to engage with how you match those together. This is a new problem, there is no answer here, but I think it is worth reflecting upon, if you like, the political economy of information, which is also about the organization of knowledge about cities and space and society, but is also about what we do as academics, it is also about the intersection between the not-for-profit and for-profit, the formal and informal, which is what academic work and publishing coming together is about. So this seems a central concern in some ways, but it is a real problem I think, a practical problem, for people that want to submit and a practical problem for journals, how they develop, and particularly, developing in new areas, and I think this is the challenge. Supposedly, academic research areas, government, etc, all want innovation, but if you try to be innovative, then you will fail invariably because the story, as we all know, is that you have to innovate, but only a tiny bit. If you innovate too far, then nobody wants you. So again, this is another challenge, how do you exist in this new world and what sort of solutions can you find? So, it is not so simple in a way that, it would be nice if it was, that simply new academic fields open up and then people write in those areas. The world is quite different from that unfortunately, and I think that is the real challenge, and it is a challenge that everyone needs to address and find the answers to.

Hiroshi Okano: Thank you, Andy. And a short but good question for Hyun, about your neoliberalism. I think that in Shanghai and Beijing, or Xian, there are many different styles of everyday lives, and it is maybe a different style of neoliberalism for the everyday lives of the Chinese people. What do you think about this?

Hyun Bang Shin: Well I think that is a topic for another symposium. It is a big issue, and I think what I was trying to do today was to show some more issues to think about and try to suggest that when researchers address these issues, which are already dominant, the existing discourse, and one example was that neoliberal urbanisation which has been around in urban studies for almost a decade, but given the length of debate and the emerging amount of literature on these issues, my understanding is that the amount of literature that actually questions how these practices are experienced and exercised in the global south is not really as much as we have expected.

And the discussion is largely focused on other cities in the global north, whereas we need to know more about how these experiences in Shanghai or Xian, for instance, can be compared not with those cities whose experiences are in the global north, but for instance Seoul, or Singapore, or Cape Town, or Rio de Janeiro. So my proposition is more about, why don't we focus more on knowing more about how these experiences can be compared between cities in the global south, while the previous discussions are largely looking, so far during the last ten years, the previous debates were more focused either on identifying neoliberal practices in the global north, or comparing the experience of the global north with the global south. And I think the second part, the comparison between the global north and the global south, that is emerging, but there is not much being done in terms of making comparisons between cities in the global south, and from my point of view that is something for *CCS* to exploit within the market without really going too far in terms of innovation.

Hiroshi Okano: Thank you very much. And for Professor Lim, finally, you talked about existing industries. So what is your opinion about the existing industries in the creative cities?

Yun-Dok Lim: Very difficult question. We know creative industries are the more important thing, the existing industries for the future. But, we need to remember, keep in mind, that in generating jobs, added values and products are from the existing industries. What I think is that we need to pay more attention to the existing industries as well.

Hiroshi Okano: Now, I'd like to ask for your opinions, or your reactions, or whatever you would like to say, from the floor. How about it? We will bring you a microphone.

Takashi Yamazaki: My name is Yamazaki and I am on the faculty of the Urban Research Plaza at Osaka City University. First of all, we have been given a lot of information from all the panelists here today, and it has been very useful and informative for me in doing my work at the URP. I want to express my deep appreciation. Next, Professor Okano has made tremendous efforts in creating the inaugural issue of *CCS*, and I, speaking as one researcher, have been greatly impressed by his efforts. And also I want to thank all the simultaneous interpreters. Actually, I can speak English, but the audience is Japanese and so I will speak in Japanese.

Probably it has been pointed out today by Dr. Pratt and by Ms. Miki, but in launching this kind of international journal, one of the problems I think we Japanese researchers have to think about is, how can we write articles and submit them so that they will be accepted? As Professor Pratt has pointed out, while, for example, this is called an international journal, basically this is an English journal, and when Japanese people who have been educated in Japan write articles for it, what form can these articles be written in so that they will be accepted? That is turning into a very big problem. There are all kinds of journals where the editorial boards have been internationalized, but if one looks at the curriculum vitae of the editors on these boards, usually the editors are people with PhD's from the U.S. or the U.K. The reviewers as well… in many cases, the reviewers are also such people, and when they are, what about for example Japanese theories of recognition, Japanese researchers' methodologies, or Japanese researchers' ways of thinking? In what form can these things be published in an 'international journal?' That is the problem that we are faced with.

When it comes to achieving an impact factor of 0.5, there is a problem of whether or not we can actually write articles that can be cited, and probably when it comes to a new journal, and moreover one that comes out of Osaka, I think that is a problem we have to confront. One thing I want to ask, I want to ask of all the panelists, what can we do to make this journal survive? Actually, already at my university, we're asking, how can we write various kinds of English articles? How does one write an article that is logical in English? I am working on a specific project for that. So for example, one thing is to do something like that. And I think it comes down giving birth to articles that will be accepted. However, what is lost in that is my own style and way of doing things. In other words, in spite of the fact that we are advocating 'culture,' there's this contradiction, I think you can call it a struggle, of how can we express our own 'culture' in that process? This is something that we have to face up to, isn't it? What I would like to ask is, with a new journal like this, do you have any advice, or something that you experienced, some way that you devised to deal with this? If there is something that you could tell us about what you have experienced at your respective universities, please go ahead.

Andy Pratt: I just would like to say, I mean I think obviously there is a language issue and translation issues, but I think that what you should know is the format of journal articles and academic writing is not necessarily native to anybody. I think it can be a foreign language for all of us, so it is a particular form of presentation that I think is one everybody struggles with. And the question of whether one can express particular cultural norms through it, I think that is a challenge that everybody faces in many ways. It is not unique, I don't think, in terms of the Japanese or someone else. I would just like to check whether, my understanding is, that in terms of citations, journals that are published in many different languages show up in the citation indexes, so it is not a language-based one, but it is a question of whether there are many Japanese journals in the citation indexes. Are they included? And that is something to ask of SCOPUS and Web Science, about what the proportion is, because clearly CCS is probably going to do better if it is able to draw upon those existing researchers' work and make cross-citations of them. Otherwise it is going to be skewed towards an English-language only audience. So I don't know, are there lots of Japanese journals in the citation indexes such as the New West or the Thompson West?

Ying-Fang Chen: I would like to respond a little to Dr. Shin's statements… Japanese and English are all mixed up in my head, but if I can, I will try ask my question in the Japanese I learned in Osaka.

I completely agree with you. The current situation in Chinese urban studies is filled with problems, yet in spite of that there is very little urban research being done in Chinese studies around the world. One of the problems in that is methodological… another professor has also said so just now, but there are currently a lot of people doing research that takes, say, urban theories from America and transports them directly to China. But what I hope for, and what we need from now on, are new things that look at the realities of China, but for those things to be instantly apprehended and theorized about, or for a new perspective to emerge right away is impossible. Another thing is, there is a tendency for critical urban research to be widely carried out not in urban studies, but in sociology, jurisprudence, or political science, and one more thought of mine is that I now want to make urban studies as a discipline, or as a subsystem of the urban development system, one of the objects of my research, but in recent articles I always, as a researcher, think that I have to research something from another aspect, as a subsystem that has a special role to perform within the system. The reason is, in present day Chinese urban development, national resources, authority, and so forth are in the hands of the government, in the hands of those technocrats, and that is a new kind of power. Urban development is one complete system, an organism. We are part of the head of this organism or system. Therefore, we must be critical, but there are aspects where we will also be criticized, and maybe that is a methodology, or else an issue for the future. That's all.

Hiroshi Okano: Thank you very much. I'm very sorry, but we are out of time and will have to end it there. Finally, I would like to finish up by asking our editor in chief Professor Sasaki for a final comment.

Masayuki Sasaki: This is not a comment, but instead I would like to sum things up. Since this morning we have had a broad range of stimulating discussions, and I want to thank you very much.

The work itself of putting out this new journal, *CCS*, is a very creative business. And, as Lily Kong has pointed out, it is an extremely precarious problem, and as Mr. Yamazaki has just said, putting out a new creative journal for the English-speaking world presents us with a very big dilemma, a creative dilemma I think. Actually, I think that in itself will give us the energy to open up completely new research horizons, and in that sense, while our dreams may be too big, we are launching a boat to begin an ambitious journey. In this venture, we would like by all means to ask for help from all of you, and while accepting your harshly honest criticisms, we would like to move forward. Thank you very much for being here today.

Hiroshi Okano: Thank you very much. Well, our discussions will continue tomorrow and the next day, and I hope you will participate actively in those discussions. Thank you all very much for coming today.

Session 3 *10:00-12:30 December 16th, 2010*

Roundtable

Rethinking Urban Creativity

Creativity has attracted much attention both in scholarly and policy-making circles. Creative cities, creative class, and creative industries are the fashionable keywords in urban studies in the present century. Interactions between urbanization and creativity, however, have not always reflected positive tendencies. In this session, after a close examination on creative industries in advanced countries, urban creativity and changing economic base are discussed.

It is difficult to provide a brief definition of the city. The Urban Research Plaza at Osaka City University adopts the notion that the city is a site of agglomeration and communication. Locational agglomeration generates benefits for efficiency, creativity and innovation. Cities have always played an important role as centers of economic and cultural activities.

Cities in advanced countries have played the role of regional motors of the global economy. Agglomeration economies linked particularly with the manufacturing industry have thus generated large industrial metropolises. The creative industry is expected to be the new growth engine. A critical assessment of the agglomeration economies of the industry would provide new insights for urban environments.

Luciana Lazzeretti Professor, University of Florence
Prof. Lazzeretti pursues research on creative industry clusters, culture and creativity in regional development. She is a person of many talents, active not only as a researcher but also as a writer.

Seiji Hanzawa Lecturer, Meiji Gakuin University
A URP graduate and rapidly emerging talent, Dr. Hanzawa has done empirical research on the factors related to concentration of cultural industries and presents evidence that is critical to existing theory

Patrick Cohendet Professor, University of Strasbourg / Visiting Professor, HEC Montréal
Prof. Cohendet has developed new methodologies in urban research using frameworks of knowledge management, innovation management, and organizational theory.

Andy C Pratt Professor, King's College London
Recognized around the world for his research on culture, creative industries, and policy, he is a leading theoretician in the world academic community.

Coordinator: **Kenkichi Nagao** Professor, Osaka City University
As an economic geographer, Prof. Nagao brings a spatial view to economics and attempts to analyze global economic activity while looking at local contexts.

Kenkichi Nagao

Current academic position
Professor, Graduate School of Economics, Osaka City University

Academic experience
1992- M.A., Geography, Osaka City University
1990- B.A., Yokohama City University

2010- Professor, Graduate School of Economics, Osaka City University
2003-10 Associate Professor, Graduate School of Economics, Osaka City University
2000-03 Associate Professor, Institute for Economic Research, Osaka City University
1997-00 Lecturer, Institute for Economic Research, Osaka City University
1996-97 Special Researcher, Japan Society for the Promotion of Science

Research interests
Uneven Geographical Development
Industrial Cluster and Regional Development
Localness of Global City-Region

Major articles and papers
Industrial Cluster and Regional Industrial Policy under the Global Divisions of Labor, *Regional Economic Studies,* vol.20, 2010. (in Japanese)
Guest Editorial: Cultural-products Industries and Asian Metropolises, *Japanese Journal of Human Geography,* vol.56 no.6, 2004.

3-0. Opening Remarks

Good Morning, everyone. We would like to begin the second day of the international symposium. The first session on this the second day is Session 3, and its title is "Rethinking Urban Creativity." I will be serving as coordinator of the session, and my name in Kenkichi Nagao of Osaka City University's Graduate School of Economics. I ask for your kind cooperation. Today's and tomorrow's meetings are aimed at specialists, and on the podium at yesterday evening's reception, at the end I made a plea for the attendees 'Not drink too much'. I am very gratified to see that an appropriate number of attendees for this specialist conference have assembled here today. Thank you.

The goal of this session is to enter deeply, and also critically, into consideration of creativity which is the advantage of the city, the wellspring of its preeminence. Actually, at the beginning stage of this international symposium the overall title was "Towards the Century of Cities," and from now on the concepts of the creative city and creative industries will be important as an economic base and also that evolves together with social developments. It has been said that policy responses are also necessary, but there is a tendency for such talk to biased towards a somewhat rosy view of the future. At this venue, our organizer is a university and not a local government, think tank, or circle of policy makers, and I think we need to consider the topic deeply as academics, so I have planned this session with that in mind.

Yesterday's conference as well included some critical insights, such as in Director Sasaki's opening remarks when he observed that just because concentration of creative class does not mean a creative city will necessarily be the result, and in Professor Sharon Zukin's talk about spontaneously arising creative districts in New York. They themselves flourish, but if they flourish too much, then the price of the urban commodity which is land gets too high and such creative districts undergo a kind of destruction. Such problematic points were discussed. And in Professor Lily Kong's talk, there were insights into how a good deal of uncertainty and precariousness comes attached to the creative economy, and so it is very difficult positioning it within a planned economy like Singapore's. While including those points as well, I would like for us to discuss these topics more deeply.

We have four speakers who will each have a slot of 30 minutes, with about 20 minutes each for their presentations and about 10 minutes for discussion and questions in response to those presentations, and then at the end we would like to take some time again for an overall discussion.

I will now introduce the speakers, and the first speaker is Professor Luciana Lazzeretti who has come here from Italy. If you ask, why from Italy? It is because, for one thing, there is the fact that Director Sasaki, who has spread the ideas of the creative city and creative industries in Japan, got the inspiration largely from Italy. Also, in yesterday's Session 2 there was some talk about whether it was alright for Japan to just follow Anglo- America, and in thinking about the positioning of Japan and East Asia, Italy, while it is part of Europe, is not Anglo-American… so we ended up having a report on a case of cultural heritage and technological problems in Italy, which will include how we should think about Italy.

After that, the second speaker will be Seiji Hanzawa, a graduate of the postdoctoral program at the Urban Research Plaza, representing younger researchers, and he will be making a presentation that will serve as an example of how the ability to communicate internationally has risen at the URP. He has some very critical views, and says that creativity will not necessarily emerge simply through concentration in an industry. He will be talking about what is necessary in order for creativity to emerge based on a Japanese example.

Next, the third speaker will be Professor Patrick Cohendet. He comes to us from Montréal. Previously, he has written pointedly in articles that the creative city concept has become excessively popular in policy circles, and he will be speaking to us today about the three levels on which he thinks creativity is born, the level of the individual, the level of the city, and since Professor Cohendet is an expert on organizations, how creativity emerges in organizations.

And then finishing it off will be Professor Andy Pratt, who has frequently come to Osaka. He discusses creative cities and creative industries in the most comprehensive way. He also spoke yesterday, and wrote about creative concepts in the inaugural issue of *City, Culture and Society*, confronting both negative and positive aspects. And so, fittingly for our final presentation, he will be giving a talk which should lead to a holistic, comprehensive discussion at the end.

Session 3

Luciana Lazzeretti

Current academic position

Professor, Economics and Management of Firms at the Faculty of Economics, Department of Management Sciences, University of Florence

Coordinator, the Doctorate Research Program (Ph.D.) in "Economics and Management of Enterprises and Local Systems" (EGISL) at the University of Florence

Director, Postgraduate Program in "Economics and Management of Museum and Cultural Goods"

Associate Professor, the Institute of Applied Physics "Nello Carrara" CNR-IFAC, Florence

Academic experience

- 1999- Full Professor, Economics and Management of Enterprises, University of Florence, Faculty of Economics, Department of Management Science
- 1994- Visiting scholar, the 'Snider Entrepreneurial Center', Winter Semester in Wharton School, University of Pennsylvania (Philadelphia, US)
- 1994-99 Associate Professor, University of Florence, Faculty of Economics, Department of Management Sciences
- 1991-93 Associate Professor, Faculty of Economics, University of Molise.
- 1983-91 Research Fellow, University of Florence, Faculty of Economics, Department of Management Sciences
- 1983- B.Sc. in Economics, University of Florence, Faculty of Economics.

Research interests

- Industrial districts, clusters and local economic development
- Creative and cultural industries, cities and clusters
- Innovation and innovation policies

Major articles and papers

- (2010). *"Technological innovation in creative clusters. The case of laser in conservation of artworks in Florence"*, IERMB Working Paper in Economics, n. 10.02, April (with Capone F. and Cinti T.)
- (2009). "The creative capacity of culture and the New Creative Milieu", in Becattini G., Bellandi M, De Propris L. (eds), *The Handbook of Industrial Districts*, Cheltenham (UK), Edward Elgar, pp. 281-294
- (2009)."Governance-specific factors and cultural clusters: the case of Florence", in *Creative Industries Journal, Special Issue on 'The Drivers and Processes of Creative Industries in regions and cities'*, n. 2.1December, pp. 19-36. (with Cinti T.)
- (2008). *Creative cities, Cultural Clusters and Local Economic Development*, Cheltenham (UK), Edward Elgar, (eds with Cooke P.)

3-1. Technological Innovation in Creative Clusters: The Case of Laser Technology in the Conservation of Artworks in Florence

Summary

The use of laser in the restoration and cleaning of cultural assets is among the most exciting developments of recent times. Ablative laser systems are able to clean and protect inestimable works of art that have been subject to atmospheric agents and degradation over time.

This new technology, in development over the last forty years, is now available to restorers and has proven successful throughout Europe. This important contribution to laser innovation has been carried out in Florence by local actors belonging to a creative cluster. Our analysis explores the genesis of this innovation in this local Florentine context and the relationships among the main actors who have contributed to it. Our study investigates how culture can play a role in the generation of ideas and innovation and considers the creative environments that can favor them. In this context, we discuss the use of laser technologies in the restoration of cultural heritage by examining techniques developed by the Creative Capacity of Culture (CCC) as a case study.

The paper is arranged as follows. After our introduction, Section 2 details the main characteristics of the model of the creative capacity of culture. The research scheme and the methodology of our investigation are the object of Section 3. Section 4 examines the history of laser innovation, from its genesis to its international diffusion, with a focus on the Italian and Florentine experiences. In Section 5, we analyze the creative cluster of restorative laser technologies used in a series of research projects financed by the Tuscany Region; we also explore the relationships among the creative actors involved, with the help of the Social Network Analysis. In Section 6, some concluding remarks and notes on policy implications complete the study.

Introduction

Thank you very much for your introduction, and thank you very much to Professor Sasaki and Osaka City University for inviting me and making it possible to participate in the symposium. It was very stimulating for me. I will try to give you an idea about what creativity means for us and how it is connected with culture in cities of art, such as Florence. Furthermore, I will attempt to demonstrate that Florence, as a city of art, is maybe also a creative city. The idea is to try to connect the past with the future and to understand a city of art, which may also be useful for creativity in this new sense. My presentation is about a specific case study, i.e. the development laser technologies for the conservation of artworks in Florence.

Object and Research Questions

Well, the object of the research is to discuss the new phase in the relationship between culture and economics that I call the cultural enhancement of the economy, wherein we have seen that everything can start from conservation and lead to economic enhancement of culture, in this sense, culture is mainly interpreted an asset. I will try to demonstrate that culture is also a stimulus for social innovation and that the theoretical model that I applied involves a creative capacity of culture. The case studies are examples of cross-fertilization and serendipity, which are two parts of creative capacity of culture.

We can now draw the main research questions.

Is technological innovation an example of the creative capacity of culture?

Is the art restoration cluster a creative cluster?

Is the city of art of Florence, also a creative milieu?

Generally, in cultural enhancement and economic enhancement of culture, you can see culture, as a factor of production. Now, I will try to consider culture as a social innovation. The other point is that we now stress the role of human capital and of the creative class instead of the artistic culture heritage. Consistently, the focus goes to the innovation process and not exclusively on local economy development. In the same sense, we also stress the transition from cultural cluster to the creative cluster, considering urban creativity as the main object of analysis,. In synthesis, the model of creative capacity of the culture is an ability, a capacity that is able to renew places, sectors and professions and generally renovate ideas and innovation through post-Fordist processes of urban economic renewal and cross-fertilization or serendipity. The point is that the two paths create relatedness. The innovation comes from the ability to create new relatedness and recognize unusual relations.

From Lateral Thinking to Lateral Proximity

The theoretical idea that I develop is that the creative capacity of culture promotes searching and lateral thinking and it is advanced by a lateral proximity, which is basically a cognitive proximity and not just the geographical co-location of creative actors. This concept is connected with the shift from close innovation to open innovation: my reference does not go anymore to vertical thinking rather to lateral thinking and to the capacity of finding unusual relations. Let me give you some idea about these issues.

The concept of lateral thinking was developed by a psychologist, Edward De Bono, who stressed the idea that lateral thinking tends to explore all the different ways of looking for something rather than accepting the most promising point of view, and proceeds from that. In this case, the change of cognitive perspectives is considered a source of innovation. Well, in clusters, we usually use the idea of physical proximity but Ron Boschma has underlined that different kinds of proximity coexist (cognitive, social, organizational). I want to introduce yet another idea of proximity i.e. lateral proximity, that connects different sectors through different paths that are prone to cross-fertilization and serendipity.

Paths of Development of the Creative Capacity of the Culture (CCC) between Renewing and Novelty: Cross-fertilization and Serendipity

Here you have the main path of creative capacity of the culture. The distinction between renewing and novelty corresponds to the difference between incremental innovation and radical innovation. In this conference, we have discussed about urban regeneration. The economic renewal is not so developed within this discipline and is related to the idea that culture can renew places, products and sectors. The example of design is one of the main important transversal technologies, and also that of typical wine&food products is another example of renewing through culture. Yet, what I want to stress in this conference are two different paths, which are cross-fertilization and serendipity, through which the city of art is also able to produce ideas and innovation. I prefer going to the next example of art restoration. What does cross-fertilization mean? There is a lot of possibilities for analyzing this concept, as cross-fertilization can take place inside a cultural cluster or among cultural clusters which can be mutually related or unrelated. The case study that I am presenting is that of relatively unrelated sectors clustered inside a city of art, i.e. a case of cross-fertilization between bio-medical technology and art-diagnostics: in this sense the city is able to produce an unusual relation between unrelated sectors and can become a new creative milieu. The different case of cross-time cross-fertilization is represented by the BHM Jewelry District, a Marshallian industrial district that I have studied wherein a traditional production was renewed by an Indian community. This is also an example of a conceptual model that has been widely used in the past decade, that of cultural district, but we can now pass to discuss about creative districts. What is serendipity? The case of Coca Cola is a clear example: it was originally a market failure because it was originally sold as a medicament, but then it became the most famous cold drink worldwide and its formula continues to be a secret. Again, the lesson of posterity is another case of serendipity.

The evolution of Laser innovation for conservation in Florence

My case study is represented by the application of laser technology to art conservation, whose opportunity was discovered by chance while using them for an archival recording of statues and monuments. Restorers tried to produce holograms and they found that the laser was useful for cleaning artworks: this is a case of serendipity.

The research that I am presenting is connected with the Florentine cultural cluster. I have studied this cluster along about ten years in order to develop a model of the cultural and social networking process and to see if this cultural cluster may be also a creative cluster. So when I saw the story of the Gates of Paradise of Ghiberti being restored through laser (Figure 1), I realized that perhaps the model cultural capacity of the culture was working. So the research question that I tried to answer in this case is: is Florence, the city of art, also a creative environment,? So, in other terms, is the city the most important factor to produce cross-fertilization? Well, I have worked in the last year in the Department of Applied Physics in Florence, a challenge for an economist, but for strategic innovation we have to do that. Then, I discovered that in 1972, John Asmus, who was in charge of an exploratory project aiming to achieve a hologram of a church in Venice through a ruby laser , discovered the possibility of removing incrustations by using the same instruments. And this was the start of the story.

Creative Local System

And the beginning of the story occurred in a city of art. In this sense, one of the new concepts that I want to introduce is the idea that the city of art may be a kind of creative local system. It took about 20 years before this idea could be developed, and we waited until 1995 in Florence to have a network of actors focusing on laser technologies, including the CNR, the National Council of Research, and Opificio delle Pietre Dure (a very important institute for conservation), El.En Group the leading firm in the field, and the Tuscany Region, that finances the operation and tries to convince all this groups to use laser technologies. Before, restoration was done only with chemical tools, then with recommendation also of the directors of the museums and of Santa Maria del Fiore, we plan to

Figure 1: Laser technologies in conservation: the case of the Gates of Paradise (source : IFAC_CNR)

do this experiment. This is the case study of a human network because the leading actors introduced to everybody to see the thing by different perspectives and to change the previous ways of working. And it is plain that such kinds of things succeeded thanks to a cultural system of values that existed inside Florence: this was the reason why so many different people – managers and technologists, and laser systems people, people working in very different sectors like in diagnostics and design – would all try to share efforts to achieve the same goal.

Creative Cluster: A network of economic, non economic and institutional actors

After this, we can talk about the rise of laser restoration communities, so we have a really radical innovation in this case. Here I have tried to describe by an economical point view this model. The creative capacity of culture about which I talked before and the two paths of creativity, i.e. cross-fertilization and serendipity, were pursued by what I call a creative cluster, i.e. by a network of economic and institutional actors who are able to generate ideas and innovation across the two paths. Well, here you have the cluster that I studied and in yellow the creative actors, because not all actors in the cultural cluster are necessarily creative actors. The ones in yellow participated in this projects to generate this innovation. Here you have the incipit of the story: the restoration of the Gates of Paradise by CNR-IFAC (the Council of National Research) and that of Santa Maria del Fiore (the Cathedral of Florence) by the El.En Group. So, the innovation is represented by the new use of laser technology and the path of cross-fertilization goes from biomedical diagnostics sector to cultural heritage.

In this sense, I have tried to demonstrate there is some kind of innovation that can happen only in a place where you have a lot of artistic and cultural heritage. The laser used formerly was too big, and this new type of laser was very useful for the restoration as shown by the example of bronzes that begun in 1982 and then continued. The last case was the story of Donatello. Do you remember that two years ago the David by Donatello was exhibited around the world? That was an example of a successful application of this technology. Now, the community of applied lasers is working on other materials to try to see if this technology is also useful in other cases.

I have applied the social network analysis to this work. Here you have the list of projects that I have analyzed and this is the result. This is the CNR-IFAC, you can see that the National Council of l Research is a bridging actor. If you consider more than four projects, you can see very clearly the creative cluster: the university, Opificio delle Pietre Dure, CNR-IFAC, so my model in someway demonstrates the idea that the creative cluster is here. The economic and the institutional actors, so it works.

Conclusion

Florence, the city of art, is also a creative milieu able to develop innovation among the path of the creative capacity of the culture. The innovation is represented by the laser cleaning technology and conservation as a successful example of the creative capacity of the culture between cross-fertilization and serendipity: you remember how the story started in Venice, and cross-fertilization occurred again in another city of art, Florence. The two unrelated sectors, biomedical diagnostics and cultural heritage were connected by a human network, and a creative cluster arose wherein there are economic, non-economic, and institutional actors. Thank you.

Kenkichi Nagao: Thank you very much Professor Lazzaretti. I forget to mention it in my introduction, but she also edited, along with British Professor Philip Cooke, the book "Creative Cities, Cultural Clusters, and Local Economic Development", and this keyword "cross-fertilization" used today, how we mutually enrich each other, is very important in the research praxis that we do at the Urban Research Plaza. Also in that book, Professor Lazzeretti, in writing about whether it is better to specialize in a particular industry or to have a wide variety, together with an economic geographer, offers the keyword "related variety" to talk about industries that are related, but have a variety in the parts where they are related. Also, for the meaning of proximity, that is not just a physical proximity based on physical distance, but cognitive distance is also important. And then, in this really good example, she talked about how the cultural elements that are extremely important for the creative economy interact with the economic elements, and concerning actors, she also talked about how economic actors interact with non-economic actors. Today we have some time for questions, responses, and replies, so if there are any questions from the floor or from the other speakers, please raise your hands. How about it?

Hiroshi Okano: First, one question is this. You seem to have used the methods of what shall I call it, social network thinking, but recently there has been a spreading influence of the thinking like Bruno Latour's that we should consider the relationships between both human actors and non-human actors rather than just actor networks, but Professor Lazzeretti, rather than social networking, are you sticking with the older method that is not that of Bruno Latour? Or do you think you are using it as one way of doing things but that it is not your ultimate goal?

Luciana Lazzeretti: I used network methodology to try to check if there are relations among the creative actors and defined the concept of creative cluster. I have not yet written about the general idea of the city as a creative city. I have decided to present a contribution for the new journal. The idea is to consider culture as a social innovation. There is not so much research on this. And this is an example that really, culture is a social innovation. My point was mainly not about the network but about the creative milieu in the sense of the global of Latour that you are speaking about is not the Latourian proximity. No, it is the other one, because the old approach is more connected with the Technological Innovation in Creative Clusters: The Case of Laser Technology in the Conservation of Artworks in Florence network approach. What I have studied is an industrial city approach. The unit of analysis is the city. In this sense what is important is the territory, not the network from my point of view, because my question is: Can Florence be an informal, creative environment? This is one of the possibilities, obviously. The firm El.En in this case was useful to develop the technology, not to invent it, OK? This is the point.

I don't know if the interaction in the human network was enough, instead of the institutional net, for me it is not so important in this case. For me what is most relevant is that there is relatedness among the actors in the cluster. So, the analysis went on for 12 or 20 years, and finally I think this is the result.

Kenkichi Nagao: Thank you very much. Well, she is saying that deeper development of network theory is not her final goal, but she is using it in her research goal of finding out what kind of thing the city is. Are there any other questions?

Sharon Zukin: I would like to ask Luciana a question that goes outside of the methodology that she used. I noticed in the last slide that financing was provided by the region of Tuscany and I am interested in, how can I say, the marketing of the cultural innovation of laser cleaning. I mean, I would think that it is a technology or a set of practices, maybe not of special equipment, but a set of practices with universal application. Does this cultural innovation depend on financing by the state or can it sustain itself by some kind of market sales?

Luciana Lazzeretti: The point is the cluster. And the Tuscany Region is part of the cluster. So the funds come from the territory because the region was persuaded to finance this sector as an opportunity for the territory. In this sense the region sustained the group of actors by helping them to access to European funds, but you may be able to find the same things without this initiative. What I want to stress is that everybody was connected in this place around new ideas. Without these, it would not have been possible to succeed. Laser technology began in Italy but then was developed a lot in France, Greece, and in Germany, but no place succeeded as much as Florence.

So my question was, why in Florence and not around Paris? My thinking is that this succeeded in Florence because there were a group of people that were at that moment in that institution and the design begun because they took care of the Gates of Ghiberti for instance, there is a local value in this sense. And if you would live in Florence, cultural heritage is something that you should understand, you can learn it from when you are a child, you continue to live in this sense, like you live in Kyoto, no? I saw Kyoto on Sunday. So the culture in here is the Marshallian idea of creativity. This is my point.

And the projects and the network for me is just a tool to verify in an objective way if this net exists, whether this cluster exists or not. I mean this one is just a bridging actor, the CNR, and the discussion was, who is the innovator? The firm? The university? So that was the question, and I have done the interviews to get different points of view and recombine them into the story. The top manager of the firm that I discussed with engineer Masotti is a fantastic man. He is also a professor of technology. He told me, "I have just done this because I like it." When I have to present this case study to the stakeholders, I present it like a promotion, but for me it was not that. I think I have told you everything. This is the beginning of the story, then it is economics, before it was culture.

Kenkichi Nagao: Your reply has led us into a discussion of institutional sickness that is like an organizational or systemic disease in certain localities. We are running out of time, but Professor Sasaki, could you please speak briefly?

Masayuki Sasaki: Thank you for a truly excellent talk. I also think that Ghiberti's Gates of Heaven is a splendid work, but I have two questions. One is about the concept of serendipity that you used in your talk today. About this concept, for example the American urban researcher Jane Jacobs in dealing with cities like Bologna and Florence introduced the two concepts of innovation and improvisation as working together mutually. I feel that this concept of improvisation and the concept of serendipity that you used today are relatively close. So, my first question is, what do you think about that? My other question is, in today's discussion, I understood that when cultural assets meet new technology, they become cultural capital. In other words, Italy is very rich in heritage, but this is not living capital. Many cultural objects are lying dormant, and their cultural value is rapidly declining, but when they met the new laser technology, by being developed into goods manufactured by laser, cultural values were attached to them and an economic value was added, so I think this is a process of turning cultural assets into cultural capital, but I want to ask you what you think about that kind of cultural capital.

Luciana Lazzeretti: I will tell you what I have understood. Everything comes from the idea of innovation. At this moment the focus is on the end of the process, on the transfer of technology. Someone defines the case studies that I have done as an open innovation case study. I have changed completely the meaning of the innovation because I am not looking for the end of the process, but for the beginning. This is what culture means as a social innovation. The focus is on the beginning of the process. Please, I am so sorry if I not arrive until the end but if I am speaking of this kind of innovation, it is completely different about the other one that you have done inside the paradigm of close innovation.

My question was, what does open innovation paradigm mean? When I met Michael J. Piore two years ago it began to come in my mind, the story. I have to understand what is open conversation, but what does this mean? The conversation was, about these four actors, they discuss where, in an informal environment, like yesterday. We have the opportunity to meet stimulating people. And then what succeeds? Perhaps I invent something. So, yes, improvisation. You can call it whatever you want but this is a sort of lateral thinking. This is creativity in our sense of the kind of people who stay here, not in the other sense of the last paradigm. You have to begin to think, perhaps we won't find it now at this moment, or maybe we can find it afterwards. For it to become a technology you need time, but we have Mr. Masotti who is also a professor, and what is interesting in the Gates of Paradise is that he liked it. But in a very simple way. And the laser was done by a creative group of PhDs, without funding, again as he was a PhD coordinator in the engineering faculty. It is not something you do in research and development, but with a group of young people that want to invent something. In lateral proximity, chance is considered as a source of ideas.

And I give this example of Venice and John Asmus. He was a student in Applied Physics and he wanted to come to Venice, just to work because of 1966's flood, money for this came from Hollywood, because he went to a party and there was a director, he said: "I want to go to Venice." "Well, take the money for the scholarship." So, there was first a creative district in the United States that financed his idea that was happening in a city of art, Venice, and another city of art developed the innovation. I know that the story was insane but I think that it is funny to speak in this term about the story of innovation. Thank you.

Kenkichi Nagao: You have put forth ideas that are connected to innovation, creativity, and reform, and from relationships of proximity, from openness, will lead into our final discussion. At this point I would like to close off the questions and discussion on Professor Lazzeretti's report. Thank you very much.

Seiji Hanzawa

Current academic position
Lecturer, Faculty of Sociology and Social Work,
Meiji Gakuin University

Academic experience
2007- Ph.D., Arts and Science, The University of Tokyo
2003- M.A.S, The University of Tokyo
2001- B.Sc., The University of Tokyo

2009- Lecturer, Faculty of Sociology and Social Work, Meiji Gakuin University
2007-09 GCOE Postdoctoral Research Fellow, Urban Research Plaza, Osaka City University

Research interests
Economic geography
Industrial agglomeration of the creative industry
Innovation studies

Major articles and papers
The Japanese animation and home video game industries: locational patterns, labor markets, and inter-firm relationships. *Japanese Journal of Human Geography* 56-6,pp.29-44,2004
Reconsideration on the agglomeration factors of cultural industries. *Journal of Economic Geographical Society of Korea* 11-3, pp.375-388, 2008

3-2. Redundancy, "Creative" Innovation and Agglomeration: Japanese Home Videogame and Television Program Production Industries

Summary

The recent rise of the cultural industry accompanied with industrial agglomeration phenomena has attracted enormous academic attention. However, most researches have underestimated the nature and importance of uncertainty in the cultural industry. In addition, it is "creative" innovation, not "efficient" one achieved by imitation, that increases commercial value of cultural products; therefore the "learning" concept, which considers the diffusion of "best practice" as agglomeration economies, is an inappropriate method of analysis.

Using reflexive consumption as a key assumption, we argue that a theory of cultural industrial agglomeration must account for the tolerance for redundancy and "knowledge¬-verification" costs that are required at the interface of production and consumption. For firms in information-dominant cultural industries to remain viable and creative, the tolerance for inevitable "inefficiency" of products is essential for creative products to emerge, and that an agglomeration may provide a means to absorb and spread the costs of knowledge-verification, which may be unbearable by individual firms in the short-run.

This presentation provides two case studies of Japanese cultural industries, home videogame and television program production, to illustrate our theoretical propositions. The case studies indicate that the "traditional" benefits of agglomeration, such as efficient transactions and trust-building, are not absent. However, we find that these benefits do not necessarily culminate in increased creative capacities of the firms in the glomeration, and we believe that the degrees to which spatial clusters of firms offer the tolerance for redundancy are the most critical factors that explain the difference in creative capacities between the two industries.

I will be talking about Redundancy, creative innovation and agglomeration: Japanese home video game and television program production industries. Additionally, this work is a result of co-research with Dr. Yamamoto at the Colgate University. In this presentation, first I am going to talk about the background of this work and review some of the early studies. And we articulate three biases in the existing theoretical accounts of cultural industry agglomerations. Then I will argue our theoretical proposition. It is tolerance for redundancy and regional resilience. After that, I will show you some of the empirical evidence. Finally, I will discuss the agglomeration benefits of these studied industries and derive a conclusion from the discussion.

Early studies on the agglomerations of the cultural industry and their problems

As you have already known, the cultural industry tends to cluster in particular places. For example, Tokyo, Los Angeles, London, and so on. Additionally, although Tokyo and Osaka are top two representative metropolitan cities in Japan but there are far more firms in Tokyo than in Osaka. The issues of early studies from the empirical viewpoint are that there are few number of comparative studies. Rather, findings of one cultural industry, especially the film industry, are over-generalized in recent studies. So we compare the two cultural industries. They are Japanese home video game and television program industry. Then, from the theoretical viewpoint, we believe that existing accounts of cultural industrial agglomeration suffer from multiple "biases" and contradictions, including extensive focus on efficiency benefits. There is insufficient account of how creativity materializes as an innovative product, and a narrow conceptualization of learning. First, concerning the efficiency bias, contemporary economic geographic studies of industrial agglomerations have been strongly influenced by flexible specialization theory, which set a high value on production efficiency. However, there is a trade-off between cost saving and creativity in innovation phenomena. Of course, creativity is more important than efficiency in the cultural industry. Nevertheless, in economic geography, this disproportionate attention to the manufacturing industry shows there is an excessive focus on production efficiency, even in the cultural industry, from the viewpoint of cost saving. About the creative values, another strand of agglomeration theory focuses on the role of metropolitan areas as the magnet of the creative workers. The presence of creative workers is surely a precondition for innovative cultural industries agglomerations, but this theory generally overlooks the fact that creative ideas do not immediately materialize to the production and distribution of marketable cultural products. In other words, although there is the severe conflict between cultural value and economic value in the cultural industry. This agglomeration theory fails to account for how this conflict is resolved. We call this predisposition "creative bias." The third bias, what we call a "learning bias," requires a more elaborate explanation. Learning has been one of the key concepts in the recent studies on geography and innovation. Learning and learning region literature has two problems: first, an excessive focus on the efficient communication of knowledge: second, the lack of consideration on knowledge verification and justification. These problems arise from learning concept's neglect of reflexive consumption in the cultural industry. Reflexive consumption makes it practically impossible for production firms to predict and grasp consumers' consumption patterns a priori.

Let me explains the two learning problems in detail. The first problem is that the predominant learning concept especially focuses on efficient mechanisms and routines for the absorption and application of knowledge, rather than the organizational capabilities of coping with unforeseen challenges. In other words, learning is concerned with the problem of not adaptability but adaptation, in order to facilitate efficient knowledge sharing and help spread the existing and established knowledge among the agents. However, due to the reflexivity, sharing knowledge is limitedly useful. In short, learning concept does not focus on the organizational capabilities of coping with unforeseen challenges. The second problem is that the learning concept tends to overlook the tremendous "knowledge-verification costs" that are required for verification of whether certain knowledge is truly valuable or not. Knowledge creation process involves four phases: socialization, externalization, combination, and internalization. Although the importance of these four phases are equivalent, learning only refers to a form of the socialization process of sharing tacit knowledge. In the externalization process, shared tacit knowledge is converted to explicit knowledge, for example, a cultural product, so that the value of the knowledge is verified; if it is truly valuable, we can say it has been justified. In short, learning literature overlooks the other knowledge creation phases, although especially knowledge-verification and justification is not free. In addition, due to the reflexive consumption, in the cultural industry knowledge is verified and justified through the result of products sales rather than through an organizational consensus. This means, in our view, the knowledge-verification and justification of new products also needs to occur at the interface of production and consumption rather than only within a firm. The value of a cultural product is determined to a large degree by how it is perceived by consumers regardless of how "creative" the production firms believe the product is. In this case, the perception by consumers may be in the form of critics' reviews and ultimately as the price that users are willing to pay. In traditional manufacturing industries, the verification of the value of the product could be more reasonable done within the firm. For example, what firms believe to be a strong product sells reasonably well; in other words, the perceived value of the product does not differ significantly between firms and consumers. But in the information-dominant cultural industries, this verification is increasingly difficult to be done within an organization. Additionally, most cultural products are destined to fail in the market. Therefore, the cost of knowledge-verification/justification requires larger expenditure in the cultural industry than in the manufacturing industry. In short, there is no effective way of verifying the product value except by putting it in the market at an enormous cost of knowledge verification-justification.

Theoretical Proposition: tolerance for redundancy and resilience

So in the industries where there is reflexive consumption, fundamental uncertainties prevail. It is essential that firms put a large variety of products into the market, knowing that many will fail. In other words, the firms must have a certain level of tolerance for redundancy and bear the costs of knowledge-verification. One of the potential benefits of agglomeration is to provide a means of spreading such cost among firms over time. For example, if a game software company has failed to produce a "big hit" for an extended period of time, it may lay off some of its workers, but these workers may find employment opportunities in other successful companies. When the company finally makes a smash hit and its revenue stream restores, it may then rehire the former employees again. In short, our theoretical proposition differs from flexible specialization and recent literature on learning in that we do not focus on cost saving and efficiency but conditions (that is tolerance for redundancy) for the continued existence of firms that will be blessed by creative and innovative products once in a while. Redundancy is inevitable inefficiency which is a necessary precondition for creative innovation to occur. On the other hand, intellectual value of regional resilience literature is currently under scrutiny in economic geography. Redundancy is one of the key attributes to enhance systemic resilience. Therefore, we can show an example of how social scientists can "contribute back" to the resilience literature through our theoretical proposition.

Empirical illustrations: Japanese videogame and television program industries

Here I would like to show our survey findings on the Japanese videogame and television program industries, in order to illustrate our theoretical argument. What you see here is outline of our survey. I don't have enough time to explain so please confirm it with the presentation materials at hand. That is, I conducted a questionnaire and interviews survey. Interestingly, location patterns of these two industries in Tokyo are very similar. The Tokyo Metropolitan Area has by far the largest concentration of both industries. However, as is shown in the following section, their agglomeration benefits are very different.

Now I will move on to the videogame survey. We categorized videogame firms into four types based on their function. First, "platform holder", firms like Nintendo, Sony, and Microsoft, manufacture console hardware as well as videogame software. These firms are also supplied with videogames from other videogame production firms. Indeed, non-platform holder videogame firms must purchase machines and software tools to produce videogames, and are required to consign the manufacturing of the game media to the platform holders. This unique power of platform holders, as a distributor of software products, enables them to monitor the market trends and to regulate the entry of software firms. This software distribution function is not highly profitable, however, and one of the surveyed platform holders confirmed that the reason for maintaining the unprofitable distribution sector was to market its consoles. In fact, compared to the subsequent case study of the television program industry, the distribution sector exerts considerably marginal influence in the videogame industry. Second, so-called "in-house publisher", essentially caries out the same functions as the platform holders except it does not provide consoles and manufacture media products themselves. They raise funds on their own responsibility, develop game software in-house, act as their own sales agency, and possess all intellectual property rights. Moreover, some leading firms are also distributors, this is the most common type of Japanese videogame firms. Third, "outsourcing publishers" raise funds on their own responsibility and market the products, but they outsource all game software development to other firms. The main reason for outsourcing the development function, is to avoid high fixed costs and maintain flexibility. Fourth, "developers" only develop videogame software on the basis of outsourcing from the other firms and their funds. There is a relatively low business risk because they can secure a certain development funds regardless of the product sales. Now, videogames firms are not always small. The large game production firms are also common. Interestingly, their functional types do not strictly determine the size of firms. Both in-house publishers and developers have large and small firms.

To summarize the characteristics of the videogame industry, first the distribution sector exerts considerable marginal influence. This is different from other cultural industries including television program industry. Second, concerning the labor market, although the Japanese videogame industry is characterized by a high proportion of permanent workers, but also by relatively high turnover rates. As a result, labor market of mid-career workers prevail. Videogame firms prefer hiring not unskilled new recruits but skilled mid-career workers who favor working within Tokyo Metropolitan Area. This is one of the agglomeration factors. Third, concerning the inter-firm relationships. Inter-firm relationships in the Japanese videogame industry can be categorized into two types: "whole-outsourcing" and "partial-outsourcing." The use of "whole-outsourcing" is to break the growing rigidity in organizational innovative capacity. Because outsourcers are having a hard time judging and determining the market trends, and are in need of fresh and original ideas from the other companies. On the other hand, "partial-outsourcing" requires intimate face-to-face communication and their close proximity is certainly advantageous. As a result, partial-outsourcing is more common among the developer firms in the Tokyo Metropolitan Areas, as opposed to those outside. Fourth, concerning the non-videogame businesses, most of videogame firms have entered other industries. For example, PC games, mobile phone software, and system software development, or the manufacturing industry. The studied firms generally consider that non-videogame businesses provided them with more secure sources of revenue than videogame business does, because of the "high-risk, high-return" nature of the videogame business. Interestingly, the dependency on videogame production is generally higher for "in-house publishers in the Tokyo Metropolitan Area than those outside; conversely, the dependency is generally higher for developers outside the Tokyo Metropolitan Area than those in the area.

We suspect that the Tokyo Metropolitan Area may enable in-house publishers to remain committed strongly to videogame business because they are able to adjust their workforce more readily and take advantage of outsourcing. Developers in the Tokyo Metropolitan Area, however, have difficulties in enjoying such agglomeration advantages because there is a large uncertainty about their videogame businesses due to the unfixed their outsourcers and partial-outsourcing orders accounting for majority of their relationships in general. Unlike them, all developers outside the Tokyo Metropolitan Area have fixed and prolonged whole outsourcing orders with leading firms; moreover, 4 of the 8 developers have only one leading outsourcer. In short, they can keep committing to videogame business with relative ease because of stable orders. As time is not enough to go through, I would like to omit in-depth explanation of tolerance for redundancy by category. If you take interest in that explanation, please refer to our discussion paper. To summarize it, tolerance for redundancy is offered through external economies in an agglomeration, on the other hand, through internal economies outside agglomeration.

Next, and this is an outline of our surveyed television program firms. Over half of the production firms have annual sales of 500 million yen or less and less than 20 workers, indicating the predominance of small and medium firms in the industry. Compared to the videogame industry, explanation of agglomeration mechanism is simpler. In the sense that strong distributor exists, this industry is a typical cultural industry. Broadcasting stations hold considerable strong bargaining power over production firms because of oligopoly resulting from limit to airwaves. In other words, this disproportionate power is derived from broadcasting firms' complete control over the distribution channels of television programs, which is essentially protected by the current Japanese broadcasting administration. Because of restrictive competition, broadcasting firms have little incentives to require creative television program. As of now, broadcasting firms usually hold the copyrights of television programs, even if the programs were primarily planned and developed by production firms. Moreover, the current economic slump and the recent start of digital broadcasting have been squeezing the profits of broadcasting firms, and they have been passing the cost pressure to production firms. There are structural factors that place less significance on creativity than on profitability in the current Japanese television broadcasting industry. The characteristics of labor market reflect such broadcasting attitudes. Creativity and sophisticated technical skill are not currently the most important consideration. Instead, certain personal characters, such as "can-do" attitude and communication skills are important. Concerning the inter-firm relationships, creativity is unimportant. One of the interviewed managers, commented that without any prior acquaintance with a producer at a broadcasting firm, proposals for a new program will not be even read, but once business relationship is developed, the relationships tend to be long-term and bring a steady flows of contract work. In other words, production firms must maintain close and frequent communication with their main client broadcasting firm. They tend to transact with well-acquainted firms with a long history of business partnership.

Comparative discussion

The two case studies show that the "traditional" benefits of agglomeration are not completely absent. Indeed, the benefits of proximity for efficient transactions and for sharing tacit knowledge or building trust are similarly important in both industries. What distinguishes these case studies is how agglomeration may or may not facilitate clustered firms to remain viable and creative in the long run. The Japanese videogame industry is characterized by a weak distribution sector, which allows the videogame production firms to maintain a relatively high degree of autonomy and freedom. The unpredictability of consumer tastes and preferences is assumed, and currently little efforts are made to control them. Given creative videogames do not come by all the time, it is critical for production firms somehow to stay in business, rather than adopting the existing best practice or minimizing production costs. Agglomeration benefits offer firms a higher tolerance for redundancy to produce a large variety of products, many of which are destined to fail in the market. High mobility of workers, convenience of partial outsourcing and flexibility to specialize or diversify their business result in dynamic capacity of creative innovation rather than static efficiency. In the television production industry, broadcasting firms, acting as oligopolistic distributors, command strong control over the program production firms. Broadcasting firms send signals to production firms that they need reliable sellers with the least possible costs. The risk avoidance behavior may be partly attributed to the nature of the market itself, where the broadcasting firms can stably make profits without creative programs due to the oligopolistic distribution channels. There is also little question that Tokyo offers urbanization economies that benefit individual firms in the television industry. Nevertheless, this agglomeration does not have the same level of tolerance for redundancy as in the videogame industry, and thus does not cultivate the creative capacity of the production firms in the long run. In other words, agglomeration benefits offer static efficiency rather than dynamic capacity of creative innovation.

Conclusion

Lastly, concerning characteristics of highly reflexive markets, the costs to market destined-to-fail products are the inevitable expenditure, in order for firms to continue producing creative products. So it is no use in decreasing expenditure and creating partial efficiency. Under these circumstances, agglomeration benefits for creative innovation are to provide firms with a tolerance for redundancy, not to provide maximum efficiency of management, which also erodes the capacity of creative innovation rather than encouraging it. Our theoretical proposition is relevant to regional resiliency literature because of our focus on the function of spatial agglomeration to accommodate a long-term viability of constituent firms rather than to maximize their efficiency.

Kenkichi Nagao: You have posed that problem that agglomeration in a cultural industry, with the cultural industry including its creative content, is different from agglomeration in manufacturing industries, and while there are some of the 'traditional' agglomeration effects, the part that cannot be explained by that you call a 'tolerance for redundancy.' In Japan we often talk about the 'content' industry, but you have a bit too much 'content' and our time has run out. So those of you who really want to ask or say something to Dr. Hanzawa, I hope you will catch him during the break and talk to him so that his reply can be heard during our general discussion at the conclusion. Dr. Hanzawa, thank you very much for a very substantive talk.

Patrick Cohendet

Current academic position
Professor, HEC Montréal Business School,
Affiliated Professorship at the University of Strasbourg

Academic experience
1979- Ph.D., Economics, Strasbourg University
1971- Master in economics, University of Paris
1969- B.A., Paris University

2006- Professor, HEC Montréal, International Business Department, Canada
1985-06 Professor, Department of economics, Strasbourg University
1979-85 Associate Professor, Strasbourg University
1974-79 Senior Lecturer, Strasbourg University

Research interests
Economics of Innovation
Technology Management
Knowledge Management
Theory of Film
Economics of Creativity

Major articles and papers
"The Anatomy of the Creative City" (2010), *Industry and Innovation*, P. Cohendet; D. Grandadam; L. Simon, vol7, No.1, pp.91-111

"Playing across the Playground: Paradoxes of knowledge creation in the video-game firm", P.Cohendet, L.Simon, *Journal of Organizational Behaviour*, June 2007, pp.587-605

Geographies of Knowledge Formation in Firms, Ash Amin, P.Cohendet, *Industry and Innovation*, No.04, vol.12, December 2005, pp.465-486

Architectures of Knowledge: firms, capabilities and communities, with Ash Amin, Oxford University Press, Oxford UK, 2004

Technology transfer revisited from the perspective of the knowledge based economy, F. Amesse, P. Cohendet, *Research Policy*, Vol.9, December 2001

3-3. Rethinking Urban Creativity: Lessons Learned from Barcelona and Montréal

Summary

In this contribution, we argue that creativity in a city supposes that new knowledge and innovative ideas can transit permanently through three layers: the underground, the middleground and the upperground (Cohendet, Grandadam, Simon, 2010). The underground is constituted by creative individuals (artists, other knowledge workers, who are individuals not immediately linked to the commercial and industrial world and whose culture lies outside the corporate logic of standardization). The upperground is the level of formal institutions such as creative or cultural firms or institutions, whose specific role is to bring creative ideas to the market (Howkins, 2001; Hartley, 2005).

In between the upperground and the underground, we suggest that a key role is played in the creative city by the middleground, which is the level where the work of collectives and communities is decisive in designing the grammars of use and other common platforms of knowledge necessary for the knowledge transmission and learning that precedes innovation in those geographically bounded innovative environments. We argue that successful creative areas in cities, are loci where the middleground plays a key role for the city as a key element of cultural creativity and social inclusion. On the opposite when the middleground has not yet formed, or has been neglected, there are major obstacles to the emergence of creativity.

As example, we suggest to study some areas in the cities of Barcelona (22@ Barcelona, El Raval, etc.) and Montréal (Quartier de l'innovation, quartier St Michel, etc.) to pinpoint and analyze the presence or absence of a rich middleground, to assess its critical role and to examine the practical measures that can be taken to rethink creativity in these urban environments.

Thank you for your introduction. Thank you Professor Sasaki very much for this kind invitation to this very stimulating symposium. I would also like to thank the organizers for the perfect welcome that we received, and also Professor Okano for helping me with some ideas that I will present. I would like to, maybe I raise a point from the view of an economist. Economists have problems dealing creativity and maybe I will try to see how we could cope with that, by coming back on some of the issues that have been put forward in the previous presentations. I would work on a model of creativity to interpret the creative city and my ideas are based on my observations with my colleagues in Montréal. Montréal is a kind of fantastic city to look at creativity. They are really laboratories of ideas for creative firms like Cirque de Soleil or Ubisoft, and a creative milieu and atmosphere in the streets which I think could be inspiring. So what I will present is a reflection done by three colleagues, and a series of papers is there.

Two main types of industrial clusters

To start with the economics of creativity in cities, we were fascinated by the fact that there were two models, two very different models. One was also a notion of cluster have been inspired a long time ago by Alfred Marshal and the idea is vey simple. The ideas of Marshal and his colleagues is, bring together in the same industries firms and the R&D units, and by a concentration power, you would have what economists call "positive externalities" and this would bring business opportunities. This should bring foundations for workforces. This would bring competitors. This would bring suppliers. And from the concentration, you would again experience creation of wealth in the economy. In Marshal's philosophy, but also that of his followers, there is only a vision of creativity which is given by proximity between science and industry. There is no place for art in this domain. Marshal has been inspiring two lines of people. One, along with Porter, that really enhances the fact that externalities, positive externalities, the creation of opportunities in clusters, is due to specialization. Specialization is what promotes and creates opportunities for jobs and creation of wealth.

The other line which I think is usually interesting and opens the route to many ideas and today is the line promoted by Jane Jacobs, and she states: "No, the externalities are not provoked by specialization. There are provoked by diversity, by the ability to integrate diverse bodies of knowledge. I think this is a major turn in the way of economics that are dealing with urbanization that she promoted. So this is a first line of thought. Concentrate institutions, firms, and then you would have something, called creative products, and so on.

The Anatomy of the Creative City

The second line of thought came, very strangely, from authors like Florida. Maybe it is due to his pioneering view, and even though there has been a lot of criticism. But the second line of view is to concentrate individual talents. Attract them, bring them together, and then there would be something. And so this second line of view is focusing on individuals. No more on institutions, but on the individuals. Attract, concentrate, do something for attracting creative individuals to the city, and then creation of wealth will follow. So again we have two types of different visions. One is looking at what we call "the upper ground," the institutions and the firms. The second line of thought is bringing talented individuals, which is Florida's vision. And from this we say, well, that is very interesting, but at least, these are only conditions, which are necessary conditions for there to be a creative city. This doesn't explain the dynamics of a creative city. It neither explains the process by which wealth is created. We missed something. And we have tried to find this something by trying to explain what we call the anatomy of creative cities through the process by which the creative attitudes and expressions of the individuals, what we call the "underground," and you reach and go to the market through the upper ground, which are institutions that are, again, producing products to go to the market, where there are artistic products or industrial products, and in between what we think, there is a layer that is of major importance. We have the conviction that a creative city is creative not because of the upper ground, not because of the underground, but its unique capability is to enrich, to enrich the middle ground.

And this maybe, again, a very strong hypothesis, but I will try to give some evidence of that. So let us first look at the three layers, and first the wellknown one, which is the upper ground. The upper ground is a layer of firms and institutions in let us say the Porterian vision. But when you look at creative cities these institutions and firms that face the market, and again, their idea is, they should take creative ideas and put them on the market, that is their function… in creative cities these creative industries exhibit very different characteristics than traditional ones. When for example we look at Ubisoft or Cirque de Soleil as examples of creative industries, there is no department of research. There are no research facilities. There are no big contracts with industries or universities. There are no networks of innovative activities, and so on. And nevertheless they are very creative and innovative. So for economists this is totally puzzling. This is totally the opposite of creativity. And an answer which I think is interesting is when we asked the director of the Cirque de Soleil, "But, where is your lab?", and he said, "My lab is Montréal, it is the city. It is the city where are my community of actors, artists, and scientists, yes scientists, but not departments of research." There are a lot of scientists in the Cirque de Soleil, but they work with the artists. And their lab is the City of Montréal, the bars, the cafes, the platforms for meetings and communities.

We went and asked the director of Ubisoft, the videogame company, and extraordinarily he gave the same definition: "My lab is the City of Montréal." And so there is something here which I think is important in terms of creative activities. On the other side of the creative city is the underground, the places with artists and people who create knowledge. What is important is not only all the artists. In Montréal there are lots of techno-geeks, and scientists, who are crazy about creative ideas. They work with artists, but they are not only artists. So to focus only on the artistic is interesting, but I think today it is larger, much larger. And this underground, all these talented people, which constitutes the underground, what is I think fascinating is, well some of them, they want immediately make money, but a lot of them say, "I am not interested in making money, I am interested in making a reputation," and what we like to exemplify is, because they are interested in getting a reputation, they will build collective knowledge to be recognized with communities of painters, of artists, of scientists together, but by doing this, their creative ideas would follow a path which will be more, much more understandable, step by step and this understanding would get to the market because the market could understand the creative ideas. So what I am trying to express here is, even if some of them are not interested in the market, their process will lead to the market. If the city is very creative, if the city has what we call a rich middle ground...

What is the middle ground? The middle ground again is the place where communities are, with all these unofficial and formal groups, collectives, associations, which are not oriented towards the market. There are places and platforms for the underground to build ideas, the consolidate, to validate their ideas, and then to bring them to the market. Then, the middle ground could, if it is very rich, express ideas that could be taken by the upper ground, who would have the keys of knowledge to go to the market. So this is a movement between the three layers that we have tried to understand.

The middleground of videogames at Motréal

As an example, I think most of you know the company Ubisoft. It is now the second company in the world in videogames. It was based in Montréal by chance because of tax rebates. But when they landed in Montréal, more than 10 years ago, they discovered the rich environment of Montréal, and then step by step they built what they call the middle ground of videogames in Montréal, and this middle ground is composed of very rich intermediaries of knowledge, collective intermediaries of knowledge that make Ubisoft stay in Montréal. Dubai tried to buy Ubisoft and said, "Come here, we have a lot of money, you can develop videogames and the world's biggest company could be in Dubai." They thought about that, but they said, "If we move to Dubai, our roots will be totally disconnected and our creativity would die. So yes, we could have money there, but not creative resources."

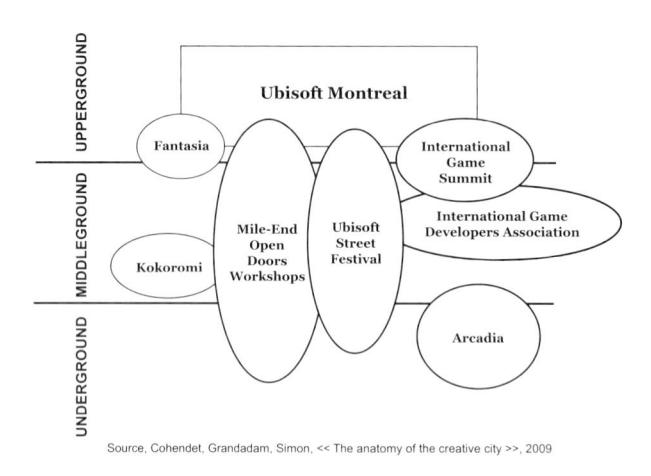

Figure 1: The middleground of videogames at Montréal

So the middle ground of Ubisoft is, for instance, a lot of festivals, totally open festivals and associations which are very important, which envision videogames that define the rules of the game of videogames. It is again not something oriented to the market, it helps all the videogames companies, including Montréal. It has a lot of festivals, it has a lot of spin-offs that try to define the rule of the game of videogames. All these middle grounds are constituted by events, by small associations, by groups of people. There are festivals of young people, 12.000 people a year, everyday for two weeks playing videogames in Montréal. And Ubisoft just looks at this festival and looks at the talent there to promote its creativity (Figure 1).

The social dynamics of creativity

So again, our hypothesis is what makes a creative city is the quality of the middle ground. This would permit the circulation of management between the underground and upper ground, and this would allow companies to stay and to do their spin-off activities there. We tried to apply this, to sum up, to this very simple graph, which is about what we think are the social dynamics of creativity (Figure 2). This is a kind of coupling between again creative ideas that come from individuals, and on the other side of the road, are the firms, the institutions, whose function in fact is to take the creative ideas and to bring them to the market and to transform them for the market. But if an individual tries

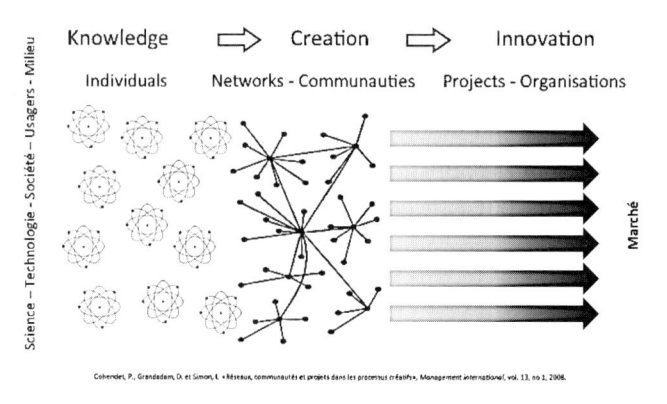

Figure 2: The social dynamics of creativity

to go to a company immediately, his creative idea is like a very fragile egg. It could break easily. He has an idea, but first of all the understanding for it is not there, and so for the creative idea to be made thicker, more dense, more viable, more expressive, more understandable, it has to go through a maze of interactions between different communities. Each one validates it, each one enriches it, each one gives more knowledge to the knowledge. And then once this is done through something which is as I said a rather codified process, even if everything is static behind it, but the creative idea there can be brought to a sufficient level to be interpreted by market forces and brought into the market. So again, this to us, and this is in keeping with the actors' theory, is a very important point for the creative city.

"22@ Barcelona" and "QI Montréal"

We tried to apply this during what we have done in summer school between Barcelona and Montréal, and this was a two week program and we proposed to the participants a project comparing two creative quarters in these two cities. Maybe one which is very well-known, it is kind of a reference to the world, which is 22@ Barcelona. It is a huge real, 100 blocks times 100 blocks, in a very nice place in Barcelona. It is nearby the harbor and the sea. It was a very industrial district, old traditional industries, which had turned into a wreck some decades ago.

The second district which could be comparable is one is which we call "QI Montréal," which is quartier innovation de Montréal. It is more a project, it started 10 years later than 22@ Barcelona, and in this real is around the school of engineering there, and here you have McGill, which is there. Around these two academic institutions they would try in another real that was always like this and very, very old industrial, traditional buildings that are closed or transformed into parking garages for cars and so on. It is terrible there and you are in the very center of Montréal. There are a lot of clusters, high tech clusters around. We have clusters in the electronic commerce, we have clusters in multimedia and so on so the idea was, let us start from the middle here, let us try to make a very innovative and creative cluster in Montréal and take the benefit of 22@ Barcelona.

So what is interesting also is Montréal tried to do something with Barcelona and imitate what was going on in Barcelona. A good question is, is the case of Barcelona a good one? They really put a lot of effort into it and said, "We will be one of the leading creative districts in the world." And they have put a lot of money into it, and to a large extent this succeeded but to a large extent only. If we look with this grid at what we tried to promote in Barcelona and Montréal, yes, we have a rich upper ground. It succeeded in building a rich upper ground. The middle ground, when we look carefully, are only structures which are top-down middle ground structures. I think non-profit institutions, this is middle ground, okay, not oriented towards the market. Non-profit institutions there are the Barcelona Activa de Vidal Foundation, and the University of Art Foundation, which are in fact top-down, decided by local authorities, and they said, "This is the middle ground, and that is it." And then if you look at the underground, the underground is composed of hundreds of thousands of creative talents there but they don't live there. The artists, they prefer to live in Barrio Gothic or Pedralbes or El Raval, and most of the techno-geeks, they prefer to live in the suburbs of Barcelona. So the people who live there are not the people who 130 work there at all. And so, as a result, when you get there, you have the impression of something very strong but something very weak. And there is a lot I think to be done to try to promote the underground and the middle ground.

It's exactly the same for Montréal. When you look at Montréal, you get the same type of result. The upper ground is very rich, it is starting, but very rich and attractive. Again, the middle ground is only universities, and nothing else, and the same for the underground. The artists and scientists, they prefer to live in Branchier Quartier and so on, and the residents don't understand what is going on. And so to us, there is a lot of work to be done to make a creative city. What could be done?, and I will stop here, what could be done?... and I think we come back to a graph that I have done with my colleague Ash Amin a long time ago, but I think for a hierarchy to be creative, a way to act is to try at the same time to activate places, spaces, events and projects.

How to nurture the middleground

It is a very simple grid based on the bar theory from Nakaya and Takashi, and derived from them (Figure 3), but I think it is important because it gives you clues to try to enhance the middle ground. Places are places to meet, agoras in the Greek tradition. And places to meet for a lot of people. For example in Barcelona today, "We have a lot of places to meet but all these places were, for instance, for the digital industries in the digital building. And for the media industry, in the media building. But as for large places where everyone can meet, there are not that many. In Montréal, there are none, not any place where all the people can meet. That is a simple problem, if you want to create a middle ground and you have no places to meet. Space is the ability to create cognitive environment where you could not only promote knowledge but absorb knowledge from the outside. This is a cognitive environment. Yes, in Montréal there are, for instance, McGill is important, and the Orchestra de Montréal, they are important players that really have the ability to emit knowledge and absorb knowledge to the world, to participate in the local buzz and the global pipelines of the world, but there aren't that many places. So you should try... for a place to be creative, you have to have spaces in terms of, again, cognitive spaces. Events are important and again we come back to what Batelt and Malbert say about events is this: they create verities to connect again to the local buzz and global pipelines. Montréal is full of events. Montréal I think is a city of events. We have events in all domains, but events in the quartier de innovation? Not that many. And you need events, and event for instance like this one, to connect people that have never met and could transform the world through

Places: the realm of near, intimate, and bounded relations, physically established
Spaces: the realm of far, impersonal, and fluid relations, cognitive constructions.

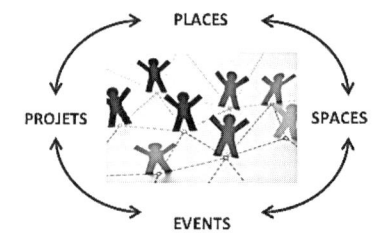

Projects: engage local communities in conversations and work together
Events: open the small local worlds to new global influences.

Figure 3: How to nurture the middleground

exchanging ideas. And then you have projects, projects are projects where you give incentives to the participants of the local milieu to do something together and in that respect, projects are extremely important for practicing, for practicing creativity in your area, and there is nothing in Barcelona and nothing in Montréal in those areas, in those domains. So yes, there is a lot to be done. These are very interesting districts, but they are not creative districts, and a lot of work has to be done to make them creative.

Kenkichi Nagao: Thank you very much Dr. Cohendet. So there are three layers that you have presented. Especially when thinking about creative cities and in that view really creative middle ground and should be rich and also of high quality. It turns in a very clear proposition and that you have given the case studies of Montréal and Barcelona, they are the heart of commercial activities together with a manufacturing factor. It has become a very large city. They are not in the capitals so they have undergone some decline stages as well, therefore Osaka feels quite close to them because they experienced a quite similar to that of Osaka in its history as well. Also the time is limited so I would like to accommodate a few questions. Yes, please.

Sharon Zukin: …quotation because it brought together some of the themes that Luciana brought up and also Seiji brought up from the point of view of place and industry. And there are so many relations between Patrick's presentation and the work of other people here at the symposium. Andy Pratt for example has emphasized the importance of what you call the middle ground, Patrick, what I called yesterday in my presentation, the theme of cultural innovations, cafes, bars, informal meeting places where people from different sectors can meet. Certainly other writers have talked about this. Just to be provocative let me bring in into the conversation an infamous comment by the architect Rem Koolhaas who said a number of years ago that his firm can only provide innovative ideas in a boring city like Rotterdam because Rotterdam is a sort of blank canvas for the firm to concentrate on their creativity and not be influenced by the urban environment. And Rotterdam, for certain economic reasons as well as the physical devastations of WWII, might be compared to Osaka, so I wonder what you think about Koolhaas's statement. But let me also emphasize something that I said in passing yesterday, very quickly, because it was not the main part of my presentation. Artists and cultural innovators who leave the production of art to create businesses of various sorts, even non-profit enterprises like art galleries and cafes for artist, play a very important role in producing this middle ground of informal meeting spaces. What happens in New York, London or Berlin is that the property developers become very interested very quickly in this kind of space. So in the smaller cities like Barcelona, Montréal, and Osaka, where at some point there is not that ravenous hunger, appetite by property developers for these middle ground spaces, is there a better chance to make a creative city?

Patrick Cohendet: So many questions! Yes, first on the question, "Could we create in a very ugly environment?" Yes. I used to do my PhD in my grandfather's farm with a lot of pigs and so on… it was the most disgusting place, but I could concentrate and do my PhD. But then, to write a book with my colleagues, I had to go to Paris to beautiful places and 132 exchange knowledge. There is a moment of specialization when you start a creative process, but there is a moment which I think is very important, a moment for the social dynamics of the creativity. And without this social dynamics of creativity, it doesn't work. I think your creative ideas are very fragile because there is not this validation processes, the exchange of knowledge that would build all the equipment which is necessary to understand creativity, forms of critique, and so on. So yes, there are moments where you can be in very ugly places, and I went and I would go back, but you know, the dynamic of creativity is something else. Now about the places, yes. What we are trying to see or to do, when you look at the ranking of creative cities, you have always cities of around three million inhabitants. Barcelona and Stockholm and sometimes Montréal, and sometimes not, but all these types of cities where it is more easy to… it is more difficult I think in New York or Paris because these concentrate in like you said in areas. Now a lot of people with whom I have been talking say, "Today, don't underestimate the virtual spaces." We can now be creative in a very different way. We meet people in creative spaces. And all the young generations, yes, they need a garage too, like our generation, but there is something very different, and then they need events, they need projects, they need spaces. The need for places is… they can move places in a given city very quickly. I don't know. An event, a dance party in the north of Paris and another one, they can meet there, they have places to meet, but it is not always the same. That is very interesting. The rest, projects, events, spaces, yes they need such things.

François Colbert: I find your work very interesting, as you know. Now there is a question that remains in my mind: first, there have always been artists in cities, all the time. I mean, it is the history of the world. But, to be creative and to build creative districts doesn't mean that humanity doesn't need products. Tables, I don't know, cars, cell phones and they have to be manufactured somewhere. You cannot live only on creativity. You have to feed yourself and so what happened with those other industries in the city? Can the city only be creative in your mind?

Patrick Cohendet: Many questions again! I think, first, creativity is not the privilege of creative industries. We worked with Bell Telephone which is a very traditional industry, even in producing electronics, it is still very traditional. And it is in Montréal, but all these very productive companies today, there are changing their mind in a very important domain. They said, "Our model of management for decades, if not centuries, has been inspired by the model of management of huge companies like General Electric or General Motors. Maybe in some domain, now our source of inspiration could be from creative industries. There are many reasons for that. One of the reasons for that is when today you employ a talented new person, this person resists any form of traditional ways of doing things in a company. And so I think, even if those big companies will still continue to produce products, the way they would produce these products would be more and more creative. I mean, changing a little bit every day, every year, the way to produce this product, from creative sources which have talents that change the world. I think creativity is not limited to creative industries. It is a movement, which is, as Lily has very brilliantly pointed out, it is a movement of the knowledge workers and knowledge workers are everywhere.

François Colbert: ... but are you mixing creativity and innovation? Because there has been great innovation in the past. I mean De Tembelque and Ford with, I mean...

... no I am not mixing creativity and innovation. Innovation has always existed and brings the creative ideas to the market. But the boiling side of creativity in these big companies is... the ways they organize, their sources of innovation, have changed.

Kenkichi Nagao: Time is pressing hard upon us. We have had questions from Professor Zukin and from Professor Colbert and discussion concerning the entirety of Professor Cohendet's presentation, and the thread of the debate has come around to the problem of urban creativity, and before all else, what form should the city take? And, for presenting this very important idea of the middle ground and talking about it, thank you very much Professor Cohendet.

Andy C Pratt

Current academic position
Professor, Culture, Media and Economy,
Head, Department of Culture, Media and Creative Industries,
King's College London

Academic experience
1989- Ph.D., Department of Geography, University of Exeter
1981- B.Sc., (Hons) Geography, Huddersfield Polytechnic

2009- Professor, Media, Culture and Economy, King's College London
2006-2009 Reader, Urban Cultural Economy, London School of Economics and Political Science
1998-05 Senior Lecturer, Human Geography, London School of Economics and Political Science
1992-97 Lecturer, Human Geography, London School of Economics and Political Science
1991-92 Lecturer, Bartlett School of Planning, University College London
1990-91 Senior Lecturer, Local Economic Development and Planning, Department of planning, Coventry University
1988-90 Lecturer, Planning, Department of Planning, Coventry University
1987-88 Lecturer, Department of Geography, North Staffordshire University
1986-87 Lecturer, Department of Planning, Coventry University
1982-83 Research Assistant, Department of Geography, University of Leicester

Research interests
Cultural and creative industries
Cultural industries; space and place
Urbanisation and culture
Globalisation and global cities
Organisation of work in the cultural economy
Cultural Policy; Urban Policy; Cultural Industries Policies
'Creative' Cities

Major articles and papers
2009 *Creativity, innovation and the cultural economy.* Routledge, London (with Jeffcutt. P)
2001 *The secret life of cities: social reproduction and everyday life,* Prentice Hall, London (with H. Jarvis, and P.C-C. Wu)
2009 Urban regeneration: from the arts 'feel good' factor to the cultural economy. A case study of Hoxton, London. *Urban Studies* 44.6: pp1041-61

3-4. The Cultural Contradictions of the Creative City

Summary

The aim of this paper is to look at the nature of urban forms and practices that would facilitate creativity and innovation in an inclusive manner. The overriding idea is that we should strive to re-make cities around how people actually are, rather than how we expect them to be. The paper is in three parts: the first reviews the current modalities of cultural work (as representative of the leading edge of change), its sociality, inclusions and exclusions. It raises the challenge that cities should actually reflect and facilitate new modalities so that creative work does not work against 'the grain' of the city; rather that the city could offer an enabling environment (social and physical). The second part explores a number of dimensions of re-thinking cities based around a series of challenges of creative practices (as characterised by those found in the cultural work): reputation and face-to-face knowledge creation, trans-localism, networked suburbs and hot-desk cities, governance via intermediaries, and the permeability of the formal and informal. The final section reflects upon the challenges and opportunities of such a re-imagining.

Contexts/Aims

Well, I really enjoyed the previous presentations and I would really like to stick to them in a way but I want to change gear, and change direction slightly, because what I want to provide in a way is another element of contrast, another facet of the story to come back to the creative city. And in many ways what I want to do is turn the rhetoric of the creative city back on itself, and so I what I have titled my talk is "The cultural contradictions of the creative city" and hopefully you will see the resonances of that term as we go through the presentation.

Basically, my point is to contradict the point that seems to be the message that everybody takes from Richard Florida, that the creative city is a win-win game, everybody wins. And I just want to raise some questions about that issue, and to look a little but more closely. What I want to do very broadly is to reexamine some of the assumptions of the creative city. And what I am particularly interested in interrogating here are issues not directly to do with the economic that have been talked about, I think that is a very productive area, but is particularly another facet of that, which is the relationship between, and the embedded notions of, creativity, liberalism and culture. These are the issue I think at stake here. And one of the points that I want to make, very generally, is that within the discourse of creative cities, there is a notion of universalism of these notions. So that all creativity is the same everywhere and it is good for us, etc., just like liberalism. So I want to question these ideas which I think then offers a fatal blow to the notion of the creative city as it has been understood.

I have previously criticized Richard Florida's work and the notion of the creative city as it has been only focused on consumption, saying that there are other dimensions to this, and particularly we need to consider production. And to a large extent the last presentation, the last three presentations, have been about elaborating that, and there is a very strong argument there. I want to come back and add another twist to that, through showing us what some of the real challenges are that actually exist in creative cities if you like, rather than just these creative cities of the imagination. And that will I think provoke some issues for thinking about this sort of policy.

So let me just come back to the standard narrative. The point I want to make here is that the normative idea of the creative city is in fact part of a long-running existing narrative. It is no different. It is the extension of an old policy of foreign direct investment and the city. And cities started off with trying to offer tax breaks, free land, free buildings, etc, place marketing, selling cities, the development of iconic infrastructure, and then more recently there have been debates about the recalibration of cities to attend to the quality of life of cities, the Mercer Index for example, that is well used by multinational corporations, and academics as well, to rank and compare cities, which talks about the value of amenity. And so I would see a logical next step here as Richard Florida's work about creativity and consumption. And to an extent, I think what this is doing continues a line of argument that aim to create 'nice cities'.

Nice Cities

When we use "nice" in English, it is an ironic term and commonly it is meant to be a criticism as well. This is not really very nice: it is too normal and very safe. So, Richard Florida offers something extra. He is offering an extension to the existing narrative of hard branding but yet it has soft edges, too. And it is entirely logical within this set of arguments, and Richard Florida's work is in a long tradition on work of regional economic development and urban development and about exogenous development, etc, very consistent with a range of theories, etc, so it fits in with that. So what I am saying is that this is actually not anything different. So when we talk about the creative cities as a new age, etc, I don't think that the argument stands. Not in this framework anyway. So this is simply the existing hard branding of cities, that is the physical structure of cities, the transformation of buildings, etc, with a slight human resources edge to it. And as I have mentioned before, it is about consumption. Remember in Ed Glasiter's work and Richard Florida's work and Daniel Bell's work, the creative city is about consumption. It is not about the creative industries, it never was about creative industries. It is about attracting the creative class to cities so that they can work in high-tech industries. It is not about the creative industries, it never was. There is nothing in Richard Florida's book about creative production. So, understood in its own terms, it is very logical, it makes sense, but it is a continuation of an existing narrative.

Liberalism under Stress

But there is something more. And before I go on, what I want to do is to dig underneath, a little bit into, the assumptions of the creative city. And one of the notions that Richard Florida uses, and it is logical within his framework, is the importance of tolerance. And tolerance is presented as a universal, and it just happens that that seems to fit very nicely with a model of liberalism. A very particular version of neoliberalism. And I think it is interesting if we listen to Lily Kong's presentation yesterday, and to the some of the more, other, work on Singapore, that we have some interesting issues here of the notion of the creative city, as exported to Singapore. And as we are all well aware, one of the elements in the economic model that Richard Florida develops as a proxy for tolerance is the socalled gay index and this doesn't fit quite so well with the administrative and governmental structures of Singapore, for example. So as Lily mentioned, there were questions in parliament, there were discussions about should the law be changed in some way to accommodate the creative class? This is a fundamental misreading of Richard Florida, I think, but also an example of the conflation of ideas about generalized notions of tolerance and creativity.

I think interestingly here we could for example ask questions about tolerance. I am quite intolerant to wealth disparities. I think that is a good thing, to be intolerant with wealth disparities. That tolerance isn't necessarily a universally good thing. Tolerance can be bad as well. Clearly the case of Singapore is a question of tolerance about particular moral codes. And that is a real cultural question about resolving those different views about those moral codes. And remember of course, the economists amongst you, that the gay index is a proxy, and in economics proxies are not the dependent variable, but a proxy seeks to track the dependent variable (tolerance?). So there is a double problem there. So there is a question in all of this, is that there are limits to tolerance. Tolerance isn't just 'everything has to be tolerant'. Tolerance is locally situated. And there is a local definition of tolerance. Always, there is the implication that we all ought to be tolerant to neoliberalism. Is that the message? I am sorry, I am being provocative here, but I think that linkage with assumptions that need to be interrogated, we need to make decisions on those assumptions rather then simply accept them as if they were fixed.

Creativity, Liberalism and Culture

Now I want to introduce a notion from political science. And I think a particularly interesting idea a couple decades ago was proposed by Iris Marion Young when she talked about justice and the politics of difference. And her point about justice, social justice, is that like tolerance, it is socially situated. And her point, and I will be very strong about this in relation to the urban, is that the imposition of universal norms, like social justice, may actually exacerbate inequalities if done in this universalist notion. So one needs to adapt and may need positive discrimination for example in order to transform situations and produce the outcome of inequality that one is trying to achieve. So there are problems with universalisms and the particularities. So there is a question about moral liberalisms, and you know we had many debates, whether it is about female emancipation, whether it is about ethnic diversity, etc, and religious diversity, etc, is the attempt and particularly of those in the West to impose a particular moral liberalism on the rest of the world. There is a challenge to that. So is it universal or is it situated? And of course the extreme of this is that everybody is different and therefore nobody can agree, I'm not suggesting that, but actually we need to investigate how the universal ideas are actually implemented in particular places. This is a very difficult question but I think it is an essential question.

Let me also think about creativity which I think suffers in many respects the same sort of formation. And about the universality of creativity and also of course it is almost entirely elided linked to liberalism. And I think we have to step back there and look at the particular history of creativity. And if we are thinking about creativity in Northwestern Europe, then we are talking about a particular period of history, of the romantic movement and romanticism, and the development of the 19th century and 20th century concepts of the artist. And this also has implications for notions of innovation because the artist was configured as an individual, and of course they lived in their garret room at the top and didn't have any interaction with any other people. This is a very strange model of innovation. This idea of the lone artist fits very neatly with this neoliberal version of the artist, and also with the neoliberal version of the entrepreneur, but doesn't link very well with the actually existing understandings of the processes of innovation and creativity. So we have some significant tensions here and of course the notion of the artist, the northwestern European artist, has an entire contradiction with the Japanese notion of artist. And there is a whole other formation there and we could go to other parts of the world to have different formations of artists. So we have to be careful not to universalize notions of artists.

I would argue that within the Florida thesis we have this neat combination of neoliberal and artist entrepreneur and this linking of creativity and freedom that is somehow necessary and sufficient, therefore you can't have creativity without freedom and without neoliberalism. That is a complex and very particular interpretation. This is a bit of a problem for China I think at the moment, and for many other countries. And this is often an argument which is used in innovation studies for any economy that is not organized around a neoliberal format. So the work by the other academic and political scientist, not the planner, Peter Hall, on varieties of capitalism, is a very strong questioning of this imposition of Anglo-American norms on Asia, for example, in terms of industrial organization. So there is a whole set of issues there and I think particularly this comes out in notions about creativity and freedom, but they appear in the rhetoric to be necessary and sufficient. I would argue that it doesn't quite work out like that.

Be Careful What You Wish for: the Actually Existing Creative City

The second line of criticism of the Richard Florida thesis is that this is a partial reading of Daniel Bell. Richard Florida's work, if you look at The Rise of the Creative Class, is very heavily dependent on the work of Daniel Bell, and particularly Bell's earlier work, The Coming Postindustrial Society, which has a number of internal criticisms that we could lay at the door, but let us put those aside for the moment okay? Interestingly, Daniel Bell himself in his later work came to realize that there are a few problems with this hypothesis and particularly in his book The Coming Postindustrial Society, he is talking about the rise of a scientific class that basically Florida renames as a creative class, but Bell is interested particularly in what he terms in his later book the "cultural contradictions of capitalism." And this was the fatal problem for the growth of the postindustrial society, which was a tension between non-work and creativity and culture and leisure, and the traditional Protestant work-ethic required of the bands of capitalism. And he saw this as the imminent and potential problem, and so yes, Bell wasn't a Marxist, far from it but he might have been in this sense in terms of inherent contradictions that he was talking about.

Now these debates, I don't follow Bell's argument, but I think the point that he raises is an important one, and it is a point which has been in the center of a lot of debates in recent years, particularly Boltansky and Chapello's work about The New Spirit of Capitalism has talked about these inherent tensions between the, if you like, the creative way of working and forms of management. These are existing tensions. Also the work, we have heard about the precariat, obviously the work of Hardt and Negri. The multitude for example… again, points about this particularly Lazzaretto's work on the link between, or the problems of the link between, art and neoliberalism. Is it a necessary relationship? Is this an excuse for self-exploitation, etc.? So there are a lot of interesting debates within this that I think are very current at the moment that I think inform these issues.

So a number of internal problems with the Richard Florida framework and some really interesting debates that I think we need to grapple with about exactly the particularities of liberalism and creativity, and their relationship.

Consumption

Let us put that aside for a moment. If you didn't buy that argument, let me try another one. Which is, instead of looking at the ideal of the creative city, let us look at some of the actually existing creative cities, so-called, and see whether they give us 'the good life', which creative cities are meant to give us. And of course as we have heard extensively, Sharon's work exemplified this, and we have heard numerous ways in which gentrification is both a gift and a curse that leads to all sorts of unintended consequences, the role of artists in gentrification for example, and the role of displacement, the contradictory relationships between market and non-market activities, and the impact this has in the development of cities, is a well-documented field. I think there is a second line here, if we reexamine the old work by Logan & Molloch for example on urban growth machines. This was an argument that they developed about the control of governance in cities. They were particularly concerned at the time about the strong relationship of interest built up between retailers and city governments. And there would basically be a relationship between them that would change the way, or control the way, that cities figured their future of investment and set their set of priorities.

I would argue that there is a second version of this. Forget retail, think culture. If you look at many American downtowns, the prospects of regeneration are about the concert hall and the entertainment center, etc. so here is another way in which city governance is linked directly to the entertainment machine or the cultural machine, and that is the only game in town, that is what governs the direction and priorities of governance. And of course, that is another way in which we might look at place marketing and the way that the priorities of place marketing are set. There is an implicit issue here of course, which many people have pointed out before, that the issues of place marketing and city branding are ones that are potentially in contradiction with cultural democracy. The tax payers who fund the city development, their priorities might be different from those that are trying to attract the foreign direct investment. Those in the city hall who are trying to attract the foreign direct investment through the building of concert halls, etc., for the elite consumers, will argue of course that in the long run the trickle down effect will be that jobs will be created for the rest of the city. The evidence doesn't quite support that point of view. But it is a nice idea.

So we come back to Sharon's point, which is, 'who's city, who's culture'? In a very real sense, it is the representation of cities, not just the symbolic representation but also the representation of them through cultural priorities, who's city, who's culture. And invariably, of course this has been said many, many times before, the reduction to an economic and consumption agenda.

Production

So it is in response to these sorts of things that clearly myself and many other people say, "There is another aspect we can look at, what about cultural production?" That is worth looking at, we can see some values there in terms of a more direct way of contributing to economies and jobs, etc. and yes there is a quite bit of evidence that we could point to there. In London for example, the third largest economic sector is the cultural sector. So, yes it is significant. And as we have heard many times already today and yesterday, the cultural sector is not like other industries, it is project-based firms, it is based on heterarchies rather than hierarchies, etc, and we have heard in great detail issues about the conditions of employment and jobs and freelancing, and informality issues.

Is This What We Want?: Is This a More Equal Workforce?

I just want to take that a step further, some of the points that Lily was hinting at yesterday, she said the data is very difficult to collect, yes it is, but the data that you can get and we have in London is indicative I think. And it is not very good, so if you look at the employment of women in the UK workforce, the data is about 46%. And in that great growth prospect of the cultural sector the audiovisual industries, it is only 36%. So they are not a very good equal opportunities employer. The concentration of women in the younger cohorts, i.e.in junior jobs, is around 44% in the overall population; in the audiovisual industries, it is 54%. So career advancement is not so good there, I am afraid. The employment of ethnic minorities, this is just for London, is something around just 24%. In the audiovisual industries, 10%. Let me tell you, in the film industries, it's 7%. So if as a city, you want to promote these industries, this is what you get: A radically more unequal society. And we know all about the ways of hiring jobs in this area. It is not through formal job applications, but it is about who you know, which is an age-old way of reinforcing discrimination. Just another interesting example about news journals, to take one example. If you look at news journalists in the UK, there are 54% of news journalists in UK that didn't go to the standard schooling system. They went to private school systems. So they are already part of an elite. Of those journalists with a degree, 56% attended either Oxford or Cambridge. That is not a very diverse group of people, quite honestly. And when you add that together with the compulsory 'free labor', and unpaid internships which are the conditions of entry to the cultural sector, then basically you need to have parents who can finances you for a number of years before you got the job. Again, quite a barrier to entry to the rest of the population. So you can find the sources of this information, I can point to these. So, 'be careful what you wish for', is my warning.

Conclusions

The creative city could be many things, but we need a situated analysis, we need to be careful in our explorations of creativity, and avoid the elision with neoliberalism. Creative cities can be about consumption. In fact, if that is what you want, they can do that. They can be about production, that is fine as well. But both of them have severe downsides, disadvantages, and they need inventive creative solutions to mitigate their worst excesses, or avoid them all together. I will just end with a point: the consequence, in a way, of this relationship of creativity and neoliberalism is that inequality is necessary for growth in creativity. I would challenge that. I would hope it is not so, as well. Thank you.

Kenkichi Nagao: I think we have heard a discussion which has on some points deepened what Andy Pratt himself has written about in the inaugural issue of '*City, Culture and Society*', and what Professor Edmond Preteceille in Paris has talked about. And I think once again the problem of the universal versus the situated, which we in urban studies must always think about, has been clearly stated.

3-5. Discussion

Kenkichi Nagao: The time that we had scheduled has already passed, which gives us very little room for discussion. But if we could impose just a bit more on our overworked translators… our time to discuss each point one by one has rapidly disappeared, but if there are a few people with questions from the floor regarding the entire set of presentations, including Andy Pratt's, please be brief… and as soon as we hear those, then I would like to hear a final closing comment from each of the speakers in order, beginning with Professor Lazzeretti, and in that way finish the session. First, let's hear from Professor Lily Kong who did not have time to ask a question before.

Lily Kong: So first of all thank you for an always stimulating talk, and I would like to bring us back to the comment that framed Sharon's talk yesterday and what I was trying to do in terms of referring to Singapore. Sharon talked about the fact that in New York there was very little of any planning and I was talking about the very contrasting situation in Singapore which had a great number of attempts at planning and management and governance and regulation in many areas. You talked about how inequality is not necessary for growth and creativity and creative activity, and the question I have is, if we were to be careful what we wish for, is it possible to plan in such a way that we avoid some of the excesses you are talking about? And when in one of you earlier slides, you ended up suggesting that you might talk about the implications of policy? I wonder what you would advocate as a way of dealing with some of the inequalities that are apparent in the data that you showed? What actions can actually be taken, if they can be taken at all by planners, to wish away some of these negativities. etc.?

Kenkichi Nagao: Thank you very much. Are there any other questions? I would first like to take all the questions.

François Colbert: Andy, if I can add to your discourse, I have been working with artists for 35 years and I love them. But what you could have added is that because there is a diverse supply on the market of cultural products, cultural lobbies try everything to justify the role of art in society, including help, education, social integration, and so on. And they try to give the idea that art is a religion, while in fact it is a leisure pursuit. It is a leisure activity except for the artists. So the lobbies were very fast to accept the ideas of Florida, because they could use them to put pressure on governments to get more money, more funds. But, and yesterday Sharon said that artists like to criticize society, which is totally true, but if you tell them that that is what they are doing, they don't like to be criticized. They like to criticize, but not to be criticized. They hate that. So, just few ideas to add to your account.

Kenkichi Nagao: Any other questions?

Hyun Bang Shin: It is not really my area of research but I just want to talk about what Andy was saying which I really liked by the way, so this is nothing like criticism, but an additional thought, especially regarding the other session this morning, which is about when this creative city issue is exported to other countries, especially in the global South, I think there is one thing which hasn't been touched upon, which is basically many of these subcontracting cities in the South where, for example the animation industry in which The Simpsons, the TV animation series The Simpsons... Many of these episodes are actually produced in South Korea, for instance, and they are exported to America to be broadcast over the whole country and whole world.

And I think there is a kind of, especially because Andy was touching upon the issue of inequality and etc., I think there are different layers of creative cities and a hierarchy in this neoliberal world being established, and I think those inequalities are being produced and reproduced. Not when in those so-called creative cities in the developed world, but also in developing countries or less developed countries where they are trying to promote these creative cities and industries, etc. but what they are actually doing is being more subordinate to existing industrial leaders in the developed world. I think those issue probably need to be more talked about, it may be interesting to explore more of these issues in the discourse of creative cities, I think. Thank you.

Kenkichi Nagao: And last but not least Prof. Sasaki, would like to ask a question?

Masayuki Sasaki: Andy, thank you once again. I am gratified that you gave us a very comprehensive presentation. What particularly impressed me this time was the relationship you talked about between the arts and neoliberalism. In that, I too have taken a critical stance towards Richard Florida. Concerning that, my question is, cultural production, that is something that takes place within a worldwide market, so naturally cultural production first takes place within the huge market of a major city, and then a strong cultural enterprise industry emerges, and it enters the world market. There are exports, and it creates employment. At one period, the Hollywood film industry was dominant throughout the world, and there was a tendency for it to try to rule the world. Then UNESCO issued a declaration in favor of cultural diversity, taking a stance against monopoly systems, that is to say, in the film industry, they tried to stop the monopoly of Hollywood, and tried to make a treaty, and in the midst of that movement, UNESCO proposed the Creative City Network. In other words, I think one can say that in the relation between cultural and neoliberalism, cultural diversity emerged as an opposing concept.

In that case, what we have to think about is that now, in some senses, while cultural production in the global creative cities is very effective as an engine of growth and in providing employment, for somewhat smaller cities, for cities with a similar ranking to Osaka's, this problem is much more difficult. In other words, in the global competition in the cultural industry, it's a question of what kind of strategies should second or third tier cities adopt, or in the case of even smaller cities, for example cities of the size of the Italian cities, what forms of production do they have? On this point, I was very impressed by Professor Lazzeretti's talk today, in other words, they managed to create a fusion between the cultural heritage that the city had historically kept and new technology, and from that new cultural products were born. This process, through which the new technology and the old cultural assets were tied together, became a new engine of growth for the city, so this relates to the question, how can a middle-sized city effectively utilize its own historically held cultural capital? If one thinks about it this way, the middle ground that Professor Cohendet talked about is very important, but for me, the question is, how can the cultural heritage of the city that has accumulated historically, and the creativity that each and every person in the city has, be brought from the underground to be reflected in the middle ground, and then to the upper ground as well? That is what struck me as the problem as I listened to this impressive talk. Thank you.

Kenkichi Nagao: Thank you. Your comment has served to sum things up, filling in for me as chairman. Time is really pressing in on us now, but we would like to hear from each of today's speakers their impressions, or their opinions about the last thing they were asked, or things that they didn't finish talking about… in tomorrow's Session 6 we are also planning to talk about these things… but to conclude today, we would like to hear from each of the speakers very briefly, I apologize but it can only be a very few words. Let us begin with Professor Lazzeretti, please.

Luciana Lazzeretti: Add new work to another one, said Jane Jacobs. This is my point to play what it is, but if I can I want to say a couple of things to my colleagues. Middle ground, the story of creative meetings' capability effect, that is the first one. The second one, I table Oxford and Cambridge much… So you try to put together like me, Marshall and Jane Jacobs. I think you are in a right place. So I think I really care about your idea about middle ground, about Montréal. I have too on the similar one about that, but we have these two pieces on the table… And social capital, the other point, there is a difference, but we have no time to discuss. Thank you Andy.

I started the creative city according to the industrial, because of the creative industry approach, so I have criticized Florida. But for this case I want to think of one thing that is very important about Florida and that is connected with Prof. Colbert. Florida has done a very important thing, focusing on human capital, and has put human capital in the same place as heritage. So when we discuss in terms of creativity in very large terms, all the economy has to be taken into inconsideration, the human capital, and the creativity. So it is a very important thing, for instance, for a new generation. In this sense we can criticize Florida in terms of liberalism, but we can also resurrect Florida in another way, because don't forget that his first book was in 2000. In that period we didn't discuss about that, so we need to contextualize the thinking. Obviously then, we continued on from there, but that was useful, and then the concept of situating creativity by Stabel, you know, that is useful in your research. Thank you.

Kenkichi Nagao: Thank you very much. Dr. Hanzawa?

Seiji Hanzawa: The problem of inequality is one that can be seen in particularly in the animation industry that I researched and in the television industry as a whole, where two classes have emerged, one that makes a lot of money, and another that is barely subsisting on their work. I wonder if this problem of inequality can be eliminated, but as one possibility, Professor Sasaki just asked, "What can be done for medium and small sized cities?", I think the medium and small sized cities can be a kind of 'backup' for the number one centers of industry agglomeration, or they can exist as a counterpart to it.

For example, in the television industry, Tokyo is filled with so many companies that there has emerged a kind of competition that resembles dumping, and where working overtime is taken for granted. In order to become number one, you have to keep being successful in Tokyo, but there are cases of creators who get tired of that and go back to the places they came from, like Osaka or Hokkaido, and while they are there they try to create what they themselves like at a more leisurely pace. In the animation industry as well, while it isn't the mainstream, there are animation companies in, say, Kyoto, or Toyama, and they do business pretty much they way they want to… it's a different style of business than in Tokyo, but in terms of quality and culture, what they are creating is high quality. There are cases like that.

Certainly, from the standpoint of the industry, a lot of these people haven't made it into the mainstream and made money, but as far as culture goes, there is nothing that is superior or inferior, so if some creators get tired of the competitive environment, go to another place, and can make the things they want to, I wonder if that isn't a way of taking positive advantage of the disparities in the system? Not all of the money is necessarily concentrated in the number one location of agglomeration, rather, one can see both light and shadow there, so, maybe this is a strange way to say it, but living a more-or-less OK life in a medium or small sized city and making cultural products may be one perspective that confronts the disparities in a positive way.

Kenkichi Nagao: Thank you. You made me remember that in Seattle, in the United States, there are a lot of cases of people who came there looking for a different environment after getting tired of Los Angeles or the San Francisco Bay Area. I think that would be a good topic for us in Japan, whether it would be good to pursue possibilities like that in Osaka or Hokkaido. Well then, Professor Cohendet, if you please.

Patrick Cohendet: A very pressing situation, and as Sharon said, very connected to what was said yesterday. I need to say first, thanks to Luciana, I can now understand that I was in despair with Florence or Sienna which I found beautiful but not creative. And thanks to her speech I can understand now that a cultural city, which is not creative, could become creative just because it is cultural. It has its assets, which can ignite creativity if you trigger it. And I think that is very interesting. I think that was very stimulating.

Concerning Seiji, I think he said something very important, which is what we lack in creativity, in artistic activity, is all these incentives of validation and structuration of the knowledge, and I think this is important. In contrast to the scientific milieu where you have all these institutions that validate knowledge, the difficulty with the artistic is, and this is the road of the middle ground to me, the middle ground is to provoke the building of structures ad hoc, to build this validation process, and if you don't have that, then you have problems with not being legitimate.

On Andy, yeah I like your talk and this is very welcome. There is something, if I could add on to the dangers of the creative city that was not expressed, and that is what I call the risk of a creative divide. It means that if you put too much emphasis on some areas in the city or some areas in cities, and not the rest of the country, you would institutionalize something like a creative divide which is a very big danger for the society. It is another form of inequality.

Kenkichi Nagao: Thank you very much for your talk, and the creative divide-related issue was pointed out, thank you very much. Now last, but not least, Dr. Pratt, would you give us your comment?

Andy Pratt: I just think the whole session was really interesting, and like Patrick, the idea of the lateral innovation transfer, I think it is really stimulating, really important. Also the verification and validation issue, and the context in which that happens, which is the middle ground. Anyway, I think those all fit together really nicely. I think what I was partly trying to say was that this challenge of the divide in a way is the, what I am trying to point out, the institutional asymmetries of the organization of the cultural sector and the innovation system. So to advocate that industry as a solution, it has its own internal problems, like all other industries, but particular to them that need to be addressed. And this is Lily's point, really. So we need policies that attend to those issues. But we can't have policies that attend to those issues without the knowledge of them, and that is partly what we have been doing as academics in these recent years, is to actually understand these industries. Because if we don't understand them there is no chance that policy makers are going to understand them, because actually the knowledge comes from us invariably. So there is a really significant issue there.

And to just widen this out, this is precisely the point that, when David Crosby and I were drafting the creative economy reports for UNCTAD, we were trying to address, which is the problem of creativity and global development. And you have massive asymmetries, particularly instantiated through the intellectual property rights regime, for example, but not exclusive to that, we can consider this many ways, whether it would be through the structure of the film industry that we have talked about, about the structure of the domination of Hollywood, etc., and you can repeat this in different ways in different industries and one has to understand those specificities if one is going to respond to them to have a less unequal outcome. And that is the policy impetus, it is how do you think about the less unequal outcome. And we need specific information and research from particular industries, and particular cities I think, in order to that, to respond to that issue. So my general point, I think, is that this generalized idea of the creative city could be dangerous. But, you know, creativity, creative industries in cities, there are a lot of good things about them as well, but they have to be applied very carefully, I think.

Kenkichi Nagao: Thank you very much. That is it for Session 3. Today's discussion has been about urban creativity, and as part of our symposium this has been a particular focus, at session that we made that is indeed aimed at specialists, but as chairperson I am relieved that the discussion has been very lively. Without necessarily taking the findings of previous research for granted, and while injecting new perspectives into existing research, and with particularly assertive criticism of Richard Florida's creative class, from the aspect of human capital, we have to offer credit on that point. There is a plan for the fourth issue of *'City, Culture and Society'* to have Richard Florida, and maybe some people from the University of Toronto, act as guest editors and make a special issue. That is supposed to be posted on line next week. In that sense, I think that Osaka City University's Urban Research Plaza, can make a contribution 'towards the century of cities' as in this international symposium.

Also, for tomorrow afternoon we have scheduled a great session for Session 6 that will run for three hours with no formal presentations. That is something the Director Sasaki himself, who will chair the session, creatively planned, and in tomorrow's session, there were things today that we didn't get a chance to fully discuss, in tomorrow's session we will be able to discuss them. Through this conference and through the new journal, I hope that the Urban Research Plaza can make a contribution by providing an environment that allows for comprehensive discussion about cities and a cross-fertilization between people of many different specialized disciplines and different academic backgrounds. Let's have one more round of applause for our speakers. Thank you.

Session 4
14:00-17:00 December 16th, 2010

Roundtable

"Networking the Asian Urban Studies" Overseas Sub-Centers

The leaders of all seven of the Overseas Sub-Centers (Overseas Plazas) operated by the Urban Research Plaza will gather together and talk about the network between the Sub-Centers, the sharing of academic research information, and their participation in CCS and the AUC. To begin with, in the first half there will be 10-minute presentations from each of the Sub-Centers, and a number of topics emerging from those will included in the discussion, and then we will produce a session recommendation concerning this network's prospects and the contributions that it can make in the future. Each of the Sub-Centers began under different circumstances and have different backgrounds, and they are not based on a single consistent policy, but that is not seen as a minus, rather the variety of resources is seen as a plus. How could the issues of, for example, Hong Kong (homelessness and other forms of social exclusion) be pressed into the same mold to match those Bangkok (energizing the city through the arts)? What kinds of strategies can the Sub-Centers employ in ringing a warning bell against globalization that has gone too far, and in building a new framework for urban renewal? Answering these questions is a big challenge, and we hope that we will be able to discover key concepts that link together this diversity, and offer proposals related to the problem of the soft infrastructure for the information that binds this diversity together and transmits it.

Jong Gyun Seo Senior Research Fellow, Korea Center for City and Environment Research, South Korea
Specialist in Urban Planning

Ying-Fang Chen Professor, East China Normal University, China
Specialist in Urban Sociology

Liling Huang Assistant Professor, National Taiwan University, Taiwan
Specialist in Urban Planning

Wing Shing Tang Professor, Hong Kong Baptist University, Hong Kong
Specialist in Urban Geography

Bussakorn Binson Associate Professor, Chulalongkorn University, Thailand
Specialist in Ethnomusicology

Nicolaas Warouw Lecturer, Gadjah Mada University, Indonesia
Specialist in Political Anthropology

Suzy Goldsmith Senior Research Fellow, University of Melbourne, Australia
Specialist in Management

Coordinator: **Shin Nakagawa** Professor, Osaka City University
Prof. Nakagawa's range of expertise extends from soundscape art studies to ethnomusicology (especially Asian), and art management studies. He is especially concerned with the potential of the arts in urban and community renewal.

Sub-Centers

Seoul
The Seoul Sub-Center was established in 2009 at the Korea Center for City and Environment Research which is a non-profit and independent research organization. Today the aim of KOCER is to analyze domestic urban issues scientifically and to develop reasonable policy alternatives in order to find better solutions while advocating independent urban grassroots movements.

Shanghai
Set up in East China Normal University in Shanghai. Since 2003, collaborating with the staff of the Center for Modern Chinese City Studies, we have investigated the slum evictions caused by the redevelopment of Shanghai, the conditions of social exclusion in a densely settled area of immigrants, and policies for responding to these challenges.

Taipei
Beginning its operation in cooperation with the Research Center for Globalizing Cities, National Taiwan University, the Taipei Sub-Center pursues alternatives in solving urban problems, collaborating with the Taipei homeless support network and other organizations.

Hong Kong
Opened at Hong Kong Baptist University in 2008, the Hong Kong Sub-Center collaborates with the university's Dept. of Geography, and the Hong Kong Metropolitan Planning and Environmental Management Centre and conducts surveys and symposia related to urban renewal, citizens' movements, homelessness, and social exclusion.

Bangkok
Located within Chulalongkorn University, Thailand's leading educational institution, since 2003 the Bangkok Sub-Center, together with the university's Dept. of Arts, has held an annual international forum on urban cultural creativity and tourism, and has been active in exchanges of personnel.

Yogyakarta
Established in cooperation with the Indonesia Institute of the Arts (ISI) and the Gadjah Mada University. Since 2003, we have been holding international forums annually at the Yogyakarta Sub-Center, jointly with the ISI and the UGM.

Melbourne
Opened at the University of Melbourne's School of Management in 2008, this Sub-Center is expected to be a stronghold for efforts in investigating practical means of social inclusion in a multicultural society and to create new urban visions from the fusion of both academic knowledge and "civic wisdom."

Session 4

Shin Nakagawa

Current academic position
Professor, Department of Asian Culture and Urbanism, Osaka City University

Academic experience
2001- Dr. Science of Arts, Osaka University of Arts
1981- M.A., Osaka University
1975- B.A., Kyoto University

2001- Professor, Department of Asian Culture and Urbanism, Osaka City University
1991-01 Associate Professor, Faculty of Music, Kyoto City University of Arts
1986-91 Senior Lecturer, Faculty of Music, Kyoto City University of Arts
1981-86 Research Assistant, Faculty of Letters, Osaka University

Research interests
Arts Management
Soundscape
Sound Arts
Asian Music

Major articles and papers
"Heiankyo – Oto no Uchu (Heian-kyo as Sounding Cosmos)" (revised ver.), Heibonsha, 498p, 2004
"Saundoato no Toposu (Topos of Sound Arts)" Showado, 239p, 2007
'Socially inclusive cultural policy and arts-based urban community regeneration', Cities, Volume 27, Supplement 1, pp.16-25, 2010
'A cultural approach to recovery assistance following urban disasters', 'City, Culture and Society', Volume1 Issue 1, pp.27-36, 2010 (with Koichi Suwa)

4-0. Opening Remarks

Good afternoon everybody. Now may I start our session 4. This session is called Networking Asian Urban Studies. And we invited 7 people from Asian Pacific countries and from the Sub-Centers of the URP. I don't like that word "Sub-Center." Really, these are not Sub-Centers, these are really partners of the URP, not Sub-Centers. Each of the centers have their own history and relationship with the URP. There is not one center, there are 7 different Sub-Centers.

The title of this symposium is 'Urban Regeneration through Cultural Creativity and Social Inclusion.' So I will say a little bit about our purpose, it is an attempt at urban community revitalization from the bottom-up, with the utilization of the arts as a medium for social inclusion, and attempting creatively to rebuild the city focusing not on the elite strata but the lower strata in the society. I think that is the second stage, that creative cities theory will move us towards. Now what is the second stage? Not attracting bohemian-like human resources with a lot of times and buildings and high-tech industries, but rather focusing on the local resources and bringing to the market products that emerge from them.

In doing that, especially using the creativity of the socially disadvantaged, it will make a path for them to participate in society and to reduce social disparities and create a truly tolerant and inclusive community. And this is a very basic, not new, but very basic and fundamental point, and this is the starting point of this session. But in any case, perhaps each person has their own idea about social inclusion and cultural activity, and we want to make it free.

Jong Gyun Seo

Current academic position
Senior Research Fellow,
Korea Center for City and Environment Research

Academic experience
2003- Ph.D., Urban Planning, Chung-Ang University
1990- M.A., Seoul University
1993- B.A., Yonsei University

2007- Research Fellow, Korea Center for City and Environment Research
1994-02 Researcher & Senior Researcher, Korea Center for City and Environment Research
1994- Researcher, Seoul Development Institute
1993- Researcher, Seoul University

Research interests
Housing Policy
Community Participation
Urban Regeneration
Social Entrepreneurship

Major articles and papers
2009, *Human Rights Conditions of Non- Housing Dwellers*, National Human Rights Commission of Korea
2009, Tenant Support Programs in Social Housing, Korea Land and Housing Corporation
2009, The Tasks of Housing Policy for the Independent Living of Disabled People, *The Korea Spatial Planning Review*, Vol.61, Anyang: KRIHS

4-1. Hybridization Can Create Strong Species

Summary

The planning of a large-scale redevelopment project in Anyang, which might include seven or more smallerdevelopment projects, has been ongoing for a few years. Many people feel excluded from the property-centered development process. They feel that they and their abilities are being ignored by planners. This frustrated group includes small businesses. Their businesses have not been included in the future post-redevelopment social composition. The major stakeholders of redevelopment projects do not value existing businesses, especially small ones, until they become strong enough to resist the redevelopment process. In many cases, the voice of small businesses has not been organized until the very last stage of the decision-making process, by which time they can just ask for more compensation; this describes the situation in Anyang.

We face many challenges, and there are many reasons why situations like Anyang's don't change. There are few hopeful cases to be found. This disappoints us and often leaves us dispirited and apathetic. Different circumstances lead to different results, though: we might find that progress has been made in other circumstances and that we can learn from those successes. There is no need to wallow in disappointment: we need to discover those successes in order to foster a more positive attitude.

The Anyang Public Art Project 2010 was a melting pot of various people's ideas on ways to rethink Anyang's problems and potential. It was a large collaborative project consisting of many small projects. Small Business Big Change, a competition for small business innovation, was one of them; it was designed to bring attention to the potential of small businesses, especially in the context of redevelopment. A wealth of lessons and ideas came from many people from many countries. The projects from which we learned most include the Sham Sui Po project of the Community Museum Project in Hong Kong, the Row Housing project in Houston, the local business support services in Bristol (England), and the Idea Village's business plan competition in New Orleans. Influenced by these challenging projects, we drew various elements from them and mixed them into our own project. We also forged links with various groups, including small business owners, academics, researchers, artists, activists, students of business administration and art, consultants, and city government officials. What we achieved required their ideas and assistance. If our project continues, we will organize the voice of small businesses, help to realize their full potential, change the local entrepreneurial culture, and take urban regeneration into a new direction.

Introduction

Thank you for having me here today, and I am quite glad and happy to be a part of the Sub-Center group. And today I will talk about the project which I have been doing this year. It is called "small business, big change." The title is quite fancy, isn't it? When I have problems to sort out and when I try to find the solution, I think it is the right time to learn something from other people and other cases. Last year, when I was at the Hong Kong conference, the whole conference was very impressive. And especially in the field trips, I learned quite a lot about community development projects in Hong Kong. But, when I started my project in Anyang, I started to learn even more from Hong Kong. And I met some other Hong Kong guys who work for the Community Museum Project. They told me about Li Tung Street and Sham Shui Po. It was quite good to rethink about what I have seen and what I have heard in Hong Kong. So I started googling them, and I found a lot of materials. So now the

Hong Kong cases are very familiar to me and this Hong Kong is not the Hong Kong I used to know. Hong Kong is now one of my textbooks, it is a "Living Library."

Small Business/Big Change began like this

I will now talk about the 'small businesses and big changes.' It begins like this: during the summer last year, a man came to my office and he is an art director of the Anyang Public Art Project (APAP) and my project is part of this bigger project. And he was quite worried about the redevelopment project which was going on in Anyang, and he especially was worried about the process and the results, and the redevelopment project had bulldozed not just buildings, but also social relationships as well. And the people could not participate in the process. And then I met another nice guy, who is named Rick, and he was in charge of another project of APAP. We joined two projects and took part in the competition together. And his projects in poor communities are quite impressive. He tried to make the poor people proud of themselves. They can have that kind of pride when they confront their problems.

My problem in Anyang is like this: the people, small business entrepreneurs, think like this: "Small businesses are not a part of mainstream." "Traditional markets will disappear eventually." "It is inevitable for big companies to dominate the market." "Most shops will not survive after the redevelopment project." When we asked if they want to come back after the redevelopment project, most people said no, they can't. Even when we saw some people who said yes, they may not be able to come back because of many kinds of reason, like higher rents. So there are a lot of groups against the project, and some of the opposition groups are based on the traditional markets. And in this kind of situation, we tried to collect some ideas from Korean cases, but unfortunately we cannot find very much, so we looked outside and found some good ideas from the UK, Japan, Hong Kong, and the U.S.

To sum up our ideas, it is like this: we need innovative entrepreneurship. Secondly, to promote it, we can use a competition. And small businesses need networking, definitely. The networks can be important resources to innovate their businesses. Finally, to continue this process, we may need some organizational infrastructure.

The competition

As for the competition, I will show the numbers first. Ten participants went through the whole process, and we had four winners. The total prize money was US$20,000. Initially we arranged US$10,000 for prize, but in the process we had a generous donor who added $10,000 more. And we have 17 professional helpers and 14 student volunteers, who work in the arts and business sectors. We had a competition, a workshop and lots of long meetings. We visited the participants' shops and factories many times. I think we did too much. We arranged many kinds of support, like business consulting, designing and so on. We planned our time for a pre-study survey, competition preparations and a one-day competition workshop, and developing business plans and supporting businesses. Here are some pictures. In the workshop we had three small group discussions which were led by 3 professionals a consultant, a city officer and an artist (Figure 1). Mainly student volunteers visited working places and investigated the businesses and helped participants to develop their business plans. They worked together like this (Figure 2). We considered the business plans quite seriously. Then we chose four winners.

This is one of the winners (Figure 3). He makes tofu in a traditional market, and he wants to make organic tofu so we arranged a trip for him to go to a place to meet an organic tofu maker. And we refurbished the shop as well.

Sharing Experience & Afterwards

Then we tried to have a chance to share our experiences, and we also wanted to make other people, like city government officers and small business people in the community, continue this kind of process over next few years. So we had a symposium which was organized by our team and KRIHS, which is a public research organization. This organization was the generous donor. Then we organized a forum, which was called the Anyang Local Economic Forum. We hope this group can be a strong pressure group pushing the city government to make policies to support small businesses. We also had a party, called Small Business Day, and at the party, and also throughout the whole process, we liked to say: "small businesses are important in the local economy," and "they can be the center of innovation", and most importantly "they should not be neglected in policy making and planning processes".

The results, at the moment, are not very good because the city government doesn't want to continue this kind of process next year. But it is very true, when small businesses are connected, they can be more creative. And we also need to be connected, just like them. Thank you.

Figure 1   APAP Foundation

Figure 2   APAP Foundation

Figure 3   APAP Foundation

Ying-Fang Chen

Current academic position
Vice-Director, The Center for Modern Chinese City Studies,
Professor, Department of Sociology, School of Social Development,
East China Normal University

Academic experience
Ph.D., Osaka City University

2003- Professor, Sociology Department, East China Normal University
1999-03 Associate professor, Sociology Department, East China Normal University
1992-94 Visiting Scholar, Institute for Research in Humanities, Kyoto University
1987-92 Lecturer, East China University of Politics and Law
1982-84 Teaching Assistant, History Department, Su Zhou University

Research interests
Urban studies about urban development and social inadequate, housing exclusion.
Historic sociology of youth, youth culture in modern China.
Chinese studies.

Major articles and papers
Urban Development: Political Economy of Space Production, Shanghai Guji Publishing House, 2009.
"Youth" and the Social Change in Modern China, Beijin: Social Sciences Academic Press, 2007.
"Punhu": The Life History in 157 Memories, Shanghai: Shanghai Guji Publishing House, 2006.
Children in the Image: Analyze From A Sociological Perspective, Jinan: Shandong Huabao Publishing House, 2003.
Moving to Shanghai, Memoirs of 52 Person, Shanghai: Xuelin Publishing House, 2003.
Requisitions of Land and the Urbanization of Suburbs, A Research in Shanghai, Shanghai: Wenhui Publishing House, 2003.
Roles Playing or Not : Youth Culture in China, Nanjin: Jiangsu People's Publishing House, 2002.

4-2. Help Systems of Housing / Residence Life in Shanghai: Our Survey and Ideas

Summary

Using ethnographic research on the residential lives of poor urban immigrants and the providers of cheap rental housing and shelters in Shanghai, this study offers observations on and analyses of the residential lives of people who cannot afford to use the formal housing rental markets or obtain essential support from local government. Focusing on their methods of acquiring shelter and the mechanisms of the informal/illegal housing rental market, we seek to understand the logic of the state-market-society relationships and appeal for social rescue on behalf of the homeless to NGO/NPO in China. Our paper should also lead to a discussion about societal possibility: through our observations on residential support networks for the urban poor, we seek to find an existing system of social solidarity and morality in today's urban China.

Introduction

Thank you. I am very glad to be here to give my presentation at Osaka City University, my alma mater. So to me, this conference has a special meaning. Well, let me begin. In Osaka I dealt with research objects that came from my advisors, Prof. Mizuuchi and the assistant professors. They are involved in research about the homeless in Osaka. But even after I returned to Shanghai, they asked me if I could do the same project in Shanghai. So, they think that in Shanghai there are many urban programs, but I always thought, we can't see so many homeless street sleepers, so I had no interest in doing the same kind of social survey. But, some years passed, and now I think I can maybe see from another side, because this is my path, my research question. Because in China there is now a population of about 200 million people who have emerged without public support. That means they have no public housing guarantees or any other necessary social guarantees from the state or local government. But how is it possible for the migrants to make a living in the city? Besides the migrants, even the local residents, in recent years, they have experienced changes, dramatic changes of space and in communications. So, they too have moved out of the central city. So, so many are moving, but the current urban life in China still shows an unusual order. How could this be true? Maybe this question is our problem.

System of housing exclusion

Because of the time limit, I will go to my Power Point slides. So, there is systematic housing exclusion. First, in the mix of housing available. This system is very cheap for migrants and some of the urban poor. So now in China there is a system of housing, social exclusion around the housing guarantees, through the different household registrations and other identity documents. Their guarantees are different. Nowadays in China, urban development is like a tank, I think. Here are some points: One is the land-based violence, and others are differential land rents and the restructuring of social space.

So, in these systems, there are differential rents that create an excessive price for housing and high rent prices in the downtown area. If the original residents in the central place have no corresponding purchasing power, they will be pushed out to the far suburbs. So this is all the residents, now they live in the far suburbs. For the migrants, housing prices are just limited to prices. One is in the shanty district, the others are in peasant houses, so now if the peasants and the urban poor have to relocate, they will go to other places. So these are the local peasants. Their houses are now regularly located. If the peasant houses are relocated, the migrants will be dislodged.

Another system is concerned with rental houses and regulations. So this work and these regulations limit strictly the poor residents and the migrants. In our surveys in the last few years we found that almost half of the migrants are living in the cities illegally. They are in reality breaking out of the regulated sites. So that situation has changed. So, first to our survey. Where are they living? Besides the migrants, there are many other groups, maybe they were living in the city for a short time for example, maybe they are parents of the students looking for jobs, and other groups who are seeking better medical care in bigger cities and some jobs. So these places are the living places in the central area and worker's places in the suburbs.

Figure 1: Low-cost apartment

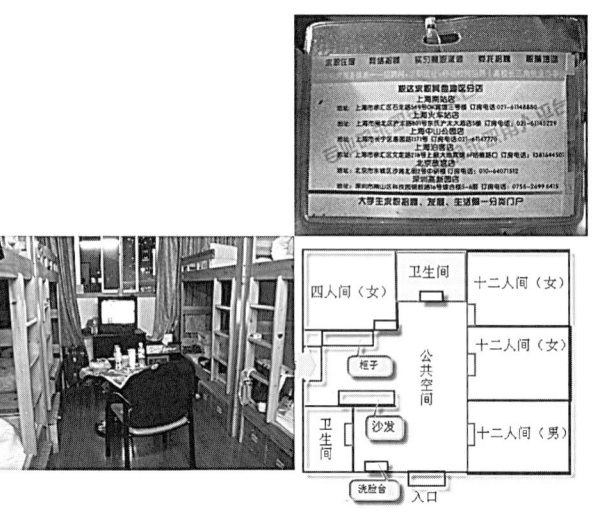

Figure 2: Fake hotels: apartment for job seekers

How could they make their living life well-ordered?

These are the apartment towers. This is a cheap apartment, a shared collective apartment (Figure 1). This type has been abandoned by the government (Figure 2). These are some fake hotels, so they have just changed places. There are many that have changed places. These are the street sleepers (Figure 3). So our question is, "How could they make their living?" For one thing, there are the socalled illegal but very active markets in the city's economic life, markets which are embedded in the society. There are also family bonds. The family bonds were weakened by modernization and urbanization, but now in Chinese urban society we can find family

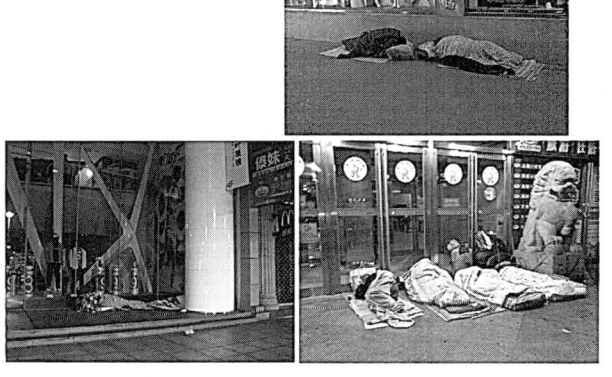

Figure 3: Street-sleepers

bonds working again. There are some existing family charities, and there are some traditional private networks for mutual help. So in the political area, for the urban citizens… there is a certain buffer zone between the state and society.

Conclusion: Social risk we concerned

The important thing is about the social risks. That is what we now are worrying about. So, there are some problems. One is the lack of public labor guarantees, and another one is the system that limits social groups in helping people. There is a problem with crackdowns on the informal markets by the local government, and the last is about the urban exclusion of young migrants. The second generation of workers have to establish their lives in urban China. So this spatially organized migrant society, how can it exist in the China of the future? That is the social risk that has awakened our concern. Sorry, my time is up, so thank you very much.

Liling Huang

Current academic position
Assistant Professor, National Taiwan University

Academic experience
- 2008- Director, Research Center for Globalizing Cities, Graduate Institute of Building and Planning, National Taiwan University (Taipei, Taiwan)
- 2007, Assistant Professor, Graduate Institute of Building and Planning, National Taiwan Univesrity
- 2003-07 Assistant Professor, Department of Architecture and Graduate School of Media Space Design, Ming-Chuan University (Taoyuan, Taiwan)

Research interests
- Globalization and Development
- Urban Studies
- Community Building and Place Making
- Theories of Planning and Design

Major articles and papers
- Forthcoming, "Taipei Metropolitan Development: Dynamics of Cross Strait Political Economy, Globalization and National Identity", (Co-author, Reginald Yin-Wang Kwok) in Stephen Hamnett and Dean Forbes (eds.) *Asian Cities: Risks and Resilience* (Working Title), London: Routeledge.
- 2008, "Against the Monster of Privatisation: Qing-Tien Community's Actions for Urban Livability in Taipei" *International Development Planning Review*, Vol. 30. p293-306. Nov/ Dec., Liverpool University Press.
- 2007, "Globalizing the City in Southeast Asia: Utopia on the Urban Edge: the Case of Phu My Hung, Saigon", collaborated with Mike Douglass. *The International Journal of Asia Pacific Studies.* Vol.3. No2. pp.1-43. Published by Penerbit Universiti Sains Malaysia.

4-3. Cultural Practices, Urban Redevelopment and the Marginalized Urban Poor in Taipei

Summary

As one of the former "Four Asian Tigers," Taiwan had created its world renowned "Economic Miracle" by the mid 1980s. However, unlike the governments in Hong Kong and Singapore, the national and local governments in Taiwan invested extremely little in public housing to facilitate economic and social development. In 2010, public housing for the urban poor represents only 0.08% of the total housing stock in Taiwan, a fact criticized by activists as "a shame on the government."

This paper aims to analyze the housing situation of the urban poor in Taipei. It will first examine the history of Taiwan's approach to housing policy and show how it has always excluded the urban poor. Then, it will analyze the recent urban redevelopment policy of Taipei and describe its impact on the housing market, especially for the urban poor. Moreover, it will address the difficulties attending political activity in the inner city and contrast those difficulties with the way more affluent communities have easily obtained resources from the city government over the past two decades. We will show that some NGOs committed to urban policy and social welfare have recently mobilized in Taipei to address housing issues and have pushed the governments to respond; their appeals will be introduced in this paper. Lastly, based on the situation in Taipei, this paper will offer collaborative research and action plans formulated by the Urban Research Plaza (URP) at Osaka City University.

Introduction

Good afternoon everyone. I am very honored to be here. And my topic has changed a bit to better echo the theme of the conference. Now, it is about cultural practices, urban redevelopment, and the marginal life of the urban poor in Taipei. I will try to bring in more the cultural factors as the medium for reinforcing the grassroots, the urban poor in Taipei, but I would like also to talk about some recent challenges.

Urban Policies in the 1990s

Let me begin from the urban policies in the 1990s in Taipei. In 1997, our government abolished martial law in Taiwan, so it meant that Taiwan started to become more democratic, and we have had a lot of new policies. In parallel with that, in the planning area we have seen some new changes happened which are more socially inclusive because we have participatory planning, historically for the first time, in producing community spaces. So, in this picture you see the planners (Figure 1). At that time most planners stayed at the government of-

More Socially Inclusive by
- Participatory planning in producing community spaces
- Historical Preservation for new urban identity
- Government-community partnership: Community Empowerment Project, Community Planner Scheme', 'Community Culture and Art '

Figure 1: More Socially Inclusive

fices, but these are planners in my department and they went to the park, visit people and talk about the project and how to make the park design better. And also we have historical preservation as a massive movement. It was mobilized by the NGOs, local historians, and also the government. Later the local government responded to this approach, so it is very important in shaping a new urban identity. And we see that there is a government community partnership in the so-called community empowerment projects and community planners' scheme. The idea is that you don't need to be professionally trained as a planner, but if you are interested in bringing people together in community design, you may join the short period of training, and then you can get a kind of certificate, and go to work with the community. And we also have a community culture and art program, initiated by the local government.

Example: Yong Kong Park in Da-an District

An example here is from the Yong Kong Park in Da'an community. Many Japanese tourists, when they visit Taipei, will visit this area. And by the park you see is a different form from what it used to be because before 1995, it was like this: in the middle the red spot you can see the political statue of Chang Kai Shek, which was very normal at that time. But after the park redesign, never, because the people thought they wanted some new things to replace the old symbol of the park. So there were NGOs and people working together, and their kids also joined in the workshop. And here we see that the statue was moved from the center to a corner of the park. So people no longer need to pay so much attention to it, and have replaced it with a small stage because people wanted a community center with a little space, so they built the stage to host some activities. And when there is no event, kids can play on it. So they turned this place into a very lively spot. And also we can see the art work. The fence was torn down and after discussion, community people decided to do the mosaic design on the fence. You can see the design that people shared together, and also the design of the telephone booth which is quite unique and you won't see it in other places in Taipei (Figure 2). The street furniture also expressed its local identity.

Figure 2: Yong Kong Park in Da-an District: Volunteers, residents & NGOs came together

Dali community in Wan-hua District: derelict area turned park

Another case is not located in a middle class community, but where had more people with lower incomes. Here the place you see used to be vacant land, but when people of Wanhua wanted to have more neighborhood parks, they started talking to the national government who owned the land, and the local government who designed and planned the urban space. After a very long time, about ten years of negotiations, a park was born.

This one you see is in the early design. The older design was decided by the community people, especially the housewives. The trees were kept there. What I want to show here is how people rediscovered local history and turned it into a mural on the wall. And this used to be the warehouse of a sugar factory. And kids come here to have their local education about the history of the neighborhood. So it expressed the characteristics of this community. And what I have shown above has shown that culture and art can become a tool to bring people together and to define them as new citizens in the city.

But, on the other hand, we have the squatter settlements being demolished almost at the same time. There were poor people and also planners working together to advocate for letting them remain there, even for having an alternative planning program, but it failed. I was part of the group of planners at that time. And the city government decided to develop it into an urban park. All the people were dislocated. But after that we had a case called Treasure Hill. At that time we tried to bring in a new approach. We tried to persuade the government that the squatter areas, the so-called illegal settlements, were part of the urban history. And at that time Taipei had a very progressive chief of the Bureau of Cultural Affairs. She tried hard to turn the Treasure Hill into a historical settlement, so the government discovered a new term or category 'historical settlement' to let the squatter area stay the same. And some of the original residents were allowed to stay. They even got some small amount of compensation. So this is Treasure Hill.

At the beginning of the idea the planner wanted to turn it into a social welfare area, but because the chief was in charge of cultural affairs, in the end we saw the so-called cultural approach to keep this area. We had artists who came together to work with the local people, and there show the artists' project. He said to the residents, "Bring one of the things you treasure most to the community garden, and I will take a picture for you." So the artists did a lot of these pictures of the community people, that's how they got involved. Someone brought there a lovely cat, or their parents or their grandson, or they took a wedding photo there. On the left side shows the local artist who lived in the village for a few decades. But he didn't really want to communicate with other people until this event.

Some features

So the point was the participatory democracy at that time, orchestrated together with the discovery of local culture, shaping the new urban identity in the late 1990s, and we also saw community culture and art activities worked as ways of advocacy and self-expression for the community of middle class people as well as poor people. But here is the one question: "What's the limit of art?" We see it cannot solve many things in the poor community.

Recent Trends

And, as for recent trends or recent challenges, the first is from the local identity project as well. I see more of the phenomena of city branding or so-called cultural industries taking place, and making a once very progressive approach more conservative. And we also saw more historical sites not becoming public spaces but being designated as creative parts of art districts. At the same time, places suitable for public space were sold by the government and bought up by developers. And we also see mega-events promoting the new urban beauty and the culture. The whole discourse now is more about the market approach. On the other hand, more and more, elite artists are replacing community artists, and they dominate the whole discourse and practices, and the events there are not locally relevant.

This shows the Taipei Flora Expo, and through this project the government heavily redeveloped the old district. This shows a movie, and the film industry promoters recently are saying that Taipei is such a big, charming film studio. And the last example is from the Wanhua area, the day-laborer area. We saw a building trying to show off its old style to promote the movie called Manga, but on the other side we also saw homeless people sleeping near the

Figure 3: historical sites designated as creative parts of art districts

park (Figure 3). Besides, the park design is trying to bar homeless people from sleeping there. I think this is not a good trend, and that we need to think about that. Thank you.

Wing Shing Tang

Current academic position
Professor, Department of Geography,
Hong Kong Baptist University

Academic experience
2004- Ph.D., Department of Land Economy, University of Cambridge
1981- M.Sc.Pl., Department of Urban and Regional Planning, University of Toronto
1976- B.A. (Hons.), Department of Geography, McGill University

2009- Professor, Department of Geography, Hong Kong Baptist University
2005-09 Associate Professor, Department of Geography, Hong Kong Baptist University
1998-05 Assistant Professor, Department of Geography, Hong Kong Baptist University
1989-98 Lecturer, Department of Geography, The Chinese University of Hong Kong

Research interests
Urban development and planning in Hong Kong and mainland China
Interrogating Western theories in the Eastern context
Urban utopias
The methodology of spatial stories
India-China comparative urban studies

Major articles and papers
Tang, W-S. and F. Mizuoka (eds) (2010) *East Asia: A Critical Geography Perspective.* Kokon Shoin, Tokyo.
Tang, W-S. (2008) Hong Kong under Chinese sovereignty: social development and a land (re)development regime. *Eurasian Geography and Economics* 49, 341-61.

4-4. Networking within Asian Urban Studies: An Inside-out Perspective

Summary

There are at least two related perspectives on pursuing and networking within Asian urban studies. One is the usual approach: area studies. The other can be called the "Western approach," for lack of a better term. The former usually highlights an in-depth knowledge of particular places and the elements of their distinctiveness. Networking premised on area studies connects the areas being researched on equal terms in order to elaborate their pros and cons. The latter perspective usually takes the West as the origin of development and assumes that Asian countries are empirical objects of the theories developed there. Networking is thus dispatched from the center to the peripheries, which usually have a minimal, subsidiary role in the network. Examples of both processes are abundant in the short history of urban studies: an example of the former is the call for ordinary city-based analyses driven by post-colonial studies; an example of the latter is the search for the "world city(s)" of each nation.

I argue that neither perspective is fruitful for understanding Asian cities, with their unique pasts, and that they both hinder any substantive, meaningful networking. Instead, I propose an inside-out perspective that takes into account the distinct historical dynamics of Asian countries and provides codetermined observations among the multiple dynamics of these countries as well as those between Asia and the West (Tang and Mizuoka, 2010). It is these processes of development, linking Asian cities together, that should be the crux of networking. I elaborate this argument by investigating Hong Kong's urban development over time and across space in order to assert that we can neither understand Hong Kong in the straitjacket of Western concepts nor treat it as unique. Hong Kong is neither a world city nor an ordinary city, but something produced in the co-determination between the East and the West and between China and rural society.

Introduction

Yes, what I would like to do today is, instead of telling you a specific case study, especially from Hong Kong, I would like to address a more methodological issue, how to make comparisons, and then talk about networking. Now in an international conference of this kind, we so-to-speak lay persons are usually told how we are supposed to study our own cases and compare them to others, including our neighbors. So, what I am going to argue is that we should drop this theoretical understanding and research methodology, and instead to start with the very basics of, for example, examining everyday lives accordingly. We would stand a better chance of understanding ourselves and others.

Networking Is Dead

Now there are in the stock a lot of these kinds of comparison methodologies, for example like here is one working on a mega project called cities, and another one that I personally attended is the INURA in Europe, as the new metropolitan mainstream. Another one would be a bit less hard, it would be based on representations.

Now there are some common features among these methodologies and let me use the NMM as an example. What we usually do is to set out an overarching global framework, and then from there we do a lot of comparisons, you know, whether you have this or that. For example, in this particular example, it lists out a few things, essential features, comparisons and some regional marketing development strategies, skyline landmarks and festivals, and then you just pick which cities have more of this kind, and then which city has less of this kind (Figure 1).

What we are seeing really though is, I would argue, something like this: it started from Europe, and then we keep on doing it as well as we can. You keep on and on and then for example we also include Hong Kong and Mumbai and

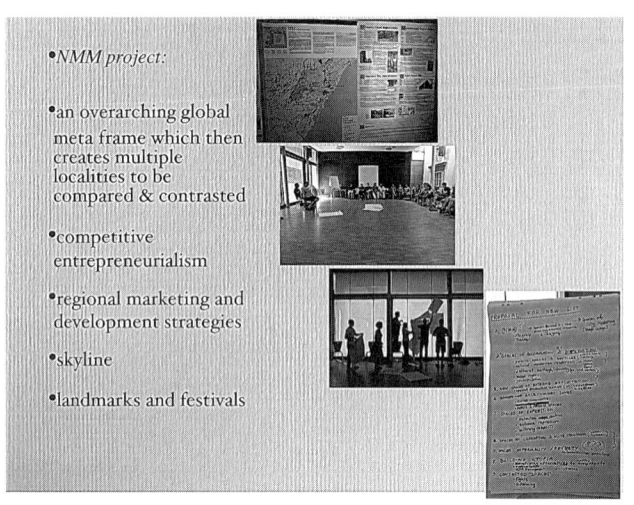

Figure 1: NMM project

then do it again. Now the issue not so much that the global south is different than the global north. As this view is problematic, it is problematic in terms of the perspective. I think for example, Andy Pratt talked about it, but I want to push the point even further. What I am saying is that what we have now observed is what I call a traditional outside-in perspective. There are usually assumptions saying that everything starts from, there is only one origin, everything starts from Western capitalism. And even if capitalism developed, and in that way, all the developed countries have no agencies, no internal contradictions.

Now what that implies is, behind it is what I would call "hegemonic production" and mainly of the Euro-American kind. Now someone, a geographer, Richard Peet, has tried to capture this, saying that there is the so-called center, and hegemony, and then there would be other countries such as the sub-hegemony (Figure 2). Now even for this, there is the problem, there is still only one center, and also, in a sense I am implying that wherever there is development, history can be ignored. Now what is the problem with this?

Let me show you another thing, for an example, what I am interested in for example in Hong Kong. For instance, this particular one is public housing in the 1950s (Figure 3). Now usually what we would do, like others recommend to us, is to do anything that is fine in the developing country, we should go all the way for example to London which is now a metropolis and look at it, look for clues about where we come from. And then according to a lot of other people, for example Bruno Latour, would call that an action at a distance, and how do we come from there, and then that might come from, for example, Mumbai. Now instead, if you look at exactly what has happened, there is a close interaction between the two which is really ignored within such a framework. Now this is one perspective.

Another perspective which is now flooding the field is called the post-colonial approach. The one statement behind the argument says that what we see now in the world is so different so that the South is difficult compare with anything. Now the post-colonial approach would argue that since there are different histories, we have alternative paths and so it is all different histories, different spaces and the issues. Then is how to compare this diversity? And I will try to argue that in terms of unit comparison we can touch on it, and just look at the city a lot but also look at the region, the nation in the world, and then in terms of theory or generalization, we talk about multi-dimensional or outward phasing. Now what this approach is trying to suggest is saying something like this: we have a lot of cities, lots of diversities. For example, here I raised only four and put in more, but I have not traveled worldwide so I could not give you all this. That is enough. Now given that Zurich is very different, I very purposely picked out photos in which differences stand out from this direction and in this dimension. Very different, and then they argue that because of that we should try to focus on each one individually. Now what I would argue is that this approach has problems, that in, for example, concentrating on the diversity we might forget that there might be some kind of center and then maybe even integration.

Long Live Networking

Well as a result, what we really should be doing is to look at all these things I call the multiple temporal spaces, at different times and different scales with a center. In particular, the whole idea about that is something I would call co-determination, one determines as well as is determined by others. We are talking about a particular country, for example, this one, developing country. You know it is developing in the world, and then is within the Euro-America sphere as well as other countries, and each which would have their own contradictions and because of that they could determine things at the same time. Now, based on that, what I am trying to argue is that we take stock of the existing literature or whatever methodologies there are of comparing different cities or doing research and see that they are problematic. Now I am not saying that comparisons are bad. Instead what I am arguing is that, perhaps we can carry on with the comparisons and let us take another perspective instead of the what I call the outside-in, and take an inside-out

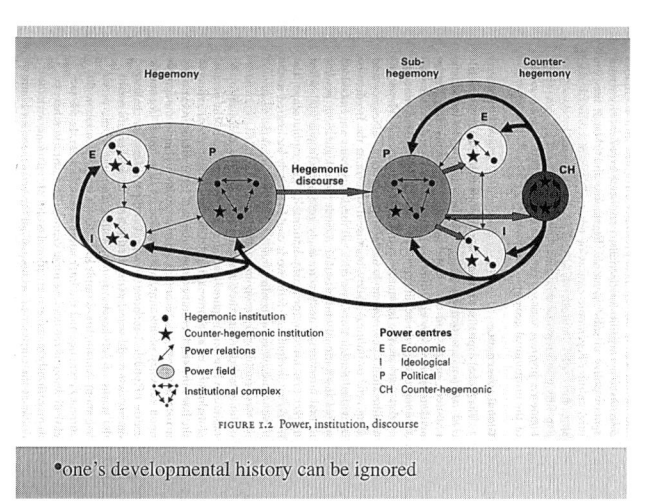

Figure 2: Power, institution, discourse
[Source:Richard Peet(2007)Geography of Power:The Making of Global Economic Policy, Zed Books, London, Figure1.2, page23.]

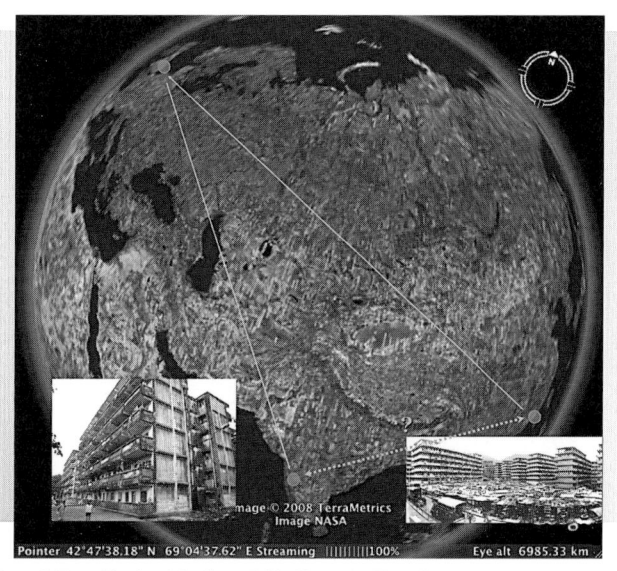

Figure 3: From Chawls in Mumbai to Public Housing in Hong Kong

perspective.

Now what is that all about? We must start with the first point that there is not one origin. There are a lot of emergences. And also some people would argue that you are arguing something depending on the vantage point. I am arguing more than that. We understand that the so-called relations will lead to determination. Now here I want to stress the point I am not arguing that every place is unique. What I am arguing is that history must be understood as some kind of co-determination. So also the emphasis is not so much on all these discursive effects, but focuses more on specific structural contradictions. Now to do that, what we would need to do is in our comparison, even in methodology, we don't care, just concentrate on several patterns instead of on interconnected processes. These are not restricted to the territorial city. It has to be related to regions, societies and nations, and even the world. And not like a lot of formal comparison methodology, using this variable and then comparing among cities. Instead we would be focusing on the processes of historical Europe around the frame of the state and land.

What I would like to do is, using Mumbai and Hong Kong, how do we compare and use that as an example? Back in the 1840s, there was the Opium War, and that Opium War links Hong Kong and Mumbai. And because of the Opium War, the capital in India would have money to build the chawls, the residences for mill workers. And then the Indians would have something in Hong Kong. So we should try to capture all these layers over time and space. And this is what I would try to draw up, like the two dimensions of time and space, and then depending on the development of each country, and at the same time which are the layers that are most related to each other?

Conclusion

So what I have been arguing is that if we really want to be networking and comparing, we should carry that out in a different way. And that whether that way is, it has a relevancy to cultural creativity, and also inclusion, and then cooperation, and this should be what our discussion is about. I know that what I have been doing is being the devil's advocate. I know that not everybody would have a free lunch, I think I will buy the lunch. Thank you.

Bussakorn Binson

Current academic position
Associate Professor, Music Department, Faculty of Fine and Applied Arts, Chulalongkorn University, Bangkok, Thailand

Academic experience
1999- Doctor of Philosophy in Ethnomusicology, University of York
1997- Master of Philosophy in Ethnomusicology, University of York
1985- Bachelor Degree in Music Education, Faculty of Education Chulalongkorn University

2004-10 Associate Professor, Music Department, Faculty of Fine and Applied Arts Chulalongkorn University
1999-04 Assistant Professor Music Department, Faculty of Fine and Applied Arts Chulalongkorn University
1985-99 Lecturer, Music Department, Faculty of Fine and Applied Arts Chulalongkorn University

Research interests
Urban culture Research, Thai Music, Southeast Asian Music, Music Therapy,
Teaching Methodology

Major articles and papers
Binson, Bussakorn. (2009) Rites and Beliefs of Music in the Thailand's Lanna Region, *Fontes (Asia Issue)*. 56(3): 299-313.

Binson, Bussakorn. (2009) The Blending of Thai-Music from the Southern Thailand, *Manusaya Special Issue* No.13: 36-51.

Binson, Bussakorn. (2009) Curiosity Based Learning (CBL) Program, *US-Chaina Educational Review*, Vol 6, No.12. Vol. 2/2009. 45-69.

Binson, Bussakorn. (2009) The Role of Food in the Music Rites of the Lanna People of Northern Thailand *Rienthai International Journal of Thai studies* Vol. 2/2009.13-22.

4-5. Deepening Urban Culture Research through the Exchange Program between Bangkok and Osaka

Summary

The Bangkok branch of the Urban Culture Research Center (UCRC) was established in 2002, in conjunction with the Faculty of Fine and Applied Arts of Chulalongkorn University. In 2006, the UCRC changed its name to Urban Research Plaza (URP). The URP has hosted eight successful international forums covering a diverse range of topics on facts of urban culture.

In addition, the URP offers a program of scholarly exchange between Japan's Osaka City University and Thailand's Chulalongkorn University. This program includes an exchange of musical culture that brought Thai graduate student performers to Osaka, Kyoto, and Nara. The strength of the scholarly ties between Thailand and Japan is reflected in the joint publication of its seven research volumes comprising pieces authored by scholars from both institutions. Additionally, a new peer-reviewed journal with a global focus, the "Journal of Urban Culture Research," was published in late 2010.

In the URP's eighth forum, doctoral students from both universities gained direct experience in delivering scholarly presentations to an international audience. Chulalongkorn University's Faculty of Fine and Applied Arts hopes to continue its academic relationship with Japan so that the current generation of Thai scholars will not only be more aware, understanding, and appreciative of their own culture but also extend the same awareness, understanding, and appreciation to other cultures worldwide. The precious collaboration exemplified by the URP assists in widening the scope of mutual respect across the world through the promotion of exposure to and understanding of other cultures.

Good afternoon, everybody. First of all, I would like to thank you for inviting me here. Since yesterday, I have learned a lot from everybody. Today, I am going to present what we have been doing in Thailand since 2003. Actually, we conducted surveys before that, in 2002, together with Prof. Nakagawa and Prof. Yamano, the then dean. Here is a picture of my university. It was the conference venue for the UCRC in 2003. The URP office is located in this building on the 14th floor. I hope some of you here will join us in March next year for the 9th URP conference, which will be the second time for the UCRC. The office is very small but comfortable, and it has a good view. We published the UCRC journals on different topics. The first one was "What is happening on the streets?"; the second was "Able Art for All" and "Cultural Heritage and Urban Tourism"; and the last was "Cultural Resources Management." We had a meeting last week to discuss the launch of our first *'Journal of Urban Culture Research,'* a peer-reviewed journal that will be online. You can Google this name or the domain name.

Scholar and student exchanges

We see each other each year, but before that, we have a kind of scholar exchange and some student exchange programs. They began with some PhD students two years ago. We have a seminar course in "Creative Cities," for which we recruit all the PhD students. We encourage them to create projects like creative economies and social inclusion projects, so that they can join us at the conference and present their ideas. Some years, we had the conference as well as a performance by a group of students. Here are some of the participants from Japan, and we have some from America and Scandinavian countries too(Figure 1).

When we were in Osaka, we explored Osaka at night, with Prof. Nakagawa as our leader. Some of our colleagues have been studying here. One PhD student has almost finished and some, like me, have been here as visiting professors. I have been here for a month now. This is a picture of when we brought the PhD students to learn about Japanese culture and to exchange their knowledge with the Japanese PhD students.

Figure 1: The 7th Academic Forum, 2008

Ongoing research of URP Bangkok Sub-Center

There are three ongoing research projects funded by Chulalongkorn University and the Department of Culture, Sports, and Tourism. I am the chairperson of these projects, for which we received good monetary support thanks to the Sub-Center. Under the aegis of this organization, we ask the government for financial support towards the creation of a cultural map of Bangkok. Instead of going to Patron's red light district, which is a renowned tourist destination, once this project is complete, you can visit Bangkok to learn about its diverse cultural heritage. What I am doing is mapping the living culture of the 50 districts of Bangkok. I want to complete this project within 8 months, so you can then Google what you want to see in Bangkok, for example, boxing or the making of art and handicrafts, and you will get the necessary directions. The next project will be music therapy; we created this program for patients in three hospitals. The third is music and healthcare in an urban park. This will be the first project funded by the Thai government and my university.

Creating a network into a true cross-cultural supportive association

I suggest that when we have the URP in Osaka, Bangkok and so on, we can make better use of our network. Take a look at this chart. While we publish a journal and conduct scholar and student exchanges, association blogs, symposium forums, and conferences, which do help a lot in our communication, instead of each center focused locally and working independently, we can work together towards a better future. For an improved and more global URP, we can create a network into a true cross-cultural supportive association. We can think about how to make the world better with our individual cultures and arts, especially in urban locations that we may otherwise forget about. We can achieve this by conducting research in a Global Center of Excellence (GCOE)—an international university of urban culture. We can share resources between universities instead of working within the confines of our country's borders. Here, at Chulalongkorn, this is what we are doing. In the future, we can say, "Hello everyone, this is our international university of urban culture; this is how we did it (cultural preservation)." We can show the world that we have many different kinds of quality journals, and we can bring people and cultures together as a network (Figure 2).

This can be achieved not just through journals but through a group of different forms of associations. We can have symposiums and online publications, for example. We want to include others who may not have the funds to support an international journal or forum individually, as these can be expensive undertakings; together, each cultural community can be supported. Thus, we can make a significant contribution to future generations, both collectively and for individual communities abroad. I would like to request that we seriously consider this. Ideally, we can have an open classroom for scholars and students from all over the world.

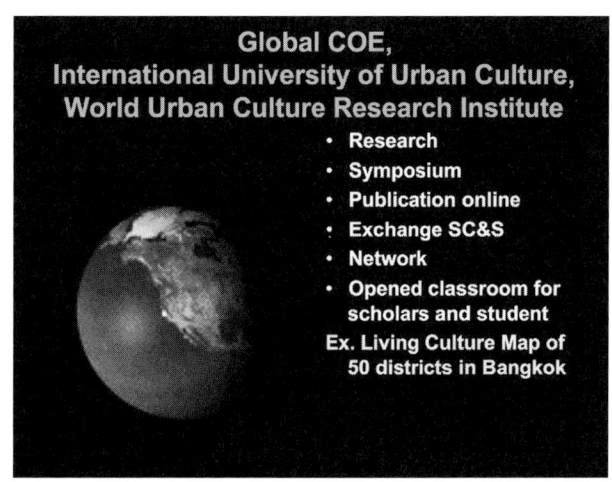

Figure 2: International University of Urban Culture

Nicolaas Warouw

Current academic position
Lecturer, Department of Anthropology, Faculty of Cultural Science, Universitas Gadjah Mada

Academic experience
2004- Ph.D., Anthropology, The Australian National University
1996- B.A. (Hons), Anthropology, University Gadjah Mada (Indonesia)

2009-10 Postdoctoral fellow. Koninklijk Instituut voor Taal-, Land-en Volkenkunde (KITLV) / Royal Netherlands Institute of Southeast Asian and Caribbean Studies. Leiden, The Netherlands
2008- current: Editor-in-chief. PCD Online Journal of South and Southeast Asian Power, Conflict, and Democracy Studies, Universitas Gadjah Mada (Indonesia), University of Colombo (Sri Lanka), and University of Oslo (Norway)
2007-09 Co-convenor. Master Programme in Human Rights and Democracy in Southeast Asia Studies of Graduater Programme of Political Science, Faculty of Social and Political Science, Universitas Gadjah Mada, Indonesia

Research interests
Labor issues, the problems of industrialisation, industrial relations, migration, urbanisation, modernization and modernity in developing countries, urban governance, globalisation, multilocality.

Major articles and papers
Warouw, Nicolaas. 2008. 'Industrial Workers in Transition; Women's Experiences of Factory Work in Tangerang'. In Michele Ford and Lyn Parker (eds.). *Women and Work in Indonesia*. London: Routledge, pp.104-119.
Warouw, Nicolaas. 2007 (reprint). 'Community-Based Agencies as the Entrepreneur's Instruments of Control in Post-Soeharto's Indonesia'. In Peter Holland, Julian Teicher, and Richard Gough (eds). *Employment Relations in the Asia-Pacific Region: Reflections and New Directions*. London: Routledge.

4-6. Struggle for Inclusion: Residents and Citizenship in Urban Marginalized Neighborhoods

Summary

It is difficult for residents living in the peripheral areas of provincial towns to gain access to the welfare schemes provided by the state and thus to fully enjoy the rights of citizenship. Despite their efforts to improve their lives, urban citizens gain only limited access, if any, to the rights and public services enjoyed by those in metropolitan cities. This political and economic distance from the center and the sense of isolation it produces have spurred urban residents to formulate compensatory strategies, including initiatives to promote welfare and other community-based issues. In so doing, residents in marginalized neighborhoods seek to narrow the distance between themselves and the state by creating and participating in techniques that could better their unfortunate circumstances and get their concerns heard. People have engaged in local cross-class alliances based on personal relationships and local intimacy, as is typically found in Indonesian urban neighborhoods, with all their heterogeneity. This paper highlights the potential arena for contestation in order to demonstrate the nature of residents' political entrepreneurship as they rally for solidarity within a town-based social network despite their hardships.

Thank you Prof. Nakagawa and also thank you for the invitation which made it possible for me to be part of this initiative of the URP, although I might not be the best person from the Jogjakarta Sub-Center to report about the work and the progress in our Sub-Center. The fact is that it was only earlier this year that I was asked by the faculty and university to be part of the Jogjakarta Sub-Center of the URP. However, this afternoon I am trying to come with some possible research agendas and also an agenda for future networking, but I am going to let you know what the background is of the agenda that I am proposing.

Introduction

While some participants in the symposium have addressed the urban issue of the metropolitan cities, even global cities, which in case of Indonesia is represented by the metropolitan city of Jakarta, a city with a population of almost 12-13 million, rather, my discussion will highlight the middle-sized city which some scholars define as a city with up to 500,000 people. And with a national population reaching about 213 million, according to this year's population census, I think that it is safe to say that almost half of the population in Indonesia live in the so-called middle cities. I would call it a 'middle town.' So there is some significance of the middle city in the Indonesian context.

However, despite the growth of the Indonesian middle cities, the urban residents of these cities experience some kind of, I am just borrowing the term from Diane Davis, from her work in 1999, people are experiencing a distance from the sources of power in metropolitan centers. So distance here refers to the degree of access of the people in urban centers to the state's institutions, practices, policies, procedures, and discourses. And this distance is lived through geographic, institutional, and cultural experience, and well as in terms of class. So here I am talking about the lack of access of women residents to the welfare schemes provided by the local government, as well as by the central government. We are talking about the local government in the provincial towns, in the provincial capital, or the central government in Jakarta. So in one sense we are talking about you might call social exclusion, but on the other hand this kind of distance experienced by the local residents also gives some space to the local people, the local communities, to come up with initiatives, and to connect their own world, their own initiatives to the government.

Two Cases of Indonesia's 'middle' city: Cilegon and Yogjakarta

I am going to use two different cases of Indonesian middle cities. One is Cilegon. It is located to the west of the town of Serang in West Java. It is called Cilegon. It has been a growing industrial center since the 1970s, and before the industrialization in the 1970s, it was only a rural county. And here the local people, in spite of the industrialization of the town, have less access to the state and public policy. I will tell you later about the form of that lack of access. And the second town is Jogjakarta, the town where the Sub-Center is located, in Central Java. So Serang is in West Java and Jakarta is in Central Java. It is an old Javanese town which has been traditionally ruled by the sultans of Jogja. And this cultural significance allowed them, after independence in the late 1940s. the city has received a special region status which means that the sultan of Jogja became the governor of the area. However in the past two or three months, the status of this special region has been undermined by Jakarta, which I will also tell you about later.

Experience of exclusion

In Cilegon, despite the industrialization since the 1970s, there is a fight over the fact that industrialization only gives benefits to migrants. As a result, the local people don't have access to industrial employment. And also, because the government puts too much emphasis on industrialization, then the other traditional economic sectors are being overlooked. We are talking about the fisheries economy, and we are talking about the agricultural economy. So industrialization is what matters most to the government. And here it shows that government's, the state's, failure to come to terms with the semi-urban characteristics of the town. They put too much emphasis on the industries. Mainly they have yarn spinning industries and chemical industries, but they neglect the traditional sector, which at the bottom shows that the boats owned by the local people have been neglected. People are not allowed to go to the sea to catch fish because the waters have been crowded by ships related to the industrial activities.

And in Jogjakarta, following the trend of regional autonomy and political decentralization, Jogjakarta could be similar to other administrative regions, that means that the head of the local government, the governor, should be directly elected by the population. So the taxes are no longer going to the sultan. So here we can see the state's failure to recognize the cultural rights of the local community and the cultural particularities of the region. Here we can see that distance can also take place in a cultural form. So, here experience of exclusion can be experience first in their access to government procedures, state procedures, policy and institutions, and also what I call the cultural distancing as shown by the central government in not understanding the local characteristics which are shared by urban residents in urban development.

However, the experience of exclusion can also give rise to initiatives by the local community. Here I will just show you three pictures. Two are images of local communities in Jogjakarta, and people in the local community are taking part in a protest, they are coming to the parliament and the local offices to show support for the sultan and they don't want the government to be directly elected by the population (Figure 1). The image is not so clear but they are actually high school students deciding to leave their schools (Figure 2). Instead, they are marching along the main road of Jogjakarta to come to the government's office and to continue their learning process. They are studying in the governor's office just to show their support for the sultan. And this is a picture from Cilegon (Figure 3). Here is actually an industrial worker who probably in the past, when we talk about the industrial workers, he may only have thought about industrial relations or working conditions, but, he is now involved in advocating the right of the local community to have access to public facilities and also welfare schemes provided by the state and the government, and there are numbers of organizations set up by him and his colleagues and other workers to encourage the local community to get access to the government.

Figure 1

Figure 2

Figure 3

Closing Remarks

Based on these brief stories, I would like to propose perhaps a few things. For the future, as a research agenda, residents' experiences of exclusion from the state's practices and distance from the metropolitan centers are crucial to 180 understanding the dynamics of cities with typical middle size characteristics. Second, initiatives and activism in whatever form it may take regarding the incorporation of local people into the urban discourse are therefore relevant to urban studies in some Asian countries, at least in Indonesia, and also this issue of the incorporation of the local community might also suggest the issue of citizenship for the least-advantaged urban population. Thank you.

Suzy Goldsmith

Current academic position

Senior Research Fellow, Foundation for Sustainable Economic Development, Department of Management and Marketing, Faculty of Business and Economics,

University of Melbourne, Australia

Academic experience

2008- Ph.D., Management, University of Melbourne
1983- M.Sc.(Eng), Water Engineering, University of Birmingham
1980- B.Sc. (Eng), Civil Engineering, Imperial College, University of London (UK)

2002- Senior Research Fellow, University of Melbourne (Melbourne Water Research Centre and Foundation for Sustainable Economic Development)
1984-02 Consulting Engineer (Partner, Sinclair Knight Merz 1994 & Goldsmiths P/L 2002)
1992-98 State Environmental Auditor under the Victorian Environment Protection Act
1983- Engineer, Severn Trent Water Authority (UK)
1980-82 Consulting Engineer (Colin Buchanan & Ptnrs, UK)

Research interests

Corporate risk and its management
Sustainable development in relation to business strategy and performance
Water resources management responding to scarcity and competition for use

Major articles and papers

Goldsmith, S., Samson, D., & Robertson, W. (2008). From Organisation to Whole-of-System Excellence: The issue of water. In K. J. Foley & P. Hermel (Eds.), *The Theories and Practices of Organisation Excellence:* New Perspectives. Sydney, Australia: SAI Global.

Goldsmith, S., & Samson, D. (2007). The Role and Contribution of Sustainable Development in Organisational Excellence. In K. Foley, D. Hensler & J. Jonker (Eds.), *Quality Management and Organisation Excellence: Oxymorons, Empty Boxes, or Significant Contributions to Management Thought and Practice?* Sydney, Australia: SAI Global Limited.

Goldsmith, S., & Samson, D. (2005). *Sustainable development and business success: reaching beyond the rhetoric to superior performance.* Sydney, Australia: Australian Business Foundation.

4-7. Is Social Inclusion Everyone's Business?

Summary

The Western Region of Melbourne is recognized as a disadvantaged region within Metropolitan Melbourne. The reasons for this include the decline of traditional industries, the higher proportion of non-English speaking residents, and the higher proportion of personal disadvantage including education, lack of support, and health and social disadvantage. There is a considerable body of data available on these issues, through the five-yearly Australian Bureau of Statistics Census, and also through many studies conducted by research organizations, not-for-profits and government.

Measures of social inclusion/exclusion account for a wide range of factors, from homelessness, through mental health to financial support and employment. The prevalence of multiple drivers of social exclusion is well documented. However, despite this knowledge, the considerable investment and effort directed at the problem has failed to halt, let alone reverse the slide.

While financial support (essentially, access to income from employment) is the only consistent item across the many social inclusion studies conducted, there has been limited research on the role of employing organizations and the relationship they have with regional support, such as training and skills development. Our research proposal asks why, and seeks to develop a broader and more nuanced understanding of the relationship between individual and regional social inclusion/exclusion, business and industry prospects, practices and performance, and regional initiatives and investments, such as skills and education.

Thank you, it's a pleasure to be here. I am going to talk about a rather different city from all these Asian cities we have been hearing about, but maybe not as different as we might imagine. This paper also involves Prof. Danny Samson, my colleague Samantha Boorn who is here today, and Max Ogden. So what I am going to cover is the work we have been doing in the Sub-Center in the Western Region of Melbourne. Really, we are trying to frame up a project and build a network for future work starting with the components of the problem and the understanding of the problem of the western region, what sort of research gaps we identified, and the nature of the contribution that we hope to make there. But first, it is my pleasure to be here because Melbourne and Osaka are actually sister cities, a relationship that was built I think originally around the two ports, each city has quite a significant port, and they have been sister cities since 1978. Melbourne now has a few other sister relationships, but Osaka was the first and that was built around similarities, so I think I bring modest greetings as a sister city.

Introduction to Melbourne and the Western Region

The western region is around this area here, and then it depends on how you actually draw it, whether you draw it close in, or whether we actually look at the corridor all the way down to Geelong, a manufacturing center here. So there are different ways of looking at Melbourne's West, but if we just look at the close-in area, which is six local government areas, it is an area of about 1300 square kilometers. It houses about 600,000 people out of Melbourne's three-and-a-half million, and that represents 12% of Victoria's population, that is the State of Victoria. A quarter of those residents are from non-English speaking backgrounds, migrants. Historically this area has had higher unemployment than the average for Melbourne, historically about 1% or 2% above, but pockets of the region are extremely disadvantaged. For example, Braybrook has an unemployment rate at the last census of 17% compared with Melbourne's rate of 5.4%, and the Western Region generally at 6.8%, so there are pockets of very high unemployment which is now seen as a youth problem and also an intergenerational problem. So the Western Region is in the bottom ten in Australia regarding work force participation and unemployment. However it is in the top ten in terms of manufacturing industry, so perhaps it epitomizes this shift towards service industries and an area perhaps that has rather been left behind in that transition.

Problem components

So we started by looking by at social exclusion, how it is measured and what it can tell us. We want to understand a bit about the current discussion in this area. Samantha Boorn did this work (Figure 1). She was comparing different projects which have been measuring social inclusion, and the sorts of factors or domains that those measurements included, finding that there was a lot of diversity among these measures. So although measurements are well advanced, there were a lot of problems about the measurement. The single common factor really is around the bottom here, material resources, income, employment.

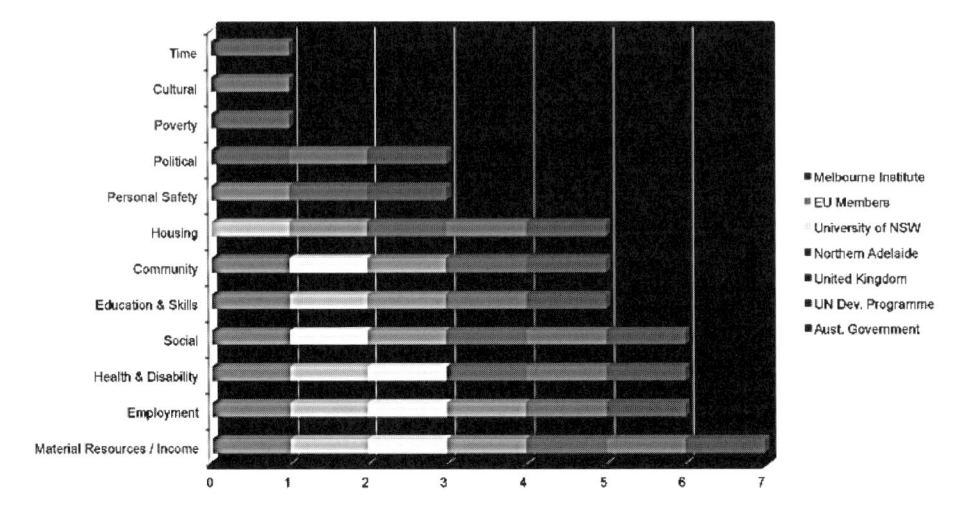

Figure 1: Social Inclusion Domains

That is what most people or most systems of measurement focus on. But the link between measurements and actions of these kind of items is quite unclear. Many people have observed this in a workshop on the launch of the Sub-Center of the URP a year or so ago in conjunction with Victoria University, which also identified that there was a fragmentation problem across these domains, that there was work going on in each separately but not together. And the same sort of observation has been made in the United Kingdom. I heard someone just speaking recently about the investment on the order of twelve billion pounds over ten years in deprived areas and yet the indicators are not moving at all. So I want to look at these efforts in terms of scale, initially, and Wing Shing Tang was talking about scale just before.

Current Practice – Research Gap

There have been quite a lot of efforts at the individual scale. This is an example of the Elizabeth Street Common Ground Project that has just been constructed:, it is focusing on homelessness, and by resolving just one of the social inclusion domain problems managing to work intensively with people on the others, so in this project there are 24 case managers. In this way, once the homeless have somewhere to live, there are people working with them intensively on the other factors in their lives like employment and mental health and so on. We are also working within our URP project which is called Braybrook Works that seeks to do something similar in terms of working with individuals, but starting with employment (not housing) as the focal problem.

There has also been quite a lot of work on regional approaches and studies, and we are seeking not to repeat this work but just to learn from it. Regional studies tend to focus on infrastructure change. What has been observed in a recent study by a group at Victoria University, is that there is essentially a two-speed economy now in the Western Region, with gentrification in some areas with professionals moving into high-value housing and working in the CBD. But the lower-paid workers are still there in progressively lower skill-level, jobs mainly in transport and storage rather than the traditional area of manufacturing.

In terms of national approaches, the Australian government has tried to emphasize social inclusion more strongly and now has a ministerial portfolio for social inclusion that tends to focus on the welfare aspects, on reducing the cost of social inclusion/exclusion, and also increasing fairness or, as the Australians say, a "fair go" for the members of the population. So that tends to focus on the underpinning or the downside if you like of the problem, and separately, a completely separate agenda. There is some expectation of an upside in terms of productivity growth and innovation, both of which are somewhat stalled. Productivity growth was 3.3% in 1998, this is Australia-wide, not just in the West, falling to 0.8% in 2008, so that is a general problem that the nation is trying to grapple with, and innovation has been the subject of many government reports along the same line.

So we identified this issue of scale as a research gap if you like. (1) Exclusion measures are poorly oriented to action, but individual attention, or working with the individual, is very resource-intensive and well, it is just helpful in dealing with the multiplicity of problems that are present in one case. It is reactive to opportunities. (2) Regional development tends to be observing and responding to change rather than stimulating change. (3) National approaches are rather stuck on these rather difficult problems of dealing with the whole of government solutions across all these domains and levels, and how to bring that together.

Business & Regional Sustainability

So, generally efforts are by their nature rather fragmented, working on the place, or the person, or the policy, and we would like to suggest that business could provide some kind of uniting theme across these scales. Also, because we are a Faculty of Business, we are trying to work in an area that we understand a bit better. So this is just a representation (Figure 2), it is not intended to be a construct, but it is a representation of what we are trying to get at here, which is that a lot of work has been around the red area on these connections, and that each of these triangles informs the next and yet they are poorly connected. Often they are studied separately and we want to be looking more at the employment domain, and how that can learn from the work of others. So we have been working hard on building networks, which I will explain quickly in a minute, and we are trying to explore questions in the area of employment and all those other domains showing around there. So we are talking about reconnecting business to place.

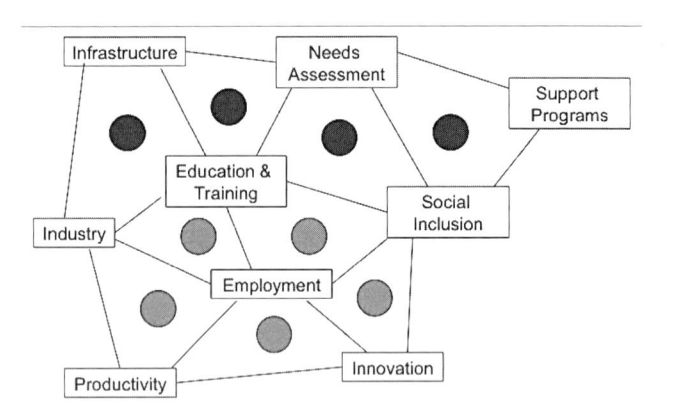

Figure 2: Business & Regional Sustainability

However, the contribution of business to the sustainability of the region is still emerging. In some industries, for example in the mining industry, working in remote regions, there is an emergent activity, as the industry is short of skilled workers, in understanding that if there is effective training and education for local indigenous people, they can also work in the industry. Yet this doesn't translate to urban regions. Business doesn't seem to connect in the same way with the problems faced by urban regions, but if we think about sustainability in a broad sense and including the economic footprint as well as the ecological and social footprint, perhaps we can understand a stronger connection between the two, and perhaps business can cover the themes of place, person and policy in a linking way. Not the only link, but a link.

So that is the sort of thing that we are trying to understand here, and looking at some of these paradoxes here of the role of small local businesses versus this idea of large multinationals. Local versus global. Globalization has meant a lot of export or outsourcing of particular activities. Maybe if we are looking for local support we value things differently. And the high road versus the low road, the idea of highly skilled work and even some sort of progression, rather than this bifurcated future where someone can start in low-skilled work but they have no way of progressing because there is no route or pathway for progression.

Network for Action & Research

We have been partnering with Victoria University, who as actually a part of their charter is also to do training and education in the West. Melbourne Mission City, which is an NGO enterprise, is connected and we are hoping to get some funding from them for some exploration of international examples. And we have some other partners as well, and we are focusing on this bottom area I showed you before (Figure 3). We are also very interested in how we can collaborate and these sorts of discussions. There are some researchers who visited us here from the URP in Japan and what we organized, and Samantha Boorn here helped organize and took them around to a whole range of interviews. They were focusing on homelessness in particular, and we held a little workshop, so that was quite a successful activity. Here they are in the very dangerous-looking Eureka Tower. This is actually a glass box that pushes outside of the tower. Only the very brave can attempt it, but of course our visitors did. Thank you.

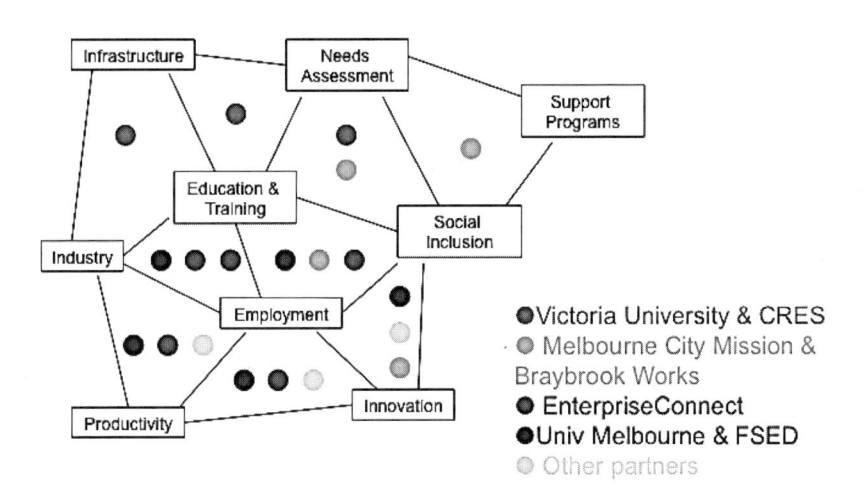

Figure 3: Networking for Action & Research: Western Melbourne

4-8. Discussion

Shin Nakagawa: After each presentation, we will discuss all together, first among the speakers here, and then I will open the discussion to the floor, so please join in our discussion, and in the second half, I would like to discuss two topics, but if there are more topics I would very much welcome them. So, the first one is to seek methodologies for urban studies which could emerge from Asian countries. Or, if possible, we could build up some Asian-style methodologies. It would be very interesting because yesterday Professor Andy Pratt criticized the hegemony of Anglo-American methodologies or theories, or something like that… So, anyway, if possible, we would like to continue on this topic. And the second one is to build up a network among the URP overseas Sub-Centers and, how can we build up networking among us? And what would be the purpose of such a network? And what can we share? And so, sorry, maybe Suzy can contribute first, is it OK, Suzy?

Suzy Goldsmith: I wasn't clear that there would be so many of us to discuss this, so you'll have to forgive me, these are just a few slides that I got together last night, mainly reflecting on yesterday's session and what we learned yesterday, and also reading the abstracts from the group here and thinking about some of what we might think about, but these are just some ideas to provoke other ideas, so they are not necessarily the best idea. So, the question I started with is how we might collaborate. Can we learn from each other? Or do we stick with the individual approach that Wing Shing Tang was talking about before and critiquing. And if we can learn from each other, what can we learn? And I've thought about three possible ways of looking at that. I'm going to go quickly through these, but won't address the third one which Professor Nakagawa has already opened up. So I was going to talk about comparison and paradox, and then of course there is the method question.

Reflecting on yesterday, in Andy Pratt's talk, he called for a new narrative for Southern cities, or this is my paraphrasing, and he talked also about for the journal, '*City, Culture and Society*' working at the intersection among urban studies, social, and economic analysis, and cultural analysis, and my colleague here, Wing Shing Tang, also spoke in his talk just now about a new approach and made some suggestions there about exploring the dynamics of change across time and space. And then, I was also seeing a parallel there to the example that Sharon Zukin spoke about in the keynote speech yesterday about a life cycle approach. She was talking about precincts in New York, but this idea that things may give birth and they may die, so this idea that we may know, we may learn, maybe from comparisons from different stages or understanding different stages. So, going back to that time-dynamic suggestion of Dr. Tang's, that was just the comparison part, and we had the talk yesterday from Takachi Machimura. He was suggesting a range of dichotomies, or paradoxes, or tensions in these urban situations, using his example of Yoyogi Park. He talked about swiftness yet inertia to change in the city, security against uncertainty, and the idea of power as being opposed to openness. So, he talked about fear, I suppose, against creativity, and he was using the example of open space as a source of creative character… this is just from my notes, I could have it wrong. So, I was suggesting… I can draw from that some notion of a tension between creativity and forms of restraint. And I was raising the question, is that really how we pose the question of social exclusion, as a form of restraint against cultural creativity, which perhaps can even be a form of innovation or freedom? Then I was suggesting that, although just working from the abstractions I may have this wrong, that there are further tensions that come or are highlighted in the observations or the work that is happening in the different Sub-Centers. So, I have just put people's names there, I won't read them out, but this idea of whether we should try to emulate or imitate other situations, or have something emergent, something that emerges, that is authentic to where we're from. And I may have taken a stretch here with some people's work, please don't be offended. Whether we work at the periphery or stay on the periphery or are marginalized, versus repositioning or forms of activism to come into the center. And whether we're working on reconstituting or reconstructing some form of existing paradigm or understanding, or even reinventing the past, or whether we're looking to redesign or explore a new future. So these are sorts, other sorts, of tensions I saw that were actually reflected in our work so I trying to suggest that maybe these might be some room for uniting themes, maybe not these, but perhaps that suggests that such a unified focus exists.

Shin Nakagawa: Can you explain more about comparisons? How can we compare these topics?

Suzy Goldsmith: Well, I'm going to ask Dr. Tang to come and help me, because it was really his suggestion! I suppose what I was, it was really following on from Dr. Tang's suggestion that there might be a new way to understand, that it shouldn't necessarily be understood according to these traditional paradigms that he actually outlined in his talk. Have you thought further about the dynamic approach?

Wing Shing Tang: I think what I have been arguing, and I think a lot of other people would be arguing too, is that there is in the literature the saying that, you know, we see things in this way, and then, you know, depending on this particular approach, some would argue that simply there are some differences that we just take into consideration. For example, a lot of people would argue for example we have something for the global North, and then you know the global South would be different, and so we just try to accommodate it within the framework of the global North. Now, I am arguing maybe perhaps even this position should be abandoned instead, because, as I argue, there is not only one origin of development, there are many parts. Now, necessarily in what I am arguing, I am not advocating uniqueness. I'm arguing that, you know, we have to take into consideration the so-called historical geography of each region. Now, that historical geography might have languages connected with others. This is how we take it into consideration. So, instead, we do comparisons, as I said, not for example, that I am personally involved in the NMM, the New Metropolitan Mainstream, and that applies to many other world city approaches or whatever, they would have, you know, somewhat like a formal comparative framework, within the framework you look at a variable, for example, high rises. You look at that variable, and then you can see, oh, for example New York would have more high rises than Zurich, and then for example, another city… I don't know, perhaps Melbourne, and then you try to do that, and then compare. And then you would say this is more, and that is less.

Now I am saying that, you know, if you really want to understand for example Melbourne or Yogyakarta or Seoul, you need to take note of the historical development of Seoul or Yogyakarta or Melbourne nevertheless, the historical has to be linked up with the rest, all the rest in the other world. So in that sense then, you know, instead of focusing on variables, a lot of the terms and concepts which have been created by the so-called Western academics, we are trying to do something really mundane and then look at what really happened in the city historically, how all these layers built up. Now, in that way, what I am proposing in my research with my colleague, an Indian colleague, is how Hong Kong is linked up in Mumbai, and then we trace, you know, how that process links up the two. And also in that process, Hong Kong was linked up with Guangzhou and Shanghai, and at the same time, Mumbai is linked up to other Indian cities, and linked up to London. And so in that way, we would have a better understanding of that particular place. In that way we are doing comparative research, but not in the so-called ordinary or normal framework that we are told we should be doing.

Shin Nakagawa: This time your explanation is very clear. I don't know if this word is right or wrong, but you would like to escape from the globalized perspective, and also you would like to escape from the post-colonial discussion. So, you would like to find a channel, varieties of channels, to make a network with each other. Yes, I just now understood. If there is anybody who has an opposite opinion to Dr. Tang…

Bussakorn Binson: Not really opposite, but I would like to give some support concerning the argument from the comparison, you know, the result of the study that you compare this town to that city, whatever, and what you discover, and what do you do next? This is more important. I think, first of all, I would like to give the example of project that I pushed very hard to get the funding for, which I was lucky to get a lot of money from the government for if I would start this in Thailand. In Bangkok, we are doing a living culture map, to see what people have done and still do and includes history with this, and we can create a network and an open classroom. If I can do this in Bangkok, how about in Osaka? Can I browse Osaka City and see the cultural map of Osaka? This will tell the tourists about it, and even the young generation in Japan can get to know their own culture, as will the tourists, to come and appreciate Japanese culture. And how about in Melbourne? What culture do you have, what is the origin of what you have in that area? What about in Taiwan, what do you have? We could do this all over, in Shanghai too. This will be a big project for the young generation, and for everybody, we can share, we don't need to argue or discuss too much in an academic way, but what you get is something that you can really get benefits from straightaway, no need to talk much. I would like to propose this idea. Thank you.

Shin Nakagawa: Thank you very much for your proposal, and in Osaka we have not yet had such a GIS project, not yet, about cultural activities. Maybe this work should be done working together with local government.

Bussakorn Binson: You have the power to encourage the local government or… is there any government that here from the city office? This is very important work, and must be done soon. Because, after I had done my work many artists died, and much of the culture is almost dead, I can tell you. But we can survive with the recognition of the generations to help in building up the community to continue with that culture.

Shin Nakagawa: How about in other cities?

Bussakorn Binson: Would it be possible in Taiwan, in Taipei?

Liling Huang: In Taipei, actually one NGO that I have been involved in, and also with one of the founding members, we have done a similar map. What we did, our approach was to invite seven communities which have been doing community planning for a few years, and then there was a project of community mapping, so they came together and learned techniques from each other about the ways they could document their communities for participatory planning. And so, on the map, what we see on one side is the investigation of the existing community resources, and on the other side we see the future vision. I think it was fascinating, but I haven't yet imagined about doing it on the scale of the whole city. But we do have some cases. But I would like to respond to what Wing Shing has mentioned about comparisons between Asian cities themselves instead of going through the central Western cities. But my thoughts were just scattered.

For example, I think some research on the urban form has been influenced by the colonial time period. For us in Taiwan, and the cities here in Japan, and cities like Seoul, I think we all were involved in this colonial power, but in a different way. For example, in Taiwan, in historical preservation as I showed in my topic, we have different attitude than they do in Seoul. We keep the Japanese houses and try to reuse them and make a different sense with them. On the other hand, when I was in Hanoi, I just got to know that when the French government was doing urban planning there, actually it quite influenced the Japanese government doing urban planning in Taipei. For example, think about the boulevards. Aside from modern urban developments, I think historical society could be one interface when we think about how they were influenced in community planning. And also the most recent urban development, like what happened in Shanghai, happened in the Taipei urban region, how this happened so fast is threatening the local urban community. I think this could also be a focus, it is something they are facing in most of the Asian cities, so we will have the political, social and political dimension, and also have cultural dimension together to look at the changes happening in local society.

Ying-Fang Chen: Everyone is talking about Shanghai, Shanghai, but when I hear 'Shanghai' I immediately get a heavy feeling. This may be because what my head is full of are its sociological problems, but this heavy feeling has an urban sociological basis. The triangular relationship between the nation, the economy, and the society… just what is its relationship now to cities, urban evolution, and urban development? Shanghai has now become what everyone around the world is looking towards now, and what does Shanghai's development, Shanghai's magical rise, show to the world? That's what I feel heavy about.

The relationship with the rise of this city, to eyes that are looking at China, it has some kind of political characteristics, or it has this and that, and judging from that, there may be a China in each of the world's countries. In such discussions I from time to time hear for example, about last year this, this year that, etc. The government of Hong Kong has come on a study tour to Shanghai. Cities in India are trying to learn from Shanghai. And the French president as well… if I were a leader of China, I'd be happy. Seen from that standpoint, Shanghai may have unforeseeable possibilities. In other words, for example Lily Kong just recently went to Taipei, and they were democratizing things, and what I talk about in Shanghai is that Taipei is great, they are preserving a lot, the citizens can participate a lot, and they can control power and privilege. So, we imagine that in the places where people live in that city, they can preserve things like the neighborhood. Part of what we imagine is actually true, but recently things have in fact been changing. So when those people from other cities, like the mayors and such, look at Shanghai and say, "Ahhh..!," there's a potential for it to be like that. Shanghai may be changing the world's cities, and that is what I foresee, but now that gives me a heavy feeling. I'm watching it. If this network can come about, I'd like to do be able to do research together with you in Shanghai on what in Shanghai makes it a problem for the world, on Shanghai as a problem for Asian cities.

Jong Gyun Seo: When I work with a certain community I try not to be very professional. I know how to make people have a fear of their problems, but actually, they don't worry a lot about their communities. Professionals can make them afraid, and then get money from them. So the professional way is not always a good way. Among professional ways, there may be some western ways, and some eastern ways. I think, even though we are in the Eastern world, the Eastern way is not always a good way. I think we can find a bit more local way. I think we can find a bit more local way.

The local way should be even more participatory. Participatory planning skills, which may have come from the western world, can be useful to make a local ways. When you get bored of using those skills, just go there and listen to the people. Then we may be able to find some better way. We can find some better ways of using the skills we have already known. I think that can be a kind of progress.

Shin Nakagawa: Thank you. And now I will ask Mr. Nicolaas. I know, we have forgotten the very local matters. You insist on initiatives and activism in communities, so can you develop this idea?

Nicolaas Warouw: Yes, from my point of view, when it comes to the discussion about urban issues I just want to emphasize that the role of the local community is very important, at least in the cases that I was using in my discussion. I can say that even the people in the past who would not have any interest at all with urban problems, you know, I was talking about workers who previously were probably only interested in working conditions, wage conditions and things like that, and also about the high school students who in the past, even during the authoritarian regime, did not have any interest at all in talking about politics, or everyday politics, but today when it comes to the urban issues, you know, the government of their city, the lack of access of the local community to welfare systems, these issues are fairly close to them. That encourages them to take part in this kind of initiatives and social activism.

In Cilegon's case at least we can see that there is a cross-class alliance among the urban population, so it's not only the citizens working, because the workers I was talking about are actually migrants. In the past there was tension between the migrants and the local community, and the local people. But when it comes to the issue of welfare, where people have access to this kind of program, then there is a cross-class alliance. The same also applies in Yogyakarta. I can show you the school students… in the past, it was only the activists, only the NGO activists, only the so-called 'politicians' who might have interest in this kind of issue, but today school children, ordinary people in urban neighborhoods, are taking part in these kinds of initiatives.

So, I see that this is a chance. The urban space is not only a space in which the state or the powerful forces can impose the meaning. But at the same time, it also gives a chance for the people, the least advantages, I use that term, to make their meaning over the urban space.

Shin Nakagawa: Are you saying that the people from different classes can make a common space in the urban area? What do you call that common space in Bahasa Indonesia?

Nicolaas Warouw: In Bahasa Indonesia it's ruang bersama, it's "common space." Yeah, the common space becomes a space for everybody. So that's why people have concerns, and take part in this issue.

Shin Nakagawa: OK, thank you very much. Now we, I agree with the term 'inside-out', and we are now approaching the idea of 'inside-out' and I would like to open the discussion to the floor about this matter, about this topic. Are there any people who will join in our discussion? For example, this 'inside-out' issue or some local space….

Wing Shing Tang: Maybe I will start the ball rolling. I've become an even more nasty devil's advocate. Now for example, Nicolaas now is working on people in Yogyakarta, and some other people working on for example Taipei… Now, there is one danger as I see it, you know usually, they might be specific to some extent to Indonesians, or specific to Taiwanese… but at the same time, we are linked to the world. But the danger is, we usually use the concepts that are so-called 'developed' elsewhere and impose them on where we are.

Now, even to some extent I would argue, like, even 'social exclusion' or 'cultural creativity,' even with that there are problems… Why? Why do I say that? Because if we look at what history is about, you know, for example, this region, the Asian region, we developed a lot like Western capitalism. We have a different way of understanding, I think some Japanese scholars have identified really long ago in the past, we had a sea trade network, and that sea trade network led to a lot of development, all these cities, and all the things that the Japanese economy, the Chinese economy, and then Korean, all these economies are very different, and because of that difference, and then seeing afterwards you know, as Liling talked about, in the early 1900s we had colonialism. And because of that, you know, Seoul, Taipei, Tokyo were connected. And then that has a serious effect on… and then you know, later on in the 1980s and 1990s because of the FDI that we talked about, and then also because of the development of culture, Japanese culture, coming over to us, and then the Koreans… so that's why we all see all this.

And so, in that sense, I'm not saying that we should not apply concepts like 'social exclusion' or 'cultural creativity,' for example in Yogyakarta or Taipei, but I would ask everyone to be cautious. Even when we start it, we should think about it, whether it is applicable. I know it's annoying but…

Hyun Bang Shin: I just want to add one more thought about, following Wing Shing's comment. Something just came to my mind while listening to the talk and the presentations, and it is the issue of concepts that have been developed this way, which I was talking about yesterday in my own talk. One example that comes to me is about the issue, for instance, the study of public administration or bureaucracy. Especially in the Western region, when you talk about bureaucracy, it is more about the government system that has been developed in the last two or three hundred years, whereas, if you actually look more deeply into the issue and bring in the history of Asian countries, especially in countries like Japan, China, or South Korea, where they have existed for at least a thousand years, civil servants' exams, which have been used as a way to facilitate social mobility, for instance, where you get relatively speaking an equal opportunity for some populations who can actually take the exams, and achieve higher or upward mobility, and enhanced social status, etc., and also which contributed to a very long traditional history of bureaucracy, established and implemented, which also again feeds into a unique way of forming a state and society, and a unique way of understanding, or establishing the attitudes towards the nation or towards the state, or towards the monarch and the leadership in given nation…

So, I think those are the kind of issues that have been neglected. What tends to happen when you have academic interpretations of history, especially a nation's history, for instance, looking at the same example, what tends to happen is, when a new monarchy or government comes in, erasing the previous monarchy's history and reconstructing it in order to justify the current monarchy coming in to replace the previous one, so you have kind of a similar situation where Westerners developed these concepts, and then they were imported, and based on these concepts, reconstructing what has already happened in the Eastern region. Which tends to… sometimes when this goes to extremes, you get a kind of very distorted view of what the local situation is, or distorted views of the local context, without really going into a more evolutionary understanding of what really has happened in places like Asia, China, or South Korea.

So, I think that's the kind of danger where the lack of local knowledge or local context, the lack of historical understanding of the region contributes to a more distorted understanding, and kind of acts as a barrier to a more open dialog between the West and the East. I'm not here to kind of suggest that we have to produce the Eastern or the Asian way of understanding, probably the more important aspect is to establish this platform where we have a more open discussion, and a constructive discussion about our way of looking at societies. I think there are… well, I'll stop by simply saying the responsibility lies with both Western and East Asian, scholars from the developing countries. You can't simply accuse Western scholars, or simply accuse the negativity of the Asian scholars for instance. We simply have to critically reflect upon the way scholars in both the developed and developing world exercise their academic practice. OK, I'll stop there.

Masayuki Sasaki: Listening to the talk just now, I really want to say a few things that are from personal experiences and my own reactions. The first point is something that President Miki of Elsevier, Japan pointed out yesterday, that in the natural sciences and medicine, the position of Japan and other Asian countries seems to have gradually become higher, but in the social sciences their position continues to be low. Therefore, people are saying they expect that *CCS* will raise the academic level of the social sciences in Asia, particularly in Japan, and I think that will happen. For example, even with the Nobel Prize, nowadays no one is surprised is there are a number of recipients in Japan. To that extent they have achieved the level of world standards. I believe that the level in South Korea, China, and other new Asian countries will undoubtedly rise. But, that is in the natural sciences whose methods are different from the social sciences and where one may show the results of experiments. However, the social sciences have their own particular problem in having to weave together social factors. Consequently, for there to be new words and concepts given to the world from Asia will undoubtedly take a lot of time and energetic efforts. We are at present trying to do that... that is my first point.

The second point is, about 20 years ago I was in a research group on the global city. Professor Kamo who will be coming here tomorrow was also a member. At that time, a group that compared the four cities of New York, Paris, London, and Tokyo came together and had debates. At that time, globalization was occurring, and the theoretical frame of the global city had been developed, and so in relation to that we were able to find criteria for comparing what the world's megacities held in common. However, at that time there was the same problem that arose here yesterday, which is that the field of finance was dominated by Anglo-Saxon methodology. Therefore, even in talking about Paris, we were forced to use Anglo-Saxon terminology. In other words, even in the nation of France which is a cultural giant, it was very difficult to explain things with the language of finance, and so France stood in a minor position. And then, as for the frame of the global city, only a handful of the world's cities fit into that. The rest of them, for example in Taylor's research, Osaka would be one of the world's third-tier cities, wouldn't it? They run from second-tier to third-tier, fourth-tier, fifth-tier, etc. Well, I won't get into an argument about that.

After a while, the knowledge economy and information revolution arose around the world, the realm of the knowledge economy spread, and as you all know, the phenomenon of the 'cultural turn' arose. From that, the earliest heavy industrial cities of the developed countries dramatically declined, and so that brings us to 'cultural capability,' the creativity that lies within culture as we are debating here today. By utilizing this in the city, cultural cities have come about. At present, I think the objects of urban research have greatly expanded. In other words, rather than a small number of giant megacities, the older type of medium and small sized industrial cities are the objects of a creative city strategy. So, suddenly comparisons within the frame of creative cities have expanded. This is the second characteristic. In that case, the doorway inward that the arts open up, replacing for example the financial economy that until now was key, have a great deal of diversity. Or, there is the history that they have. In that sense, many different value criteria have been brought into urban analysis. And if that is the case, it is very difficult, it becomes very difficult to make comparisons, there are a lot of variables. However, concerning problems of culture and the arts, if one analyzes them separately, through that it has been discovered that it is fascinating that one can make a relative ranking or order. I think that is the fascination of analyzing cities using the cultural creativity that we are now employing.

In such cases, the next thing, and this will be a big debate, is the question of whether we analyze creative cities within the framework of neoliberalism, or do we analyze creative cities in a framework that transcends neoliberalism? Concerning that, in editing this journal *CCS*, and I wrote this in the introduction, at the beginning I put an article by Saskia Sassen who is a leader in the debate over global cities. The title of Professor Sassen's article is, "It's return as a lens of social theory." In other words... it was Max Weber who talked about the bureaucratic institutions of the city. Then, there was the urban economy, then the high tech economy, then the financial economy, and now we have the cultural turn. Returning again are social problems. And in that, talk about social inclusion is also being added.

In thinking about it this way, as Asian-style problems, to give one example including Shanghai, there is on the one hand, a debate over the competition between creative cities that is the result of neoliberalism, and on the other hand there are big gaps that are expanding in Shanghai's society. That really is heavy, as Professor Chen said. How to go about analyzing this heaviness, that is now being questioned, and so for that Asian-style means, for example when we thing about creative cities, that there are these big gaps.

How we theorize from this is a big topic, and I think there are a number of methods. For example, 20 years ago the focus of urban research was on New York, London, Paris, and Tokyo, right? That was because that was precisely where the concept of the global city had been developed. Until very recently, we had London as a global creative city, replacing the global city. Yes, but we are making this into a special feature for the second issue of *CCS*. Yes, but, when someone asks, which cities we should focus on to analyze these new theories about Asian-style creative cities? Undoubtedly one of those will be Shanghai. It is at present really beset with many problems. Therefore, deeply analyzing a prototypical city or analyzing it historically is one method, that can be one axis, and the method of comparing it to other cities is probably another one. And then, different from that, analytically researching the variety of social experiments in social inclusion through the arts that have been taken up large cities, historical cities, and mid-sized cities in Asia such as were reported on here today, and then objectively analyzing their mutual effects on each other, shall I say their power of influence, can't that be used as a method? That's what I think.

Shin Nakagawa: That was quite a splendid conclusion that you reached. Would anyone like to make a response to the views Professor Sasaki just expressed? How about it? I think people are now probably ruminating about that, but we have a little more time.

Evelyn Schulz: Actually, I would like to comment on the issue of methodology. For example, I am doing Japanese studies, in German it is Japanologie. In Japan, this kind of field does not exist. If I look at the curriculum of Japanese universities, Nihongaku doesn't exist. So, what I want to say is, in my field, we always gave a very strong struggle with methodology. That means I have, for instance, I have an interest in certain sources, in certain facts, Japanese facts, I'm interested in, and I always have to communicate with certain fields, in Germany, or let's say in American fields, and in Japan. That means, if you want to present our interests, our field of research, in the international community, it is essential to use the language, to use their methods, but we always have to be very careful, to what extent, for example Saskia Sassen's theory of the global city, to what extent it really fits to the sources we have, Japanese sources. So I think, for example, I have students, I also have PhD students, I always tell them, you have to be aware that a lot of our methods have been produced in a Western field, and our job is to have a kind of careful dialogue. And that's what I would… so, in this respect, I think Dr. Tang used the expression, to what extent we can adapt Western methods? I would suggest to feel oneself as being in the position of a cultural translator, in order to bring in Asian issues, Japanese issues, into a global context. What I want to say is, we need, in brackets, Western theories in order to communicate our issues with a broader audience. And so, this is just a comment on the issue of methodology. Thank you.

Toshio Mizuuchi: The problems we are now talking about are, how should we be building a network of the Sub-Centers, and then should we debate about research methodology for that? What we are trying to introduce to all of you listening here today is, why does such-and-such a Sub-Center exist, what is the reason that these people have gathered together here? Maybe there is not really a clear reason. Honestly speaking, the Sub-Centers came about through personal associations, someone was in Seoul, someone was in Hong Kong, someone was in Bangkok, through those kinds of relationships. However, among these individual relationships, I think there were things they shared between them, and they had shared methodologies. I think that probably it would be a good thing to discuss this a bit more.

If I were asked what these shared concerns and shared methodologies are, I think there are three things, three points. The first point is, while I think you all probably have your own separate fields, in pursuing your research, what kind of attitude do you have towards the central government, the regional government, or the city government? It seems to be characteristic of the people in these Sub-Centers that they have rather sensitive and perhaps critical thoughts about political commitments or policy commitments. So, one thing that I want to have settled is, I think they all have a stance towards the government… they may be close to the government, far away from it, a counter-reaction to it, they may distance themselves a bit from it… there are all kinds of stances, but I think they probably have a stance towards politics and policy. That's one point, and the second point is, what kind of relationship do they have with the residents or the citizens who are at the opposite pole from the government? At none of these Sub-Centers are the people armchair researchers. I think they are active researchers who go outside… along with your attitude towards the government, at the same time, I think you all must have a way that you relate to the residents, the citizens, or to social movements. The third point, what it is, is about your professionalism, you are all professionals. How do you make your specialization manifest? I think that's the third point.

I think there's probably a fairly common basis as well in relation to how you all communicate about the government and the residents, and your own professional techniques and ideas. And so, I'd like to hear one more short comment about that from each of you… maybe it's not necessary to do that now. Maybe it's possible to discuss this tomorrow and afterwards, but I think it would be good to have some discussion based a bit more on these things we share in common. I may have spoken in a way that has heated the discussion back up, but I thought it was necessary to be sure and set the discussion straight on those issues, so I made a comment with the hope of straightening things out.

Shin Nakagawa: Now, could you please try to answer these questions? Please try… For me, as an example, my stance is alternative, an alternative approach to the government bodies, but my relationship with the local people is very good. I feel that my job as a professor is not jus to write academic papers but also to make some real organization in the society. It's OK, such an answer…? Not good, not sufficient? For example… So, anybody…

Suzy Goldsmith: Maybe what you are suggesting there, Professor Mizuuchi, is that these are layers on which we might work together also. So, publishing together is obviously one area, but we talked about participatory mechanisms, and I think each of us in our own way is exploring some form of increased participation, in quite different ways, perhaps, the nature of participation in urban communities, in urban society, is something for example that we all do share. I don't know how far we'll go with criticizing the government… since we generally look to the government to fund us. But I suppose that at least, if we're trying to do research that addresses new areas, we're always saying to some extent that what is now falls short of what might be. So, to that extent, there is always some criticism.

Shin Nakagawa: OK, maybe we can continue to discuss this matter. Now, we have only ten more minutes, and…

Liling Huang: Can I ask a question? A very important question. What would you do, what would the URP do, if the Japanese government stopped supporting the URP? I suggest that since we have the same interests, we should prepare for that day. For example, if we can found an association, Asian, global, whatever, about urban housing studies, we will not care so much if the Japanese government stops supporting the URP.

Shin Nakagawa: Always, always we are afraid of that. And always we are trying fund raising, trying to get funds from foundations or other sources. If we can make our own base by ourselves that would be ideal, but I think that is very difficult… in Japan now. I'm sorry, this is a very sudden jump to… for the last question. This is one example of collaboration.

The URP is now preparing this program for organizing an Asian Arts Management Research Network, so the possibility of social inclusion through arts… as Professor Sasaki said, this is a very important mission for us, and we would like to promote a socially inclusive community-based arts management, that is a very long word, in Asian countries, and if possible, if some or any institutions are interested in this program, please join us. And the second thing is, this is a shift in the paradigm of arts management from Western to Asian-style. The mechanisms of arts management theory and the way we examine arts management theory, and the methods of its application that fits in Asian societies ultimately necessitate such a shift in the paradigm that was developed to function in Western society. This is a little bit strange, but we dare say it that way. So then, as a result, we would like to establish a network for Asian arts management studies. And this system, that is capable of supporting arts management research in Asian countries continues, should be established in the setting of international urban studies. This is one proposal from us.

And please, while we discuss the philosophy of collaboration or we discuss our conceptions of methodology, on the other hand we would like to discuss such a very concrete program at the same time and if you have any ideas about working together, please propose it. And maybe we had better discuss this matter, or continue this meeting if possible next year, too, if we can get a budget for going to Melbourne, then let's everybody go to Melbourne next year, for example, and so this is a very concrete proposal, and we have already discussed this with Professor Bussakorn and also the professor from Yogyakarta… and so, then, anyway, our research subject is not seeing visible things, the object is invisible, something hidden, so we must always dig or find out things from under the ground, so… we are researchers, but sometimes we could also be activists. And sometimes we work together with the people and then the URP is always focusing on working together with the citizens. Usually, we easily use the word 'citizen,' but what is a citizen? It is quite different in Indonesia, or in Japan, in Hong Kong, too, the concept too is also very different. Of course, we always should take care, be careful of the meaning, but this time we have gathered together for the first time, and it was a very meaningful meeting for us, and I hope for you as well, but it should be continued. How about that, Dr. Huang?

Liling Huang: I agree with Professor Mizuuchi and Professor Nakagawa in their idea about being researchers and activists together, I think, to answer what Suzy mentioned about how can we confront the government. But to me, in Taiwan, we have been like this for about twenty years. I think it's because the Asian city is changing, and on one hand we have democracy and on the other hand we have a new social dynamic going on now. And for us who work in the university, we have some needs for dealing with those different forces and also working with communities, I think that is pressing, so… and as for the proposal or the three areas Professor Nakagawa mentioned, I think it's interesting it mentioned about social inclusion and also the new paradigm of the role of the arts in Asian cities. And I think it could be related to the democratic turn in those cities, especially as Suzy mentioned, in participatory planning. And now through the my experience in Taiwan, more and more I feel culture is a very useful medium for raising up issues and raising up voices, and also to connect people together for communication. Of course, it has its limits, and sometimes just art is alienated from people's daily lives, so that is something we need to be careful about. And so, I would like to continue to explore my own research and to have a network with Osaka City University and also with researchers from other cities. I fell very honored to have that opportunity here today.

Shin Nakagawa: Is there anybody who would like to make a final comment? What is this? Please imagine, so…. Manila?! There is nobody here now from Manila. We would like to construct a new relationship with Manila too. Yes, and please join us, from Taipei, from Melbourne, Seoul, Hong Kong, … This is one framework, but we can have plural frameworks. OK, is there anything more? No, nothing? So, thank you very much for your kind cooperation, to the speakers and to all the participants and the audience, and we would like to continue our discussions tomorrow as well. So, thank you very much.

Session 5
10:00-12:30 December 17th, 2010

Research Presentation

Presentations by URP Research Fellows

URP's young researchers, who have been promoting leading research as actively and diligently as any urban researchers around the world, will present their cutting-edge research results in urban studies. Dr.Hyun Bang Shin, Lecturer at LSE, The London School of Economics and Political Science, will be invited to act as commentator for each research presentation.

Chisako Takashima GCOE Postdoctoral Research Fellow, Osaka City University

Hannu Kurunsaari GCOE Postdoctoral Research Fellow, Osaka City University

Sunsik Kim GCOE Postdoctoral Research Fellow, Osaka City University

Lisa Kuzunishi GCOE Postdoctoral Research Fellow, Osaka City University

Commentator: **Hyun Bang Shin** Lecturer, The London School of Economics and Political Science
Recently, while doing geographic research on urban policy and urban problems related to the staging of mega-events in East Asia, he is very active in London's urban research network building.

Coordinator: **Hong Gyu Jeon** Associate Professor, Osaka City University
Prof. Jeon is a rapidly rising talent conducting surveys and research activities that emphasize contemporary circumstances in poverty and social exclusion, not only in the two countries of Japan and South Korea, but across the entire East Asian region.

Hong Gyu Jeon

Current academic position
Associate Professor, Urban Research Plaza, Osaka City University

Academic experience
2005- Ph.D., Urban Engineering, The University of Tokyo

2008- Research Fellow, Research Center for Asian Social Well-being and Development, Nihon Fukushi University
2007-08 Deputy Director, Housing Welfare Planning Division, Ministry of Land, Transport and Maritime Affairs, KOREA
2007- Part-time Lecturer, Graduate School of International Social Development, Nihon Fukushi University
2006- Visiting Research Fellow, College of Social Work and Community Development, The University of Phillipines-Diliman
2005-07 Research Fellow, The 21st century COE Program, Nihon Fukushi University
2003-04 Research Assistant, Seoul Development Institute
1996-98 Researcher, Korea Center for City and Environment Research & Director General, Korea Community Organization and Information Network

Research interests
Poverty and Social Exclusion / Inclusion in East Asian Cities
Regeneration Strategy for the Socially Disadvantaged Area in East Asian Cities
Housing Plus Support Program for Homeless People in East Asian Cities
Community Development
Housing Welfare Policy and Support

Major articles and papers
Toshio Mizuuchi, Hong Gyu Jeon, 2010, The new mode of urban renewal for the former outcaste minority people and areas in Japan, , *Cities*, 27, Supplement 1, pp.s25-s34.
Hong Gyu Jeon, Inclusionary Area Regeneration for Socially Disadvantaged Areas: Flophouse areas in Seoul, Korea, International Symposium on City Planning 2009 in Tainan, pp.130-139.
Geerhardt Kornatowski, Hong Gyu. Jeon, Drawing on Local Resources to Regenerate Korean Flophouse Districts: Possibilities for an Alternative Housing Safety Net, The Asian Planning Schools Association, Nov. 2009 in Ahmedabad, pp.1-13.

5-0. Opening Remarks

Good morning, everybody. Thank you for coming to this session. My name is Hong Gyu Jeon, and I am an associate professor of the Urban Research Plaza at Osaka City University. At this time, I am honored to be coordinator for this session. This session is for presentations by the GOCE Postdoctoral Research Fellows. As you know, our URP has implemented a big project as a Global Center of Excellence recognized by the Japanese Government. This program is called "Reinventing the City for Cultural Creativity and Social Inclusion." The program is an interdisciplinary examination of urban governance under the banner of "Cultural Creativity and Social Inclusion." In this program, we have established a career path building program which is the GCOE Postdoctoral program. In this program, we have opened a recruit system, twice a year, by inviting applications from all over the world. Moreover, we have doctoral research fellows and a Ph.D. candidate research program. We believe that these research programs can build their research skills and their career path. Our GCOE program consists of four units which are the Urban Theory Unit, the Cultural Creativity Unit, the Social Inclusion Unit, and finally the International Promotion Unit. Each of the research fellows belong to one unit in order to accomplish their research purposes. And the URP has supported their activities. This session is also being presented so that after this symposium, they can revise their presentation papers and have a chance to submit their academic research output for publication. For example, they may submit it to a new international journal 'City, Culture and Society', or to the URP working paper.

I would like to say thanks Dr. Hyun Bang Shin, who is a lecturer at the London School of Economics and Political Science. He is also joining this session as a commentator. He will give comments for each presenter after their presentations. I hope his comments will help presenters in their research papers to write a more refined version.

Chisako Takashima

Current academic position
GOCE Postdoctoral Research Fellow, Urban Research Plaza, Osaka City University

Academic experience
2010- Ph.D., Graduate School of Business, Osaka City University

2011-Lecturer, Kyoto University of Foreign Studies
2010- GOCE Postdoctoral Research Fellow, Urban Research Plaza, Osaka City University

Research interests
Arts Management
Management of traditional performing arts organization
Supporting industries for arts
Audience Development and Successor Training in the cultural sector

Major articles and papers
Chisako Takashima "Reviewing arts management' Studies," Keiei Kenkyu, Osaka City University *Keiei Gakkai,* July, 2005, pp.165-180.

Chisako Takashima and Takaya Kawamura "An Activity-Theoretical Approach to the Management Study of Traditional Performing Arts Organizations : A Case Study of Successor and Audience Development of Ningyo Johruri Puppet Play," *Keiei Kenkyu*, Osaka City University Keiei Gakkai, July, 2007, pp.81-104.

5-1. Audience Development and Successor Training in Japanese Traditional Performing Arts

Summary

Concern over the preservation and handing down of traditional performing arts is on the increase throughout the world, as can be seen for example in the activities of UNESCO. However, it has been pointed out that these activities for preserving traditional performing arts, by turning them into cultural treasures, make the objective of traditional performing arts the mere preserving of their past forms without allowing for changes, when they should instead be 'living' arts for both the performers and the audience. While official policy measures have been oriented towards the 'mummification' of the traditional performing arts, how have the performing bodies that practice the traditional performing arts gone about securing audiences and successors for their respective arts?

The three Japanese performing arts that have been recognized as intangible heritage by UNESCO have each adopted differing operating models in setting up a system for training their own successors and developing their own audiences. In this presentation, by explaining the operating models of the Japanese traditional performing arts, their means of training successors and developing audiences, and related issues, I will consider what kind of operating models, successor training, and audience development can make continuation of 'living' art forms possible.

Bunraku, which has adopted rewards based on actual ability, has great difficulty in securing both successors and audiences because it has no means of developing an audience premised on this pattern of handing the art down. On the other hand in Noh, which has adopted the Iemoto system, while this seems to have shut the door to the outside, by accepting many performers as apprentices, it has made it possible to train successors and develop an audience within the system. In the world of Kabuki, there are two successor training systems, one for non-hereditary actors and one for the hereditary ones, and exposure of the hereditary actors who play leading roles through the media has contributed to the development of an audience. In the current situation wherein all of the performers necessary for staging performances cannot be turned out through the hereditary system, a merit system that rewards actual ability regardless of hereditary connection would seem to be effective for motivating performers and elevating their skills. Then, the study also considers developing a participatory audience premised on successor training through a merit-based system.

Introduction

I am Chisako Takashima. Thank you so much for giving me an opportunity to present my research. Today I am going to talk about Japanese traditional performing arts. Traditional performing arts have attracted world-wide attention in regional research, and intrinsic value in themselves. Some traditional performing arts have faced decreasing audiences and successors, because of heavy competition with other entertainment and mass media such as TV or the Internet. So I set my research question, "How do traditional performing arts organizations secure successors and an audience?"

Subject of Research: Three Management Styles of Japanese Traditional Performing Arts

There are many traditional performing arts in Japan and three of them are registered as world intangible heritages by UNESCO, Noh-gaku, Kabuki and Bunraku. These are operated by each own management style. In each of these cases, this research analyzes the three management styles focused on issues about successor training and audience development. When recent issues for traditional culture are discussed, they often emphasize the essentialistic view, but this research is positioned in the constructionistic view.

Case 1: Noh-gaku

The first case is Noh-gaku. Noh- gaku is consisted of four aspects: a shite (main performer), waki (a subperformer), kyogen (a comedy performer) and hayashi as musicians. There are many schools for each aspect. For example, there are five schools of shite, and three schools of waki. The performer wears a mask and the mask shows the character.

Noh-gaku has been managed by the iemoto system. Iemoto means a grand master. The system has three primary functions. The first one is producing performance. The second one is training performance professionals. The third one is an organizer of the school. It is a hierarchical structure and the iemoto has ultimate authority. He has the power for creating new plays, producing a performance, publishing texts, and accepting professional performers. The iemoto system consists of four positions: the iemoto, the shokubun, the jun-shokubun, and the shihan. Those four positions are defined as the professional performers in the iemoto.

There are also many amateurs under those positions. This is based on the license system. Performers can upgrade their positions by taking an exam and paying the license fees. These license fees are an important income for the iemoto and the school. The iemoto system includes both male and female performers. It used to accept only males, but in 1948 it accepted female professional performers. Iemoto and shokubun adopted a hereditary system for securing successors. The other two positions did not. An amateur can be a jun-shokubun or shihan by passing exams and paying the license fees. The training system is based on apprenticeships. The hierarchy is rigid and is funded by licenses and the hereditary system. There are training programs by the government, but most of the performers have been adopted as an apprentice. Noh-gaku includes both the performances and the audience in the community. So the audiences are performers and the performers are also the audiences. It ensures the securing both the audience and the performers. This means that the amateurs support the iemoto system.

Case 2: Kabuki

The second case is Kabuki, the Japanese drama with music and Japanese dance. Kabuki stage and seating area has long narrow walk-like extension. It is called the Hanamichi and it is characteristic of the Kabuki stage.

Kabuki is operated by three formal organizations. The first is Shochiku which is an entertainment business company. Kabuki is managed by this company as a profitable business. The second organization is the Japan Actor's Association. Kabuki performers are freelancers. All Kabuki performers are registered with this organization to work as professionals. This organization provides welfare and negotiates with Shochiku on working conditions. The third one is the National Theater. It produces performances for the National Theater in Tokyo and sometimes in Osaka. And it also provides training programs for successors.

Kabuki accepts only males. There are 316 performers at present. Becoming a major performer is something achieved by inheritance. Some other performers are from the outside Kabuki and take the training program sponsored by the government. About 27 percent of all performers are graduates of this training program.

Training system is based on an apprenticeship. It is hierarchical in structure and formally divided into two positions. They called 'nadai' and 'nadai-shita'. Nadai-shita means under the nadai. They have different roles in plays. Performers with more than 10 years experience can take the exam to become a nadai. But some performers remain as nadai-shita because they have acquired versatility in particular roles which can only be held by nadai-shita. 14% of nadai were from the training program in 2010. More than 40 percent nadai-shita performers are from the training program.

In Kabuki, the audience is separated from the performers; the audience pays admission fees. The tickets cost from 5,000 yen up to 30,000 yen. Hereditary performers often appear on TV, in theaters, and in the media. It is important to interact with the audience. Most of the Kabuki performances are classical, but innovative forms of performance styles or new projects are created. One of the famous innovative performance styles is called 'super kabuki'. It mixes the western opera and the Chinese opera. There is a unique project 'Heisei Nakamura-za', and people watch Kabuki in an old-style theater. There are no chairs and the audience has to sit down on the floor. There are also educational performances for the beginners. The performance has a narration before the Kabuki performance.

In Kabuki, famous and important names are passed down from one generation to the next. When the performers inherit the names of their fathers or related performers, the anniversary performances have been held in many places for a long time. Recently this performance has taken place annually, and also memorial performances are held in the places associated with famous performers. These performances are important in getting audiences.

Case 3: Bunraku

The last case is Bunraku. This is a puppet play for adults. Actually nowadays children and young people watch it too, but the stories were made for the adults. For example, love stories or tales of vengeance. Kabuki and Bunraku share many stories in common. Bunranku is performed by storytellers, musicians, and puppeteers. One puppet is manipulated by three puppeteers. It is a very unique style. Bunraku is only national theater company of traditional performing arts in Japan. Bunraku is now managed by three organizations. The first one is the National Bunraku Theater in Osaka. The National Bunraku Theater produces performances in two national theaters, in Osaka and Tokyo. There are 60 people on the administrative staff. The second one is the Bunraku Association. This foundation produces performances outside of the two national theaters. This also serves as a trade union for Bunraku performers. Bunraku performers register with this organization and work as professionals. The performers are freelancers, the same as in Kabuki, and they have a contract with the National Theater, which they book every year through the Bunraku Association. The third one is an NPO Ningyo Johruri Bunraku-za. This is a volunteer association aimed at audience development and performers' welfare.

Bunraku accepts only males, and there are 98 professional performers. Bunraku has not adopted a hereditary system. It welcomes all young males. The training system is based on apprenticeship, regardless of lineage; highly skilled performers can take an important role in any play. The training program is provided by the government. It is in the National Bunraku Theater. This training program is an introductory one, then on the job training begins after they finish the program. Bunraku has a hierarchical structure. A ranking list is published and positions are very clear among the performers, but the criteria are not clear. Ranking is decided by the opinion of other performers.

The audience is separated from the performers, and the audience pays an admission fee to watch. The tickets cost about 5,800 yen. It is much cheaper than Kabuki. Most of the performances are classical plays. Some performers try to create innovative performances. However, they perform them outside of the national theaters. All Bunraku performances, produced by the National Bunraku Theater and the Bunraku Association, basically have to follow the classical plays. Famous and important names are passed down, but anniversary performances or memorial performances are not held on a large scale as in Kabuki. They are educational performances for the beginners. The National Bunraku Theater provides a display of some texts and brochures, because some texts are in old Japanese and they are very difficult to understand for people. Recently National Bunraku Theater offered lessons for children in elementary school and technical guidance for other companies. There are many puppet play companies in Japan, and most of the companies face some difficulties in acquiring the skills of manipulating puppets and maintenance of the instruments. So, a Bunraku NPO supports their activities for the promotion of Bunraku.

Conclusion and Implication

There are three different management styles in the Japanese traditional performing arts (Table 1). Only Noh-gaku accepts both males and females. Noh-gaku also includes professional and amateurs. While the other two arts have adopted an inheritance system, Bunraku has not and has adopted a

	NOHGAKU	KABUKI	BUNRAKU
Performer	* Male and female professional and amateur performers	* Male professional performers	* Male professional performers
Successor	* Hereditary system * Direct apprenticeship * 6-year Training Program (only for Waki, Kyogen and Hayashi)	* Hereditary system * Direct apprenticeship * 3-year Training Program	* Direct apprenticeship * 2-year Training Program
Successor Training	* Apprenticeship * Rigid hierarchy by the license system and hereditary system	* Apprenticeship * Rigid hierarchy by the hereditary system	* Apprenticeship * Rigid seniority rule * Rigid hierarchy by a merit system that rewards actual ability regardless of hereditary connection
Audience	* Audience as performer	*Audience as customer	* Audience as customer
Performance	* Wide classical repertoire * New plays * Performances with admission fee	* Wide classical repertoire * New plays * Unique performances and project * Collaborative performances with modern drama. * Performances with admission fee	* Wide classical repertoire * Performances with admission fee
Audience Development	(successor training is audience development)	* Exposure to mass media * Performances for beginners * Innovative performance style and project	* Simultaneous electronic display of chant texts during performances * Detailed brochures and books * Occasional educational performances for children and adults

Table 1: Audience Development and Successor Training of Nohgaku, Kabuki and Bunraku (Source: Drafted by the author)

merit system. And all those traditional performing arts have adopted apprenticeships for successor training, and a rigid hierarchy. In Kabuki and Bunraku, the audience development is different from successor training. In the case of Noh-gaku, audience development is the same as successor training. In Noh-gaku, the performers are the audience and the audience is performers, but in Kabuki and Bunraku they are separated. It means that we can recognize performances of Kabuki and Bunraku as commercial commodities.

From reviewing the three performing arts and their qualification, the qualification of performers define the volume of performers. If they welcome all and get many performers, the performance is suffers in quality and is for both performers and potential performers. If they limit qualifications and cannot get many performers, the performance is for audiences as consumers, and they need to attract audiences. The audience is a performer or potential one; performance is for the community. If the audience is just a consumer, the performance is just a commercial commodity. These characteristics of the audience and performances define the way of audience development. If the performance is for the community, audience development is just to be inclusive and the number of performers is important. If the performance is just a commercial commodity, a careful audience development is necessary and the performing arts survive under heavy competition with other forms of entertainment.

As a conclusion, it is clear it is difficult for traditional performing arts to survive as commercial commodities under stiff competition with other forms entertainment. So, from the three management styles, it might be necessary to change the idea of the audience development into an expansion of the performers. In the expansion of performers, the accessibility to performances and performers for potential performers is significant, and an instrument for performing much better performances and sharing skills and teaching methods is very important for expansion of opportunities to perform. If we need a lot of instruments to perform, it is difficult to take part in a performance.

All three performing arts have adopted apprenticeship, and also two of them adopted a hereditary system. This has some problems for motivation of performers and how to keep motivation of performers is also important. If it is very difficult and if takes long time to master the skills, it is quite difficult to take part in performances as an amateur or beginner. So, shared skills and styles that make it easier to learn and creating clear steps for mastering skills need to be considered to motivate performers. Thank you so much for listening.

Hannu Kurunsaari

Current academic position
GOCE Postdoctoral Research Fellow, Urban Research Plaza, Osaka City University

Academic experience
2006- Ph.D., Graduate School of Business, Osaka City University

2008- GOCE Postdoctoral Research Fellow, Urban Research Plaza, Osaka City University

Research interests
Recycling industry and the sustainable city
Cost management
Resource-based view and capability-building
Corporate social responsibility (CSR)

Major articles and papers
Kurunsaari, Hannu. 2010. *How accounting acts in capability building:* Recycling network enterprises developing their networks. Asia Pacific Management Accounting Association, Annual Forum, Proceedings, National Taiwan University, Taipei. 2010.

Kurunsaari, Hannu. 2010. *Dynamic capabilities as drivers for change:* Towards eco-target costing. European Accounting Association, Annual Meeting, Proceedings, Istanbul. 2010.

5-2. Accounting in Recycling Network Enterprises: Reflections on Capability-building

Summary

Recycling has become increasingly important as it contributes to the sustainable city by creating jobs, reusing materials and reducing the environmental burden. Many of recycling enterprises take a form of a network enterprise. These networks enable firms and individuals to get access resources and develop their capabilities but little is known how capability-building happens. The study is motivated by concerns how accounting acts in capability-building in network enterprises, especially in recycling network enterprises. Capability-building is stimulated by various needs and conflicts among network partners and the paper is an initial exploration of how accounting acts in this process. The research develops a framework to understand that accounting works through two sets of mechanisms: self-regulating and orchestration mechanisms in a network enterprise (Mouritsen & Thrane 2006, Vosselman & Van der Meer-Kooistra 2009). The cases of two Japanese recycling franchise chains are explored in order to understand how management control mechanisms maintain and develop their networks.

The study gives evidence that accounting is significant actor in contributing to capability-building in network enterprises. System builders use management control mechanisms to respond to needs and conflicts and build capabilities to overcome them. Capabilities are results of interaction between network partners and resources of the network. This interaction between organizational actors is mediated by accounting which sets procedures for transactions, integrates all relevant interests and determines accepted behavior to increase 'willingness to accept vulnerability'. Individual partners receive various complements through the networks, including capabilities in customer service, purchasing and learning. The study suggests that management control mechanisms have an active role in initiating trust in the beginning, but later trust reduces the need for formal control and mechanisms for cooperating and sharing resources and capabilities become dominant.

Introduction

Thank you. Before I start, I want to thank all the speakers for interesting presentations, which we have heard during the past two days. Today I will speak about reflections on how accounting acts in capability-building. Accounting is, of course, a human construction but it is also a non-human actor in our organizations and networks.

The background of the research

This research has its background in regional studies and surveys in the recycling sector in Japan. Then, the second stream of research is the studies on management accounting in inter-organizational space. This literature investigates how accounting is an integration mechanism bending all relevant interests towards one another. This is very important because many networks are not legal entities, but are just built when people who have got different goals, when they start to do something together.

Recycling industry

The recycling industry has become bigger and bigger in recent years and it is an interesting industry in the sense that if you compare it to the industries which use virgin raw materials, such as mining. For instance, 200 years ago when coal mining started, the unit costs were very high, but the more they mined coal, the cheaper it became. And this is the same when we think about oil production. When oil production started around 150 years ago, the oil was very expensive to pump out from under the earth. But, the more you started to produce oil, the cheaper it became. The unit costs went down. But the recycling industry has a very different kind of nature. Usually it is easier to recycle small amounts of recycled goods or recycled materials. But the more you start to recycle, the more difficult it becomes to procure all these kind of materials. Usually when recycling projects start, they have some ideas to find a lot of waste and get this idea that they can recycle these materials. But very soon the original amount material is recycled and then it becomes difficult to procure all these recycling materials again. However, during the last ten years, many raw materials have become more expensive, and it is no longer so easy to produce raw materials from mines, and the prices of raw materials have gone up. The prices of energy, such as oil and coal, have gone up as well. As a result, the recycling industry has become bigger and bigger. The recycling industry is important for a sustainable city, because it contributes to job creation and reduces the environmental burden by reusing materials and goods. It is also contributing to the economy of the city. Many people who work in the recycling industry, of course there are some very well-paid jobs, but there are also many people who are homeless who take part in recycling cardboard, metal cans, or something else. The recycling industry offers very different kind of jobs, not only for well-educated people, but also for people without much education. Many people, if they cannot find anything else, can become a kind of recycling entrepreneur. The recycling industry includes enterprises which have a business model in the following activities: collecting disposed-of materials and products from the users; processing recycled materials and goods; selling processed materials and recycled goods in the market. This is quite a broad definition but it covers those activities which can be called "recycling."

Motivation for the research

This study is motivated by concerns about how accounting acts in capability-building in network enterprises, especially in recycling network enterprises. Network enterprises attract partners by offering capabilities and resources which potential partners lack. New partners bring their own resources and help to increase the resource base of a network enterprise. And this research explores how accounting acts in the process of building capabilities in network enterprises.

Growing importance of networks

Networks are growing more important, in today's world, knowledge, intangible resources and capabilities, have an increasingly important role in economic output. This encourages firms to develop their networks to gain access to various resources. Networks help firms to build their capabilities in different areas, such as how to buy, and how to purchase more recycling materials, so that they can continue their business. It is very easy to start a recycling company but it is difficult to continue because if you run out of recycled materials, you cannot run your business.

Network enterprises

And sometimes this recycling can take the form of an enterprise network and it can be called a network enterprise. However, usually this network enterprise is very fragile as its members have different goals, and accounting for network enterprises is a set of mechanisms which help to stabilize a network and build up its capabilities.

Resource-based view (RBV) and capabilities

When I started this research, I was concerned with which kind of capabilities and resources companies need. I employed a resource-based view to understand which are the necessary capabilities and resources for recycling companies to possess so that they can carry out their strategy and run their business. These capabilities, they refer to what an organization or network can do as a result of bundles of resources working together. However, even though the resource-based view is a very interesting view, and I personally like it, it is not very explicit in telling us how resources and capabilities become to exist in the first place. Many of the studies which have been using the resource-based view overlook how organizations came to possess these resources and capabilities in the first place. Therefore, I started to look for some methodology which can help in understanding how companies and organizations and networks, even universities, can build up their capabilities.

Actor-network theory (ANT)

And I became interested in actor-network theory as it provides a methodological framework for the study of how scientific ideas and technological artifacts come into being. And this key methodological principle of ANT is to follow the actants or actors. These actors can be human or non-human actors. I focused especially on one non-human actor, accounting, because accounting acts between parties of the network and regulates or orchestrates actions between the parties. I focused on how accounting acts in capability-building.

Accounting as an actor in network

This research develops a framework for understanding that accounting in network enterprises works through two sets of mechanisms: self-regulating, and orchestration mechanisms, in a network enterprise. I employ the lens of actor-network theory (ANT) to understand how these mechanisms act. The cases for this study are two Japanese recycling franchise chains and how they use their accounting. I tried to find out what their accounting is and how it acts in capability building.

Accounting mechanisms

This slide gives a view of accounting mechanisms in capability building in the network (Figure 1). Capability-building is here on the top. Capability building is supported by self-regulating mechanisms and orchestration mechanisms. And then here are orchestration mechanisms, and here are self-regulating mechanisms. In the beginning, especially when a new partner enters the network, orchestration mechanisms initiate self-regulating mechanisms. And this arrow represents how accounting acts in which are procedures, which are practices in initiating self-regulating mechanisms. This usually happens during the training period when a new partner enters the network. These create the minimum level of the capabilities which are needed to run their own recycling shop. These

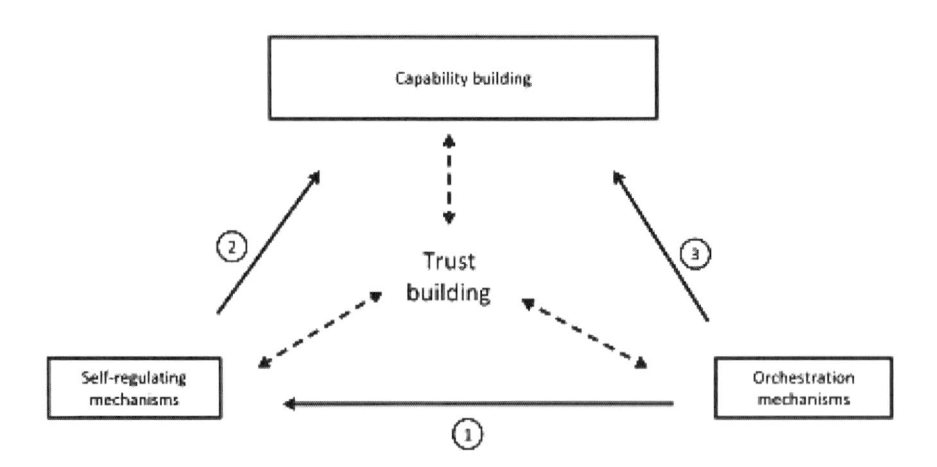

Figure 1: Accounting mechanisms in capability building in the network

created self-regulating mechanisms, when they are set, ensure that the member of the network can perform their actions at the minimal level. And orchestration mechanisms, they are also in charge of building new types of links, adding new members, new partners, and creating completely new kinds of compliments and capabilities which the network can employ. Indirectly these mechanisms, as well as capabilities, contribute to trust-building. In the beginning, self-regulating mechanisms ensure the members of the network can perform activities at the minimum accepted level, but later when their capabilities become better, when they are improved, also their capabilities start to contribute to trust-building and members can start to trust that this member has enough capabilities, and his capabilities are growing.

Orchestration mechanisms also increase trust because if there is some new kind of situation which the members have to face, the orchestration mechanism will respond to the change. This experience of problem-solving contributes to trust-building.

Following an actor

About the methodology of this research: These arrows represent the effects of accounting, and these are penetrating through the metaphors of collaboration, information and knowledge sharing, connections, hubs, distribution of resources, and conflict-solving. This means that following an actor in this research means seeking metaphors of accounting in maintaining and developing networks.

The cases

The case studies in this paper are the Recycle Mart chain and Seikatsu Soko which are recycle shop franchise chains, i.e. dealers of secondhand products. Recycle Mart has a network of over 100 franchise stores in Japan. Seikatsu Soko has over 200 shops in Japan. These shops are dealing in secondhand products, usually for everyday living. Totally, in Japan there are now over 10,000 of these kinds of shops. There are also many franchise chains of recycling shops in Japan which have at least one hundred shops each in Japan. If you compare these kinds of recycling shops to other types of franchise chains, such as fast food shops or convenience stores, a big difference is that usually fast food shops and convenience stores can rely on the headquarters if they run out of articles to sell, the headquarters can contact manufacturers, and they can supply enough new merchandise. But recycling companies cannot do this because secondhand products are not provided like that. They must gather their merchandise from ordinary households, bankrupt companies, or sources like that. The data was accumulated through hearing and semi-structured interview sessions during the last two years. All these interviews were made into transcripts later.

Member selection

Member selection is a very important stage when networks increase their capabilities. One main reason for applicants joining a franchise chain instead of setting up a shop on their own is that they can get access the brand and know-how in the forms of manuals, business procedures, and oral accounts of business processes. This is an important reason why applicants want to join a network instead of setting up their own independent shop. There is the HQ, and a new applicant and a member. There is also an older member who contributes knowledge-sharing with the new applicant. The new and older members are the both paying royalties to the HQ in exchange for capabilities and resources which they are receiving from the HQ.

Challenges

There are many conflicts and challenges in the network, for instance, the costs and time of learning and the disparity between selling and restocking. Many of these new shops, when they open a new shop, the shop is full of recycling products. Often it happens that they will become very successful and they will sell all of those items and they find out that their shop is almost empty. Then they realize that the customers won't come to see an empty shop. This is a very big challenge, how they can do restocking, in the beginning. Collective purchasing is one of the benefits which can help these shops. There is also competition between shops on the Internet, as it has no geographical limits, so shops from different regions can compete with each other. This study gives evidence that accounting is a significant actor in contributing to capability-building in network enterprises. Capabilities are the results of interaction between network partners and the resources of the network. This interaction between organizational actors is mediated by accounting, which sets procedures for transactions, integrates all relevant interests, and determines accepted behavior to increase 'willingness to accept vulnerability.'

Control technologies

This table shows different types of control technologies in recycling shop networks (Table 1). Here are some control problems which the mechanisms try to answer. Here are effects of the control mechanisms, and here are some examples of these mechanisms. There are, of course more of them. In addition, recycling shop members receive various benefits through the networks.

	Self-regulating mechanisms	Orchestration mechanisms
Control problem	Instability between the HQ and entrepreneurs and how complementaries of the network are shared.	The expansion of the network and creating new complements between shops.
Effects	Stabilize business processes. Mechanisms reduce conflicts, free riding, and install incentives.	Devising new opportunities. Develop new links. Setting up self-regulation mechanisms.
Examples	Standard procedures, royalties to the HQ.	Member selection, knowledge sharing.

Table 1: Types of control mechanism in recycling shop networks

One is customer service that they can give some guarantee with what they produce. When customers buy some secondhand products, they can return it if the product does not work. There is a purchasing benefit. This is very important because they can do promotions together and independent shops, they cannot buy all the products if, let's say, some big company goes bankrupt, but they need other shops that can absorb all the items. Let's say that some big hotel goes bankrupt and they will buy all those items from the hotel rooms. They need a lot of financial resources and space to store those items, so the chain can give this kind of benefit in increasing scale for the company.

Learning benefits

Then there is a learning benefit. If there is some problem, they usually contact the headquarters, and the HQ tries to solve the problem. The HQ also asks for advice from senior members of the chain. Internet services are becoming more important. When we speak about learning, we need face-face contacts for trust-building. There are monthly auctions which are only open to the members. During yesterday's presentation, Patrick spoke about middlegrounds, and the auctions would be considered a sort of middleground where the members can meet each other, sell and buy products, but they are also exchanging information during the auctions. From the accounting perspective, they do resource allocation there, they do information-sharing there, they do knowledge sharing there as well, as they are building trust during the auctions. However, you can look at these regional meetings from the viewpoint of other studies. There is also an annual meeting every year when all the members get together, have a good time, drink and eat something, and exchange news, especially about how things are changing their industry.

Conclusion

Here are some concluding comments on "How does accounting act in capability building in network enterprises?" Accounting mediates interaction between organizational actors by setting procedures for transactions and determining accepted behavior, which increases willingness to accept vulnerability. There are fees and royalties, and fees in exchange for knowledge, capabilities, and the other kinds of support. Or even financial support. Together they can create new kinds of advantages which they could not do alone. The developing use of the Internet is one way which is taking place at the moment, through which they can promote their own products and the chain on the Internet. When partners enter the chain, in the beginning there is very intensive reporting by new partners to the headquarters. Because they want to check out if new members are doing properly restocking, are they buying enough? And that there is no disparity between selling and purchasing, because it can easily cause the shop to go bankrupt, if they are selling too much and do not restock fast enough. Accounting enables centers of calculations, such as the HQ, and the clusters in the same regions. It is becoming more and more common that there is one successful member in the network who starts to set up his own recycling shops, because he has some skills and capabilities that he can use to run a business better than other owners.

Future directions

If I may, I will say a couple words about the future directions of this research. The recycling industry is becoming increasingly complex as companies and their networks grow rapidly. Yesterday Patrick showed us a very interesting chart about the social dynamics of creativity. In the beginning, there are individuals who have knowledge, then in the second stage were networks, and the third stage was organizations and projects. The recycling industry is also this kind of industry where people have very good ideas how they can recycle something, raw materials or secondhand items, that is the first step. Individuals have ideas, knowledge. And the second step is that those individuals start to create networks, in the beginning the networks are very loose and they have a lot of trouble but if they work very well, they can organize better and they can become real organizations and also in their purchasing channels, how they do restocking of recycled materials, they become better. Personally I think of this as a part of the narrative of industrial ecology. This means, how our industrialized society gradually learns to recycle all items which we are using. It has been too long that the industrialized products are after use just thrown away and they end up at a landfill site. If we want to create a sustainable society, a sustainable city, we must improve our recycling systems how to get rid of landfills.

There is also one more direction of research that I am working towards. I want to create a more complete form of the resource-based view which can really be called resource based theory. I want to use this methodology of ANT to understand how resources, also human resources, human actors and non-human actors, how they are translated into capabilities. I think the resource-based view really lacks this kind of methodology at the moment. Thank you for listening, and I will finish here.

Sunsik Kim

Current academic position
GOCE Postdoctoral Research Fellow, Urban Research Plaza, Osaka City University

Academic experience
2003- Ph.D., Policy and Management, Ritsumeikan University
1999- M.A., Ritsumeikan University
1995- B.A., Seoul University

2009- Part-time lecturer, Graduate School of Policy Science, Ritsumeikan university
2007- GOCE Postdoctoral Research Fellow, Urban Research Plaza, Osaka City University
2005-07 JSPS Postdoctoral Fellow, Japan Society for the Promotion of Science
2004- Strategy Research Staff, Busan Bank
2000-03 JSPS Doctoral Fellow, Japan Society for the Promotion of Science

Research interests
Endogenous Development of Urban Area
Community Finance supporting Community Design and Development
Studies of Urban Regeneration by means of Social Enterprise

Major articles and papers
Major Changes of Community Development Supports And Community Finance in Obama Administration, *Area Development* No.532, pp. 21-26, JCADR, 2009
Cooperative Bank and Community Development in Korea focused on 'Saemaul Gumgo', *Shinkin Bank Study* No.61, NASB, pp.24-31, 2007

5-3. The Experimental Investigation between Social Enterprise and Community-based Art

Summary

In most cases, community-based art, if it is tried to solve out the community problem, made impact to community revitalization as a result of play of self-sufficient play. In this case, there are a few public supports, and the results express as individual activities or movement. We can guess what structure of support system and what type of organization would be there, when the community revitalization arouse through the artistconscious plan and implementation.

In the paper, the sustainable condition of artist organizing activities are explored and other forms of something can be able to think about, dealing with the three cases of community-based art deployed in United States and South Korea, concentrated on the poor area in the big city. These cases have contents for co-work of university, NGO, financial institutions, and municipal governments; which are connected in a solidarity network. And each sector's roles are expressed in charge inquiry into the whole point of view of making sustainability of community-based art implementation to a poor area. General and sustainable conditions are also considered. In the case of South Korea, it is referred that the art enterprise or social enterprise organized by artists, or hire artists as employees and member of implementation simultaneously has an important role of example activities. In the case of the United States, it is dealt with that real estate development of the social enterprise for making the artist studios and the galleries in order to give chance to new artists in the underserved communities.

So far, public supports for the artists are deployed as an giving a hiring chance in a public art program, temporary performance art in a festival, and some kind of taxation help. But as a real, it is not implemented systemically that the giving an accessibility of the art to the poor class and the public support for fulfilling of their demand to the arts. What kind of beneficial and useful role can be played as a social enterprise of artists would be referred conditioning that deficits of public supports continued for long time, in order to obtain of equality for these kind of art and make sustainability of providing people with it.

Thank you everybody and I want to express my appreciation to my two colleagues before my presentation, and my appreciation to all the faculties and staffs of the URP for making this great meeting, and to the guests from other countries. Thanks to everybody for giving me an opportunity to show part of my recent studies.

Introduction

I would like to start from making sure again present state of art support by public administration. Until now, the way of support for the arts and culture has generally been quite severe 'Choice and Concentration' which made the public supports to art vulnerable and unstable. And it was often influenced by the political intent. In a severe fiscal condition, many politicians think cut budget for cultural programs first. This is true especially with local governments. To the community-based art, despite it is often used as a tool of community development or community revitalization, public support does not go to artists, but just for building community cultural centers, facilities or festivals.

So I became to think over the lasting support to the community-based arts and its potential of solving social exclusion. I don't absolutely mean it has to be based on public system, but this can mean a network of social support system or social capital in various ways. I assert that a small social intervention to them can make bigger effect than intervention driven by public administration. But many cases are needed about public support in Japan, Korea and other Asian countries.

The purpose of this paper is to examine the possibilities of substantial stable supports for artists at the bottom and the creative activities from the bottom against this background. We can refer case of NFF in the first. It is an abbreviation of non-profit finance fund. It is established in New York City in 1980's, but now it has become a nation-wide non-profit private organization. NFF has served more than 112 arts non-profit organizations by providing 16 million dollars in loans. It has 20 % of NFF in New York of its lending portfolio and it is delivering more than 40 non-profit businesses analyses. I mentioned NFF is one community development finance institution in the City of NY which is certified by the federal government of United States. It acquires quite big resources from donations and the investment of commercial banks and commercial firms and they reinvest and make loans to local community and community development corporations to promote community vitalization. This program of NFF can be compared to Kickstarter which is the new web-based largest funding platform for creative projects in the world. It supplies broad wide funding system focused on indie artists making network with patronages and artists through the web. But it is needed to succeed in commercial based and needs business success. Patrons, that are investors, own whole intellectual rights and article shows the business potential. But it does not appear that this is suitable for all community-based arts. I would like to examine three cases of artist organizations with the strong social mission. One is in Philadelphia, United States. Two are in Seoul Metropolitan in Korea.

The Case 1: Crane Art

The first case is Crane Art in Philadelphia. Crane Art is a new type of community art facility, located in the deteriorated street area in Philadelphia. The Building of Crane Art is called as the Crane Building. It has been a symbol for this community. It is in manufacturing section in Philadelphia. The building was built in 1905. It is concrete based with bricks used for plumbing warehouse. Later it was used to process frozen seafood.

Their principal purpose is to lead vitality within a deteriorated communities through artist's activities and provide affordable, stable, creative space for artist by establishing the community art center. And to scrutinize the process of the evolution and make junction points for the community and artists through 'Crane art' as an art center. It was a long term experiment by three founders. Two founders were professors of the Temple University in Pennsylvania, and one was a not-profit real estate developer. Crane Arts have 45 studios rented for artist with affordable fees, and five rental facilities everybody can use and common sharing rooms. This space is often used for community program and art classes or meetings, and two Art NGO's offices in their building. They are managing art Network and program of Crane and neighborhoods.

This building is highly popular and artists want to use this common space, have to reserve it three month before, but almost all cases, it is free of charge. The cost is borne by the studios of artists.

The important thing is that Crane Art raised fund through TRF. TRF is 'The Reinvestment Fund', CDFI (Community Development Finance Institution) and a nonprofit financial organization located in Philadelphia. CDFI is the widest in United States and 925 certified organizations by this

Figure 1: Exhibition and Events of Crane Arts

October. As a leading CDFI in Philadelphia, TRF has composed various portfolios and providing loans to construction community facilities of underserved communities, loans to build supermarkets for low-income families, loans to small cultural and art businesses, 30 million dollars portfolio is tied up to the creative sector. Crane Art project was perfect fit for TRF. TRF views the art to be critical for the health of a community and investment in the projects that has potentiality to catalyze revitalization of various neighborhoods in Philadelphia. Then TRF invested 4.3 dollars in Crane Arts as a loan to own their building. It is a part of 35.8 million dollars awarded to TRF 2004 from the Federal government. Besides, TRF got another allocation of 75 million dollars new market tax credit in 2006.

At this slide, you can see the shape of the Crane building, and studios. These are the facilities for them (Figure 1) . This is an art festival in their neighborhood and communities.

I must explain the system of New Market Tax Credit via TRF to raise funds for Crane Art. This New Market Tax Credit was created by Federal Government. And it is one of the most important funding systems of CDFIs. They attract the market capital using this tax credit. The tax credit is different from Tax exemption or Tax relief system. Often it can be dealt as cash. So tax credit from the Federal Government is transferred to Market equity investors by CDFIs. And CDFIs attract market money to low-income communities to return of their tax credit. And they attract additional loan investment by leverage. The 230 certified CDFI acquired 26 billion dollars New Market Tax Credit in 2002 – 2009.

This system differs from top down supporting system by the view point providing strong power in decision making and the degree of freedom of investment. It makes the system more substantial and flexible. Crane Artists is unusual and a rare case of NMTC invested in an art center. In most cases they invest in business in low-income communities and commercial facilities, hotels, affordable housing, kind of challenge to get accessibility for the culture and art and community regeneration simultaneously.

Because of this character, following conditions and limitations in Crane Art emerge unlike with traditional artist facility or art center. First, tenants and artists have to pay the rental fee, including running cost and interest, the art center has to make a profit to such an extent of paying loan for a long time. Second, it is necessary to sustain relationship with the communities. This relationship does not make profit, but it must be reconcilable for companies. It can make sustainable, independent and self-sufficient support system. It is one of the character of social enterprise and shows possibilities not depending on grants of any other private foundations and any other public administration.

The Case 2: Noridan

And the next case, it is called Noridan (Figure 2). It means "playing group" in Korean. It was established 2004, the same year when Crane Art was established. It is an employeeowned company which vitality and energy pursue the sustainable mode of life enabling their work worthwhile. They pursue the triple bottom line and they compose their business by making recycling musical instruments, public design of play ground with their recycling instruments and cultural education for socially exclusive people lack of cultural opportunities and teenagers. It deployed 170 performances going around 16 regions, 14 countries since establishment. Noridan has very highly shown high growth.

This is one instance. The growth of Noridan is very high as it is shown in this picture. The sales are 1.5billion won. It is 1.3 million US dollars in 2009. This is the number of employment, they employ 73 members.

All Noridan members are not professional artists. Surely, the core members have the background in professional arts but other members consists of high school drop-outs, NEETs, the unemployed

Figure 2: The activities of Noridan

from big business, housewives, and other young jobless. Most of them have experienced social exclusion and are inadaptable of the archetypical work systems. Interesting is that Noridan has strong effect of Haja Center. Due to currency crises threatened Korea at the end of 1997, massive unemployment was produced and also young unemployment was swollen. It was necessary to have new models, so the Seoul metropolitan government established this center, called formally "municipal youth experience and training center". And the metropolitan government deputed its operations to the department of Cultural anthropologies in Yonsei University in Seoul Metropolitan. It is because it proposes initiatives and concepts for a professor who is a leader of cultural anthropology in Yonsei University. So Haja center's work is that making creative milieus and resources to and by teens.

This center has got two important roles. The first is the birth of Noridan. The trigger of making Noridan was festival by Haja Center in 2004. After the festival 7 teenagers established Noridan with inspiration of Steve Langton's recycling instrument performance. In the development of operations of this kind of organization, it is necessary to have high creativity, and it is always demanded that reproduce milieu of emitting one's rich creativity repeatedly and continuously. This center always sustains this creative atmosphere of Noridan. The second, the important role of the universities, like Yonsei University, can never be ignored. The university served as a shield and a protector against inflexible bureaucratic intervention by the administration. As the depute manager, the university accorded the biggest degree of freedom as possible as it can to the adolescent showing around Haja Center and the program managers so that they can exert their own creativity and originality. It can be said that Haja center was a foothold to create and maintain creative milieu at Noridan and the others.

The Case 3: Jobarte

The last one is a group called "Jobarte" (Figure 3). The Jobarte is a social enterprise, artistic enterprise, which has branches in Seoul, Inch'on and Kyongggi-do prefecture aimed at peoples of low-income community since 2004. Its concept were "play is work" and "work is play", same of Noridan. Meanwhile the mission is keeping a community for low-income families and vulnerable groups and job creation for artists. This is different from the mission of Noridan, the achievement of triple bottom line, promoting ecology, equality and economy continuously.

Consequently, Jobarte consists of some kind of artists by performing artist rather than unemployed youth, retired, NEETs like Noridan. There are many young artists without stable work and support. They have risk to fall out and become marginalized. The start of Jobarte was a performance program brought by Work Together Foundation tried to support temporary job for unemployed artists. The program was making and performing an art performance by residents in 95 low-income communities in Seoul, Inch'on and Kyonggi-Do prefecture with collaboration of unemployed artists. The group of the artist finished this program made Jobarte Company even though the financial aid from Work together Foundation was cut off after this project.

And this time main target was changed into art education program for the low-income children of Community Children Center. Community Children Centers are established by the local government and their missions are providing various educational programs for the children of low-income communities. More than 1000 community children centers are concentrated to Seoul, Inch'on and

Kyonggi-do prefecture. It is accounted for 35 % of whole nation consists. Above these, Jobarte has implemented performing arts program by its own arts teams.

There are two decisive factors behind the growth of Jobarte. One is support of "Work Together Foundation" and another one is "the social enterprise promoting act". The Work Together Foundation incubates social enterprises like Jobarte in low-income communities and they provided loans to non-profit organizations. This is targeting social enterprises or preliminary social enterprises since 2003. This is one big support finance program for artist organizations. The other one is "the social enterprise promoting act" implemented from 2007. The support contents are composed with certification supports, business consulting supports, professional manpower supports and social venture supports. The support contents are composed with certification supports, business consulting supports, professional manpower supports and social venture supports. What if a company acquired the certification, it is designated as a priority support institution for the social job creation program, and get support of payroll costs during three years. In case of Jobarte, even though almost employees are put into the educational program, because the tuition fee from the Community Children Center is utterly low, Jobarte cannot help but strongly depend on the subsidy of government. Accordingly, these subsidies are very helpful to management of the company.

I don't have lot of time for more detail explanation. So it is better to go to discussion. The first is whether the form of social enterprise can be supportive or not for artistic organizations. The second is the importance of stable and constant finance system attracting market capital and making niche markets shown by the case of Jobarte which is the common point of these three cases. The decisive role of the intermediary was observed in all cases. Intermediary Art organization makes big differences in government organization systems to support art organizations. And we can talk about the possibility of making creative milieus for these communities, intermediaries and organizations. I will finish my brief presentation. Thanks for attending.

Figure 3: The activities of Jobarte

Lisa Kuzunishi

Current academic position
GCOE Postdoctoral Research Fellow, Urban Research Plaza, Osaka City University

Academic experience
2007- Ph.D., Kobe University
2001- M.Phil., Wakayama University
1999- B.A., Wakayama University

2008- GCOE Postdoctoral Research Fellow, Urban Research Plaza, Osaka City University
2007-2008 COE Researcher, Department of Architecture Graduate School of Engineering Kobe University

Research interests
Housing Policy for one-parent family and DV survivors
Studies of relationship between change of family form and housing needs
gender and housing issues in Japan

Major articles and papers
Women in the Great Hanshin Earthquake. *Women Gender and Disaster Global Issue and Initiative*, Sage Publications, Elaine Enarson and Dhar Chakrabarti, Editors, 2009, 367p.

Housing situation of Single mother households in Japan –Periodical change of tenure of single mother households and the difference of housing situation between single mother households who is left as a widow and who is divorced- Proceedings of the 1st APHR Conference on Housing and Sustainable Urban Development 1st ASIA-PACIFIC HOUSING RESEARCH CONFERENCE in KUALALUMPUR, pp.135-pp.146, 2003

5-4. Problem of Mismatch between the Process of Securing Permanent Housing and Housing Policy for Single Mother Households in Japan

Summary

Since the 1970s, the number of divorced women with children has risen sharply, comprising 1,517,000 households in 2006. The main problem created by the increase in these households is their low economic status. Single mother households in particular are among the poorest of all households, with an average income one-third that of general households. Under the profit-oriented housing provision system, it is difficult for such low-income households to secure affordable housing.

The owner occupation rate of single mothers (20.6%) in 2003 was about one-third that of the overall rate. Compared to general households, the rate of single mother households living above the minimum housing standard is lower, and their housing expense is much higher. In particular, the quality of their private rental housing is the lowest of all households. The main factor is the tendency of divorced women, particularly those with children, to move out of their marital homes immediately before or after divorce. Single mothers also tend to fall into poverty and subsequently face unstable housing situations. Currently, there are three types of housing assistance for single mother households: farther less family daily living support facilities, the loan system (housing fund, moving fund), and public housing. However, for serious housing conditions, these types of housing assistance are insufficient. Thus, improvements in housing situations and modification of current housing policy are urgently required. To clarify possible solutions, this paper examines both quantitative and qualitative aspects of single mothers' housing needs and identifies aspects of housing assistance that are inadequate for single mothers' process of securing housing.

Introduction

Ohayou Gozaimasu. Good morning, everyone. My name is Liza Kuzunishi and I am a GCOE Research Fellow at Osaka City University's Urban Research Plaza.

Today I would like to talk about the problem of mismatch between the process of securing permanent housing and housing policy for single mother households in Japan. Japanese family form has been changing over the last 30 years. Before the typical family was made up of a mother, father and 2 kids, but these standard nuclear families have been broken up, increasing the divorce rate, and the increasing number of single mother households is related to this situation. Although the typical family composition has changed, urban planning and housing policy still focuses on the standard nuclear family. We need to think about what living environment matches the new types of households.

Single mother households in Japan

First, let me explain some basic information related to single mother households in Japan. According to the latest data, the number of single mothers is 1,517,000. In the past 35 years, the number of single mothers has more than doubled. You can see that the proportion of divorced households has risen sharply. This is the divorce rate and this is widow rate (Table 1). The causes

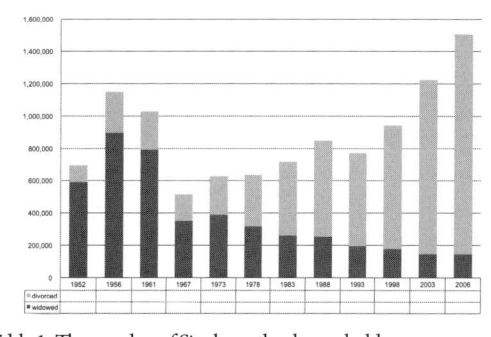

Table 1: The number of Single mother house holds
(Source: National Survey of Single Mother and Other Households 1952-2006)

of this increase are changes in lifestyle and the social awareness of women. The main problem resulting from this increase of divorced women with children is economic.

Single mother households belong to the poorest group of all households. Over 50% of single mother households live at or below the poverty line. This figure shows the average income of single mother households and of general households. You can see the single mother households' average income is about one third of the average rate of general households.

In 2006 the average earned income was 1,620,000 yen. Although over 84.5% of single mothers have a job, half of them are part-time workers. You can see that part-time workers' earned incomes are lower than those of full-time workers. You can see that single mothers' earned incomes are half of full-time workers' incomes.

Many women in Japan tend to stop working because of marriage and child care. Single mothers also did not have work or part-time work at time they were married. It's hard for those women to find a full-time job after the divorce. Moreover the balance of work with child care is hard for single mothers because the Japanese child care system is not flexible. For these reasons single mothers are more likely to work at part-time jobs.

Vulnerability of single mother's housing

Single mothers' low income status relegates them to lower quality housing.

In Japan the owner occupation rate of general households is over 60%. On the other hand, in 2003, single mothers' owner occupation rate was 20%, so the rate is one third of the general rate. Instead, single mother households tend to live in rental housing or with relatives. Of course housing tenure is not by itself an important issue. But in fact compared to general households, their housing quality is very low. And the housing expense to income ratio is much higher.

Moreover, single mothers tend to face more serious housing problems immediately before and after divorce, when about 70% moved out of their marital homes. Although housing assistance is insufficient at the time, women who move into private rental housing or relatives' houses move several times during a short time period until their housing condition becomes stable.

So, improving their housing condition is an urgent matter. Regarding this situation, previous studies have indicated that timing is an essential factor for assisting in the securing of stable housing, and assistance should be divided into several stages to adapt to their process of gaining independence. However, it can be considered that the mismatch of single mothers' housing needs and housing assistance is not only an issue of timing, but is also related to location and living environment.

To improve their housing conditions, the government must not only provide affordable housing but also holistically consider the needs of single mothers' livelihoods.

Aims and methodology

This study aims to clarify the relationship between single mothers' choice of new residential area and their neighborhood before the divorce, and the connection between childcare, work place, and residential area. The mismatch problem between securing permanent housing and housing policy from the aspect of their geographical needs has not yet been studied and there are no statistical data on it. So I would like to report about it using my own survey. Let me explain research methodology: This study is a case study of Osaka City in Japan. 400 questionnaires were distributed among 2000 members of an organization in Osaka City for mothers and children from June to July, 2005. The response rate was 71.0%.

Public housing assistance for single mother households

Next I would like to explain about housing policy for single mothers and their needs: We have three kinds of governmental housing assistance for single mother households who struggle with inadequate housing conditions. The first are facilities for fatherless families intended for emergency, transitional or temporary housing. Any single mother household that is in poverty can use these facilities but you can see that single mothers' need for these facilities is very low. Most facilities are old and small, and there is social discrimination towards facility residents. Due to these problems, single mothers tend to avoid using this type of housing assistance.

I will show you some pictures of facilities for single mother households. There are 280 facilities in Japan. And the private space of 50% of these is less than 30 square meters. So, they are very small and very old and dark. This is a typical facility for single mother households.

On the other hand, new facilities have recently been constructed or renovated. This facility was in Miyagi Prefecture in 2009. In front of the entrance, the common space, a pre-school, and a gym. This is a private living space.

And high quality facilities like these are unusual, many single mothers try at present to use this kind of household. And the next one is the loan system. This loan is available for purchasing and renovating housing, and to prepare for moving. But the need for this loan is very low. You can see that over 40% of the respondents were unaware of it. This one focuses on single mothers who own or who intend to purchase housing, but the single mother home ownership rate is very low. So the targets of this are restricted. And it is difficult for single mothers to get this loan because of strict criteria. To gain access to this loan a guarantor is required and the applicant must have an income above a given level. And also single mother households avoid applying for this loan because they are unable to repay it.

The last one is public housing. Compared to facilities and loan systems, single mothers' need for public housing is very high. However public housing doesn't meet their needs for three reasons: First, the supply is inadequate. Next, there are many vacancies in inconvenient locations but few in convenient locations, even though single mothers have specific needs in their neighborhoods, and there is little public housing meeting this limiting requirement. This point will be discussed in more details in the following section. And last, the public housing can't address immediate or sudden housing needs. As a previous study indicated, most single mother households need to secure stable housing before or right after divorce. However public housing requires time between the application and entrance, at least five months or more. For these reasons single mother households tend to live in lower quality private rental housing or with relatives.

Single mother's specific geographical needs

Next I would like to go on the main subject. In the survey, almost 80% of respondents moved out of their marital homes. Some previous studies hypothesize that single mothers move into metropolitan areas to seek job opportunity and affordable housing. But this is not the case. This figure shows the relationship between their moving situation and former residential areas. 23.4% stayed in their marital homes, and 45.1% moved within Osaka City. In fact, almost 70% of single mothers have remained in the metropolitan area. What factors do affect single mothers' choice of residential area?

As shown in this table, while most respondents who remained in the same housing did not give a reason for staying, about 40% cited their children's school or childcare. Regarding the subjects who moved within Osaka City, half of the subjects cited "because of children's school or childcare," and 36.6% of the respondents remained in the same city because of relatives. For respondents who moved to Osaka City, about 80% moved to seek relatives' support.

In contrast, few single mothers moved into Osaka City to search for job opportunities and affordable rental housing. These results indicate that single mothers' preferences for neighborhoods are divided into 2 types:

The first group remained or moved within the same city because of their children's school district or childcare. Single mothers tend to avoid making their children transfer to another school due to concern over whether their children can adapt to new surroundings. Moreover, because the number of preschools is chronically insufficient, it is difficult to find new preschools for them. Therefore, single mothers try to minimize the distance between their former and new residential areas.

The second group moved from another city or prefecture to seek relatives' support.

It is thought that the reason why single mother households rely on relatives is the need for childcare support and housekeeping. Single mothers have to manage jobs, childcare, and housekeeping on their own. Generally, preschools in Japan do not accept children who have a fever or are injured. In these unforeseen situations, single mothers must take a leave of absence from work if they do not have private support. In many cases, these situations cause them to lose their jobs. Informal support is an essential factor for single mother households who have young children.

On the other hand, regarding the reason for choosing a new residential area, only 12.5% answered "because there was available public housing" (Table 2). Single mother households faced serious housing problems due to barriers, such as economic issues, childcare problems, and lack of access to real estate agents. Therefore, it is thought that there is usually a lack of affordable housing in the desired areas. As mentioned previously, public housing is often unable to meet single mothers' specific geographical needs, and thus many single mothers often move into rental housing which is of low quality and too expensive.

Former residential area	Because of relatives	Because of Children's School and Childcare	To gain better job opportunities	less stigma toward single mothers	Because there was available public housing	Availability of cheaper rental housing	To gain better social welfare	No reason	Others	The number of valid responses
Not moved	9 / 14.3%	25 / 39.7%	9 / 14.3%	2 / 3.2%	0 / 0.0%	1 / 1.6%	1 / 1.6%	35 / 55.6%	1 / 1.6%	63
Osaka City	45 / 36.6%	65 / 52.8%	35 / 28.5%	8 / 6.5%	20 / 16.3%	14 / 11.4%	1 / 0.8%	3 / 2.4%	23 / 18.7%	123
Osaka Pref.	31 / 75.6%	16 / 39.0%	6 / 14.6%	1 / 2.4%	8 / 19.5%	2 / 4.9%	1 / 2.4%	1 / 2.4%	3 / 7.3%	41
Other Pref.	38 / 84.4%	16 / 35.6%	11 / 24.4%	1 / 2.2%	4 / 8.9%	6 / 13.3%	1 / 2.2%	0 / 0.0%	6 / 13.3%	45
Total	123 / 45.2%	122 / 44.9%	61 / 22.4%	12 / 4.4%	34 / 12.5%	23 / 8.5%	4 / 1.5%	39 / 14.3%	33 / 2	272

Table 2: Former residential area and reason for choosing present residential area

Workplace, residential area and childcare

I will go on to the last subject, which is the relationship between residential area and workplace. The responsibility for childcare is one of the barriers to stable job status for single mothers, particularly those with younger children. As shown in this figure, the unemployment rate of single mother households with children from 0 to 3 years old is the highest. Additionally, this table shows that the rate of full-time employment of single mother households gradually increases as the age of the children increases. These are fulltime workers. The number is increasing.

This figure shows the childcare problems of single mothers who have children under 6 years of age. As previously mentioned, regarding absence from work or leaving the office early to manage an unpredictable situation, about 80% responded that they have problems "when children are sick or injured." Preschools usually open at 7:00 am and close at 6:00 pm, so single mothers have to match their work time to childcare time; in the present study, 60% complained that they were unable to work overtime. These requirements restrict single mothers' choice of workplace.

This figure shows commuting times and youngest child's age. Commuting times within 15 minutes are highest in every age category. Single mothers tend to find workplaces near their homes regardless of their children's age.

This table shows commuting means and the youngest child's age. Over half of the respondents commute by bicycle. The rate of bicycle commuting for single mothers whose children's age is under 3 years is the highest, but the rate of commuting by train is the highest for mothers whose children are over 16 years old. Single mother households who have older children do not need to manage childcare. Additionally, part-time workers do not generally receive commuting expenses; thus, these workers try to find a workplace near their home. The consequence is that single mothers are more likely to minimize the distance between the workplace and home in order to manage an emergency situation, to match their work times to school times, and to save on commuting costs.

Conclusion

Mothers who prioritize preserving their children's environment and obtaining available preschools tend to not move, or try to minimize the distance between the former and the new residential area, while mothers who seek relatives' support for daily life tend to move to a new residential area. The Japanese childcare system does not adequately support single mothers who work and care for their children on their own. So, these factors are essential in allowing single mother households' livelihoods to become independent. Government assistance should thus be more flexible in providing support to single mothers regarding the location and also the timing that they have chosen for creating a stable and independent life. One possible way to offer this kind of support would be to make housing subsidies available for private rental housing. And collective housing is one option to balance work and childcare for one-parent families.

Thank you very much. Thank you for your kind attention.

Session 6
14:00-17:00 December 17th, 2010

Panel Discussion

Perspectives of the AUC and its Prospects

The broad purpose of the Association for Urban Creativity (AUC) is to tap into the creative knowledge of citizens in solving practical problems, then to absorb this knowledge and combine the accumulated "citizens' knowledge" with "academic knowledge" to create unexpected, but well-matching theories for urban studies.

In this session, we will discuss the presentations of the preceding three days and aim at understanding "citizens' knowledge" as reflected in the activities of the AUC. In particular, we will focus on social inclusion through the arts and cultural creativity as applied by the Asian Network of the Urban Research Plaza. We will also discuss potential ways of establishing a new paradigm for theories of the creative city and a vision for creative city planning and urban administration.

Coordinators

Masayuki Sasaki Director of the Urban Research Plaza, Osaka City University
Prof. Sasaki is one of the world leaders in the theory of creative cities, where there is a move away from mass production and towards formation of a flexible urban economic system through promoting the free exercise of the citizens' creative activities. He has founded NPOs, and is extremely active in issues facing local communities. He is also editor-in-chief of CCS.

Toshio Kamo Professor of Ritsumeikan University, former director of the Urban Research Plaza, Osaka City University
Based on the results of his many years of research on local government and devolution from a political science perspective, Prof. Kamo is one of the most influential political scientists in Japan, and has actively spoken out on community building.

Masayuki Sasaki

Current academic position
Director, Urban Research Plaza,
Professor, Graduate School for Creative Cities,
Osaka City University

Academic experience
Dr. Economics, Kyoto University
M.A., Economics, Kyoto University

2007- Director, Urban Research Plaza, Osaka City University
2005- Dean, Graduate School f or Creative Cities, Osaka City University
2003- Professor, Graduate School for Creative Cities, Osaka City University
2000- Professor, College of Policy Science, Ritsumeikan University
1999- Visiting Researcher, University of Bologna
1992- Professor, Faculty of Economics, Kanazawa University
1985- Associate Professor, Faculty of Economics, Kanazawa University
1980- Senior Lecturer, Faculty of Economics, Osaka University of Economics and Law

Research interests
Creative Cities, Cultural Economics, Urban Economics

Major articles and papers
Urban regeneration through cultural creativity and social inclusion: Rethinking creative city theory through a Japanese case study, *CITIES*, Volume 27, Supplement 1, pp.3-9, 2010

"Towards an urban mode of production: A case study of Kanazawa", M. Nadarajah & Ann Tomoko Yamamoto,ed. *Urban Crisis United Nations* University Press, 2007, pp.156-174

Toshio Kamo

Current academic position
Professor, Graduate School of Policy Science,
Ritsumeikan University

Academic experience
2007- Professor, Graduate School of Policy Science, Ritsumeikan University
2006- Director, Urban Research Plaza, Osaka City University
2002- Professor, Graduate School of Law, Osaka City University
1993-94 Dean, Faculty of Law, Osaka City University
1985- Professor, Faculty of Law, Osaka City University
1972- Associate Professor, Faculty of Law, Osaka City University
1967- Assistant Professor, Faculty of Law, Osaka City University

Research interests
Theory of Political Process, Public Philosophy, Theory of Local Self-Government

Major articles and papers
Political Economy of Decentralization: Japan, Asia and Europe, *Policy science,* Vol.7-3, pp.109-122, 2000
Decentralization of Tax and Public Finance in the Political Process, *The journal of the Tokyo Institute for Municipal Research*, Vol.89-1, pp.77-87, 1998
World City : On its Conceptual History, *Journal of law and politics of Osaka City University,* Vol. 40-4, pp.467-484, 1994

Masayuki Sasaki: Shall we start final session? I would like to introduce to you Professor Kamo. He is great contributor of the foundation of the URP. Please.

Toshio Kamo: Four years ago I stopped working here at Osaka City University, and now I work at Ritsumeikan University in Kyoto. Kyoto is a wonderful city to live in, but Ritsumeikan is a university that is pretty tough on its people, and because I had classes I couldn't leave the school for the first and second days of this symposium, but today, finally, I was able to show up. Consequently, since I don't have a clear understanding of what kind of discussion already took place yesterday and the day before, so, although it may seem a bit absurd, I want to try to be careful not to throw confusion into the discussion. In this symposium, the themes that have been taken up in various ways are cultural creativity and social inclusion. If one looks again at this, these are not just themes of urban theory, but they can be thought of as themes embodying issues that are transcending the deep disorder of the contemporary world.

In the history of cities, there have been many tragic times when the economy collapsed, there were large disasters or war broke out, or the social organizations of the city disintegrated and people lost their homes. For example, Charlie Chaplin's City Lights, Arthur Miller's Death of a Salesman, and John Steinbeck's Grapes of Wrath all depict stories set against the background of the Great Depression of the 1930s where, nevertheless, the intangible power of trust and cooperation between people and the strength of wisdom and imagination supported people and the cities were rebuilt. Eventually in those cities the public sector revived, and through the building of a social safety net the cities were resurrected as places for people to live. I am again reminded that the cities where a new public welfare system was created and they began to include people rather than excluding them were probably built during the time of our grandparents.

However, in recent years, there have been collapses of many kinds in these 20th century-type cities. As an extreme, revelation fantasies and science fiction movies, if one watches them, have one after another depicted the literal end of the world or the collapse of cities, such works as The Day After Tomorrow, Deep Impact, or 2012. As can be seen in such works, a vision of an apocalyptic near future for cities is being depicted. However, the themes we are dealing with here are the problems of the collapse in urban society. As a result of a market economy that has run wild, we are being revisited by an age in which there are more and more people appearing like the homeless, the working poor and NEETs, people who are being divided, and ostracized, and are losing their homes.

Last year, in fact, probably by mistake, a magazine was sent to me from the Davos Conference in Switzerland whose title was Creative Economy, which surprised me a bit. In other words, even in a neoliberalist, market ideology-driven organization like the Davos Conference, it seems that they have started thinking that it is necessary to build stability in the world by building a creative economy and using the imaginative power of culture and the arts for technology and industries, rather than just relying on the financial and service sectors. However, if one thinks about that again, tying together cultural creativity and social inclusion is not an easy task. Rather, I think it is filled with dilemmas. For example, at the level of the nation state, Sweden has for many years dealt with a 'positive labor market.' What the government's policy of a positive labor market mean is that people whose knowledge, technology, and skills have become outdated and obsolete and have been pushed out of the labor market are supported under the public welfare system, they are encouraged to obtain new knowledge and imagination, and they are then returned to the labor market. So, I think that Sweden and some other countries have created a mechanism for social inclusion that includes people socially and in the work force by literally upgrading their intellectual and cultural imaginations. However, following this case of Sweden, recently the new industrial fields that are fostered by creativity and the cultural activities fields have stopped expanding, and public welfare is been rapidly shrinking. Consequently, it is being said that creativity and inclusion have not meshed together well. I think we can assume that probably this problem has gradually been spreading in the economies of the developed countries, and is becoming a very serious problem that they all share. As for the question of how do we overcome that, I think that is the thing that we are going to be confronting. If this AUC that later today will be proposed can become an organization at the forefront of overcoming, for example, these new problems faced by the creative society, and can show the power to open up a new dimension, that would be wonderful, but in any case we here at the Urban Research Plaza have already set out the basic themes of cultural creativity and social inclusion as topics for urban research, and we have drawn together the research we have been doing related to that. We are all looking forward to the realization of this AUC in the future and the building of a concrete framework related to cultural creativity and social inclusion, but I have to say that that will probably not be such an easy task. In this session, if we can discuss things in this new dimension, and do some brainstorming about issues in urban research, I hope it will give us an opportunity for finding some hints and maybe a foothold for development in the future.

That is my take on the problem, so first of all, I would like to hear from Professor Sasaki about his take on the AUC.

Masayuki Sasaki: The structure of our symposium is varied and its contents very diverse, so shall we first take a look back to the previous five sessions? And then shall we talk about the direction and perspective of out international research status, as in *City, Culture and Society* and the Association for Urban Creativity? So, for the first session, Prof. Mizuuchi. Please.

Toshio Mizuuchi: I handled the first session of Sharon Zukin, Lily Kong, and Prof. Machimura, and these presentations were based on looking at the individual cities of New York, Singapore, and Tokyo. And as I stressed in my session, when I preside over a the session, I have to refer back to Osaka cases. Why our Urban Research Plaza was established? This is because of our experience in how to govern the Osaka City, which is the financial supporter of our university, and we are responsible to meet and respond to the government's requests. I will show why Osaka is so much in difficulty in socioeconomic situations, I will just show some evidences through maps and then we will repeat what it is that the three presentations expressed to convey their message to us.

This is a map of Osaka metropolitan area (Figure1). So I will just present these maps and show what they illustrate. Let us remember that we are now looking at the city boundaries, the contemporary city boundary is the thick line indicated in picture 1, and this JR Loop line nearly coincide with the city boundary at the beginning of the 20th century, which circles the historical core as a castle town at Edo Era. As I said that this outer thick line was the boundary in 1925, so it has already lasted for 80 years, and the city of Osaka, the space of the city, is this space. And this boundary still continues in effect, nearly 80 years later.

These are maps of Osaka, Tokyo, Nagoya (Figure 2). You can see how the condition of Osaka is worse. The blue marks are the poor residents. This is from an article in a Japanese journal whose title is "The Poor and the Rich people", and the blue means the distributions of poor people and red means those of the rich. So this is the dramatic difference in Osaka City through the years. We are now here in the only small space for the affluent people's quarter in Osaka, but based on the residents' level , and the income level, it is far lower than Tokyo or Nagoya. This is very characteristic of Osaka.

In the next picture, I can show the unemployment rate for 2000 (Figure 3), so ten years ago. It is a little bit outdated but shows conditions of very higher rates of unemployment, especially in Osaka and Kobe comparing with Tokyo. And this is also the distribution of the professional affluent people (Figure 4). There are many affluent, highly educated and professional people who are concentrated on the western side of Tokyo and live there, but in Osaka, and the suburban areas where we can see such people in sporadic concentrations. So this is a big difference.

We have also been thinking about Osaka City and Osaka Prefecture (Figure1).

This is Osaka City. And this map cover Osaka Prefecture, Hyogo Prefecture and Kyoto Prefecture. So of course we live in a metropolitan area and we have a lot of connections across the city boundaries, and we think over how Osaka was developed or coordinated by the connections of each local governments. We have been acting together with the Prefectures and the City governments. In this picture 1, the biggest event was the Expo of 1970, held outside the city boundary. And the Kansai Airport is here and all of the largest new towns are all located outside the city boundaries. So the

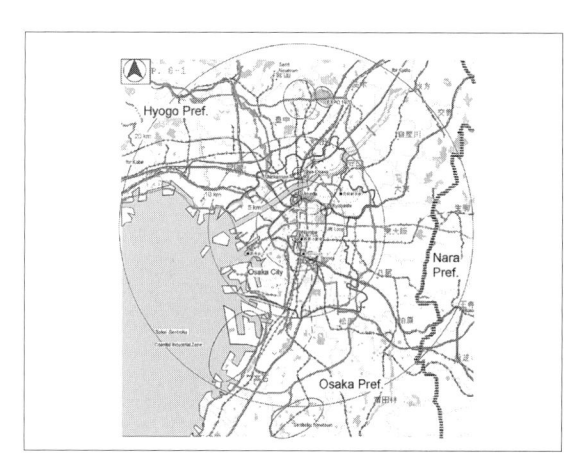

Figure1 General Image and Location of big projects in Osaka prefecture

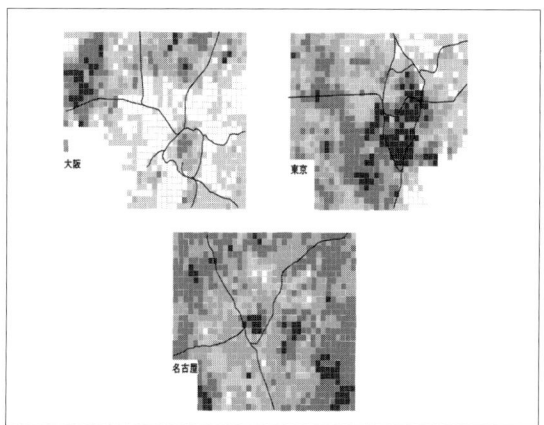

Figure 2 ↑ Osaka   ↑ Nagoya   ↑ Tokyo
Distribution of "Rich" and "Poor" Residents

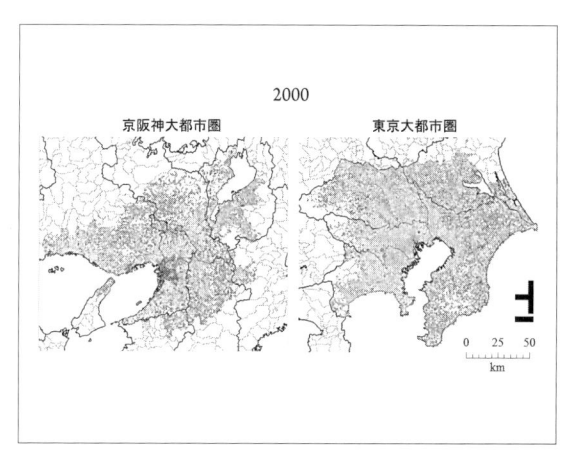

Figure3 Distribution of unemployment rate in Osaka and Tokyo metropolitan region

Figure 4 Distribution of unemployment rate in Osaka and Tokyo metropolitan region

Figure5/6 Distribution of War-disaster area and post-war rehabilitation and reconstruction works in Osaka

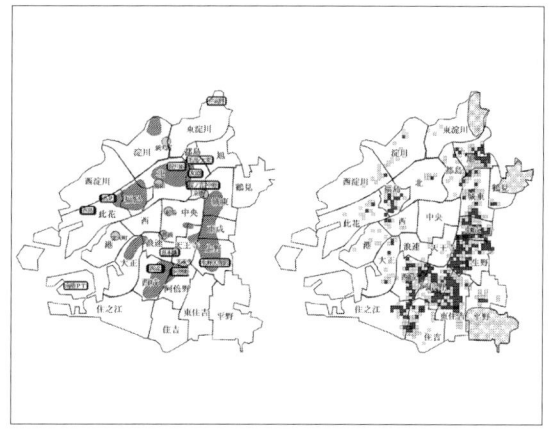

Figure7/8 Distribution of widen structure collective housing area in the late 1970s which was not damaged by air bombing

Perspectives of the AUC and its Prospects |241

conditions of Osaka should be strongly linked to the prefectural areas.

This Figure 5 shows areas damaged by the air raid bombings in 1945. There were 30 air raid bombings and this color here shows the bombing area. So physically, Osaka was once destroyed in the air bombings. And the Figure 6 shows the conditions of the post-war reconstruction work operated from 1946 through the 1960s, there are the reconstruction works mainly targeted in this area. So once the town was rebuilt after the war, this is one of the main characteristics of the Japanese cities where most cities were rebuilt after WWII.

So as for physical issues, how will government make an effort for how can it regenerate or revitalize residential areas? The Figure 7 illustrates one of the typical projects of the housing redevelopment from the 1970s to the 1980s in Osaka, and the Figure 8 shows the distribution of substandard housing, mainly the wooden houses, as this distribution shows. And these two show similar distribution, and also the city government made an effort to redevelop this kind of inner city area. Like this (no Figure), a formerly substandard wooden housing districts were renewed and apartment housing block with a welfare facility or a kindergarten or some public parks were built. Or this is (no Figure) the largest redevelopment project in the Abeno area, and is now in its final stage. It took 40 years to redevelop this area. But it is a very big, gigantic project that requires investment of huge funds.

At the industrial level, this Figure 9 shows the distribution of the decreasing rates of the industrial manufacturing sites, so many in the bay areas from 1959 to 1977, This picture shows the decreasing rates of the secondary industries, mainly manufacturing, how the decrease occurred in the bay area and also in other inland areas. So this is the great damage due to the economic conditions. And also about the socio-economic conditions, the blue-collar distribution seen in Figure 10 is surrounding the city center. Not salaried men but blue-collar people are concentrated in inner city around the city centers. And few professionals or highly skilled people live here. They are only concentrated to live on the Uemachi Upland (Figure 11). We are now here in the center of the place where professional, relatively affluent people are concentrated. And the Figure 12 shows the distribution of foreigners. About 90% of them are Korean-Japanese people and there is a high rate of ethnic segregation that we can find.

We are now focusing within the city boundaries. And here also, are the unemployment rates (Figure 13). And Osaka is highly developed with segregation of the socio-economic variables and, especially this area of Nishinari ward, out of the 24 wards or district governments, this Nishinari ward suffers greatly from unemployment. And the Figure 14 illustrates the distribution of elderly singletons. They are also concentrated in this ward. And the Figure 15 also shows the population densities. And the Figure 16 is the space for housing. So we can see the very strong segregation occurring in these areas.

And so for this background, Professor Andy Plat has made remarks on some urban studies regarding socio-economic conditions, which should be covered as a topic in the new journal of *CCS*. Seen in the Figure 17, the Osaka City government mainly made efforts to make this a kind of axis of the growth poles, with one growth pole being Midosuji Boulevard and Osaka, Umeda Station and Namba Station, they are the big three terminals, but this one is a very strong growth pole. But Osaka's growth pole is very simple compared to Tokyo's. Tokyo's is very multiple, but Osaka's is very simple.

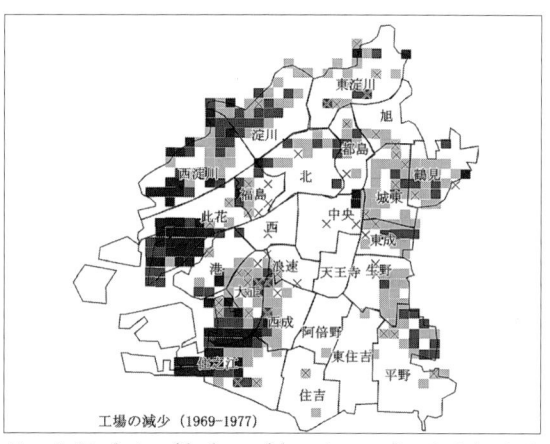

Figure 9 Distribution of the degree of decreasing manufacturing industries in 1970s

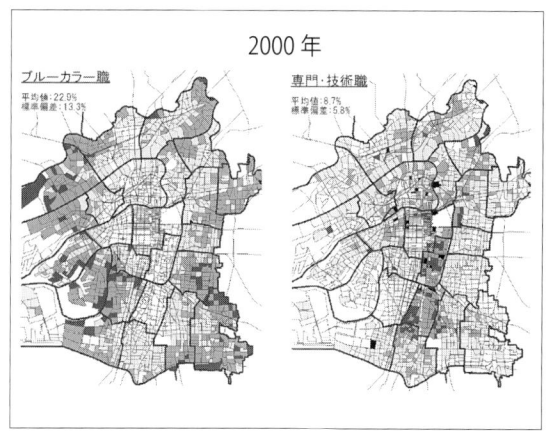

Figure 10/11 Distribution of blue-collar and professional and technical person in 2005

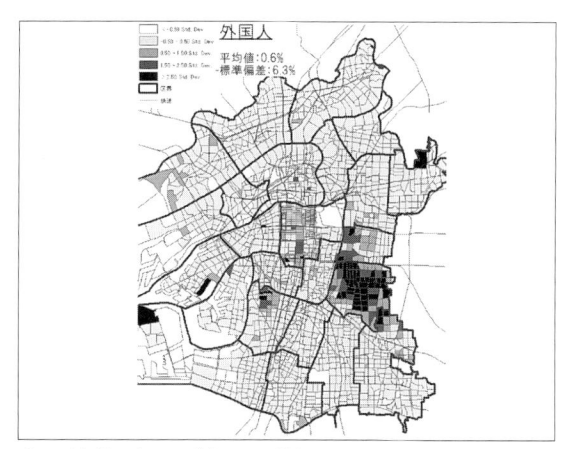

Figure 12 Distribution of foreign in 2005

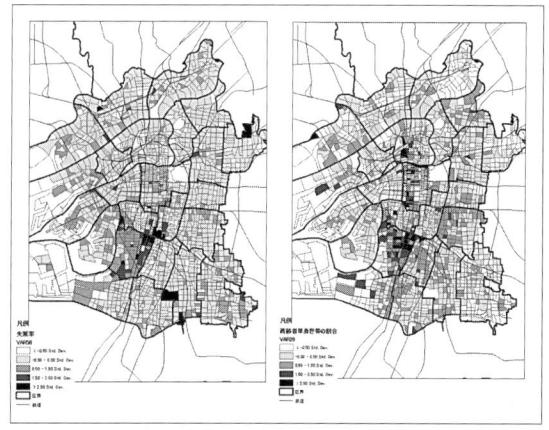

Figure 13/14 Distribution of blue-collar and professional and technical person in 2005

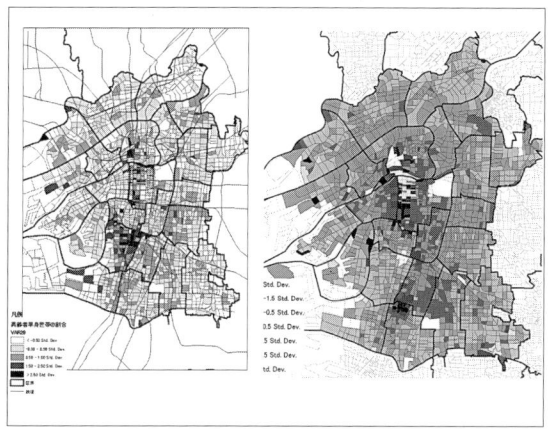

Figure 15/16 Distribution of population density and space of pre person in 2005 and 2000

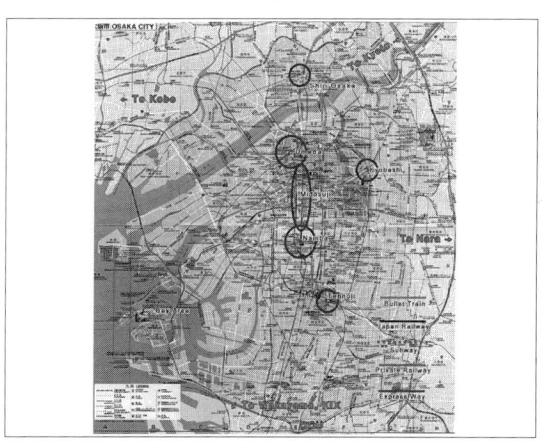

Figure 17 Location of core areas of existing urban development

Perspectives of the AUC and its Prospects

But the Osaka city government decided 20 or 30 years ago that they needed to have more variety in their growth axis from east to west and in the bay area corners. Of course there are many redevelopments through the initiatives of the city government with the funds invested here and so this is the new growth axis.

Originally, there was only one from north to south as seen in Figure 17. Now the new axis runs from Nara to the bay area shown in Figure 18 and there is a new arch from Kobe to Kansai Airport that we are imagining. Because these trends were foreseen during the bubble economy era, Osaka had many future prospects. Through the funds of the abundant tax revenues, they thought they could successfully fulfill their dreams. So these kind of plans were designed and Figure 19 shows is the bay area plan, and there were many container wharfs and new towns and amusement sites, etc. But after the bubble economy and the start of the 21st century, Figure 20 draws the distribution of the homeless, suddenly after the collapse of the economy in the middle of the 1990s. There were many homeless people emerging and distributed over the entire city.

But there are also some strong urban movements in Osaka City. Surrounding the Osaka loop line of railway, I call this area the crescent zone seen in Figure 21, and there are many strong focal points of the Japanese-Korean segregation areas, and they have unique social movements against the Japanese government or mainstream society. And there is a big concentration of day laborers who are mostly single people and they still have a unique social movement. And there are also some Japanese minority groups of the outcast peoples. And this is a large outcast people concentration area in Japan, we call it a Buraku, and they have some strong power to coordinate together with the government and to renew the area, and there are also Okinawan people from the Okinawan Islands, who experience discrimination by the mainstream society of Japan.

So there are many legacies from the social movements of minority people, and in the light of the Osaka City government policies, these social movements are not so openly reflected in the city policy and planning. So in the Figure 22, the green marks show our URP's research plazas' distribution, and we have a strong connection with these social movements, and aside from economic development, we are involved in many culturally creative actions, etc. so we have some target areas for getting involved with some local residents and NGOs, and we have organized many projects.

So to conclude, Sharon has some very unique gentrification projects. In spite of the fact that they have not had such a long duration, we have in these areas done some watching and listening and participate together concerning some kinds of gentrification issues. And also, Lily's comments are hard to illustrate in an Osaka context because she has made some remarks about education and training issues. So this is the part of our target of how the academician should develop such programs. And, responding to Professor Machimura, is one of the other open space issues, that is, we have made very strong efforts to elaborate how the homeless people living in public parks is a very big issue in Japan and Osaka.

All three of the speakers proposed some alternative ways of how to govern the city, not ordinary city policy, but very flexible, and in touch with the real changing world, I think they showed us how to tackle that.

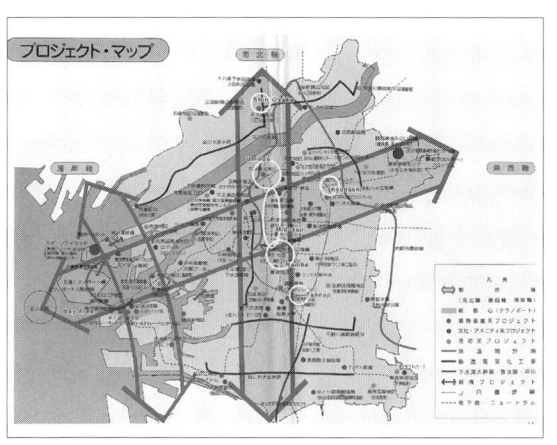

Figure18 Location of development axis planned in 1990

Figure19 Location of bay-area development projects

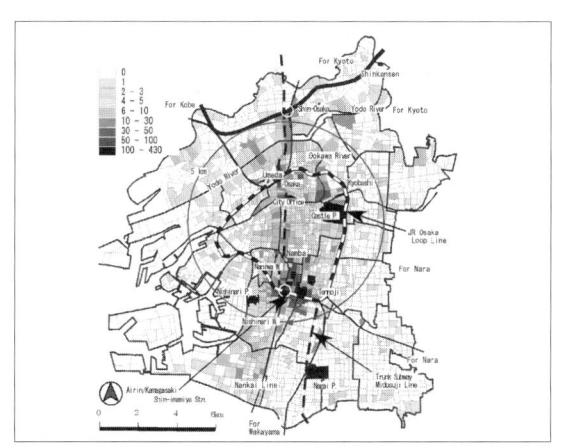

Figure 20 Distribution of rough sleepers in 1998
(homeless people who slept outside)

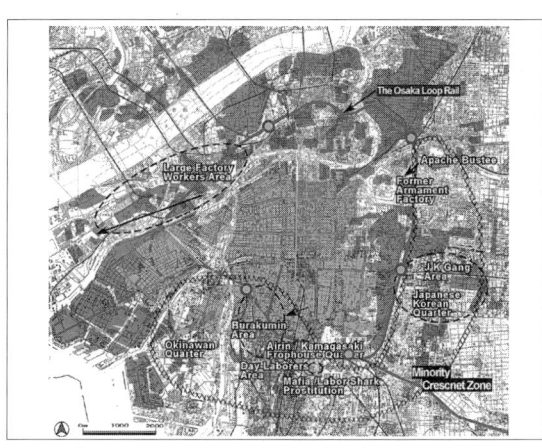

Figure21 Location of "minority" group's social movements

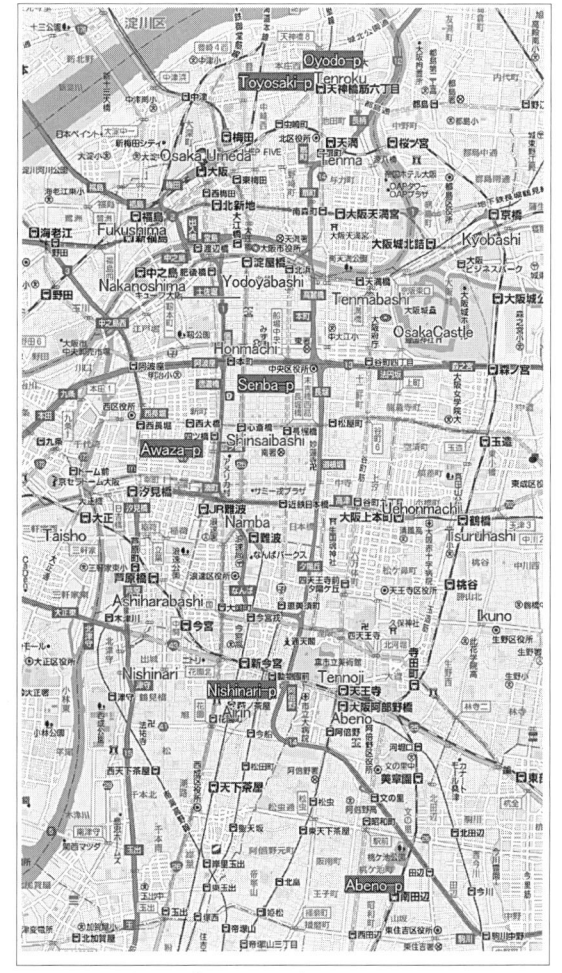

Figure 22 Distribution of URP on-site plaza

Perspectives of the AUC and its Prospects |245

Masayuki Sasaki: Thank you Prof. Mizuuchi for that very interesting follow-up, and the next speaker is Professor Okano.

Hiroshi Okano: In Session 2, we heard about the new international journal, *CCS*, from the Elsevier company, based in Holland, about ten years ago through acquisitions and mergers they took over a number of what had simply been academic presses, like Pergamon Press, and they have now built a giant academic publishing corporation that is number one in the world. So it's that kind of international journal. They have a database, it's called the ScienceDirect database, and without this database the universities in the world, including Japanese universities, would not be able to do research… I wouldn't go so far as to call it a monopoly, but it's the kind of international academic publishing company that the association of public university presidents in Japan has to come together and negotiate with Elsevier over prices… this is the company the Urban Research Plaza approached to launch the journal *CCS*. One of the reasons was, to have the strength of Japanese research, the strength of research in the social sciences, properly appreciated by people abroad. In other words, since almost none of the articles in the social sciences (in Japan) are written in English, there still isn't much Japanese presence worldwide, and this goes for the Nobel Prize as well. Really, I think more Japanese should get it. Especially the Nobel Prize in economics, not one Japanese has gotten it so far. Therefore, in urban studies, while it is a multiple discipline of various discipline fields, for one thing we wanted research results in sociology or the humanities to be properly appreciated. This may be a special situation for we Japanese. Everyone here from overseas is properly recognized in English-language research circles. There are a lot of things we could talk about, but first, as for '*City, Culture and Society*', we have a contract for five years, so from this year through 2014, four issues a year times five years. 4 x 5 = 20, right? So, that means 20 issues with about 6 or 7 articles in each issue. About 7 articles to be published, and four times a year, 4 x 7 = 28, so that means 28 articles a year. The company, Elsevier, has given us targets, and we have to achieve these targets within the first three years. One of these is called the 'impact factor,' and this is the rate of citations, how many times the articles that are published in *CCS* are quoted, used, or noticed in the other top journals. The target number is 0.5, the number of citations divided by the number of articles. That means the top journals in the English-speaking world, since most of the top journals are written in English, we need to have the articles in *CCS* cited, among all the articles that are written in English. This figure of 0.5… *CITIES*, which is one of the top journals in this field, this black thing here, *CITIES* has generally an impact factor of 0.5. So, in other words, from the very start we are being told to achieve the same impact factor as the top journal. This is really going to be hard. So naturally we have to have really good, really well-known people who right for the top journals, and who are native English speakers, write for us. Or, we have to instantly create a movement with a new direction in urban research or in cultural research in order to quickly increase the number of citations. If we don't do all kinds of things, then *CCS* is going to disappear.

And then, there are the number of downloads. 50,000 … 50,000 cases of downloads per year is an important goal. And then there are the number of subscriptions. In recent years the number of subscriptions has changed from hardcopy issues like this to mainly being in electronic form, so hardcopy subscriptions are becoming less important. But, after all, something like this that you can look at and handle will be seen as being a better journal, and with a lot of subscriptions, the citations will also increase. All of these indicators are very much linked together. Within three years we have to completely achieve these evaluation standards. After that, through 2013 and 2014, if we have achieved those standards, then we can keep on going, but in the event we can't achieve them, we will have to do a lot of negotiating with the Elsevier company. In that, our activities are in accord with the strategy of the Elsevier company. We are aiming at UNESCO for example, or international organizations related to the UN, international bodies, or enterprises, place like that. Especially, the reason we are putting out *CCS* is that we want to increase their customer audience among Asians. Especially mainland China, where the volume is so huge. Penetrating into the market of Chinese research organizations or to Chinese researchers is something that is very important to Elsevier. Therefore, while it is four issues a year in the beginning, later they want to go to eight issues. Or, our competitor, Urban Studies, puts out 13 issues a year. They put out one issue every month and then a supplement. By increasing the number of issues that come out and are read, it raises the impact factor of citations, and increases the number of downloads as well. Therefore, as I wrote at the very end, for the editorial staff the just the opening launch was pretty hard, and we have a limited number of people working, so we need people to proactively send us their articles or activities, we need to have people put together special issues, people who can do all kinds of things on the editorial staff, or even to join me as managing editor. There is even the possibility that we will have to think about having two editors in chief. In order to support that, the AUC, the Association for Urban Creativity that Professor Sasaki talked about and which we are mainly discussing here in Session 6, creating this kind of association is vital for the journal, and not just for the journal, but for we researchers, and for practitioners who are involved in urban culture. Professionals, people who are actually doing things, the staff of international organizations, or people related to the government, or various people related to state governments or to cities. Or ordinary citizens. Yes, ordinary citizens… at the beginning in Session 2, as I briefly indicated, we've come to the situation we need to have not only researchers judging whether an article is good or not, but have ordinary citizens judging whether certain research is good or not. We need an association where we can have all these different types of people involved. I have written about it as a kind of 'commons,' but that is the network-type of organization we are creating. Dividing this into Type A and Type B, As an example of Type A in business studies, I'm in business studies, Elsevier puts out Long Range Planning, and it has six issues a year. But under this, a Strategic Planning Society has been created, and they hold seminars and provide information, not just for researchers but also for practical practitioners. Their website is also filled with all kinds of information. In addition, they publish 12 issues a year of a newsletter, a newsletter every month. And then, while mainly it is researchers who are writing for Long Range Planning, there is also a magazine, it's a magazine for practitioners. It comes out four times a year. Building this kind of formidable organization is what I call Type A.

Honestly speaking, it's possible that we won't be able to build a Type A organization very quickly here at the URP, but then there is Type B, referring back to Professor Colbert for an example. In Session 2, he was the second speaker, and he talked about HEC Montréal, one of the top business schools, that pioneered in the publication of the International Journal of Arts Management, that covers arts management and arts marketing, and the organization which supports it, AIMAC, which holds an international conference every other year. It's executive group is the organization that puts that on. It's purpose is to help support the International Journal of Arts Management. Rather than looking at a Type A case, for our first two or three years, I feel that something like this AIMAC may present us with a good model to learn from.

Professor Andy Pratt talked about how things are too skewed towards Anglo-America. As for an Asian perspective, during the first three years we are going to have to have Anglo-Saxons, native speakers of English, writing articles for us so that they will be cited, so for the first three years, working on an Asian perspective will be pretty difficult. And then, as for new topics or new research methodologies, we will be rapidly producing these. And then there are the Sub-Centers. We have a lot of Sub-Centers, especially in Asia: Shanghai, Seoul, Singapore, Hong Kong, Bangkok, Yogyakarta, Taipei, and Melbourne. We have these places. We will need to have lots more support from them coming here, supporting the association, and supporting the journal. And as I said before, from *UN HABITAT*, from the UNDP and groups related to the UN, and we want people from other organizations as well to come here and help us. Therefore, I think that by all means you should create the AUC. That is all.

Kenkichi Nagao: The actual goal of this session was, it's written here as, "Critical Insights on Urban Creativity," but it began with the intention of thinking a little deeper, not just critically in the negative sense, but as a deeper critical evaluation. Four years ago at the symposium for the founding of the Urban Research Plaza, I was in charge of business affairs, and so this time I was wondering whether I needed to do anything, but after running around a bit in the planning stage of this symposium, suddenly I was included, and so, with the feeling that after all, 'creativity' is the keyword for the age we are entering, and if that has to be emphasized, how can we build a bright future with that? I can't say there wasn't an aspect to it of not allowing this to turn into the kind of atmosphere where we all shout "Banzai!" together three times. It's just that this is not a symposium being put on by a local government or a think tank, but by a university, I thought we also needed some critical insights,

Kenkichi Nagao

and then also some discussions on some more focused themes, so I talked about urban creativity. Just now Professor Okano mentioned it, but in the inaugural issue of '*City, Culture and Society*' as well, Professor Andy Pratt has written about creative cities. The creative city is being talked about as if it will solve all our problems, one might say the creative city is our wishing star, but it is also necessary to say that it will certainly not solve all our problems. In the U.K., and in Japan as well, when some catch phrase that sounds attractive to the ears of local governments appears, first of all it is thought about in the sense of being a good omen, but then gradually step by step it turns into what the British call a 'theory led by policy,' it becomes co-opted by the policymakers. Actually, in Japan as well, the concept of 'industry clusters' gradually was interpreted by a number of scholars in ways that were advantageous to the Ministry of Economy and Industry. Should we let things continue to slide in that direction, do we want this to be a symposium sponsored by the university that approves of that? It was with that in mind that this session came about.

There have been any number of concepts considered regarding creativity, but the first time debate heated up was over the idea of the 'creative class' as laid out by Richard Florida. That was referred to in Professor Sasaki's speech on the first day, and, for another promotion, there is a special supplementary issue of *CITIES*, and in the article that Professor Sasaki wrote for that as well, it says that simply having the people who fit into the creative class category gather together does not necessary lead to a creative city. This kind of problem was posed in the first session, and as for the economies that are associated with such places, Professor Lily Kong, also in Session 1, talked about how much they are accompanied by a great deal of precariousness. In Session 3, Professor Cohendet said that more importantly than asking who these people categorized as creative are, we have to ask more about what they do. In this vein, a number of criticisms were voiced in the discussion about the creative class, but at the end of that discussion Professor Lazzeretti reminded us that while there are aspects of his theory that should be criticized, we must not forget that at least about ten years ago Florida clearly stated that we have to look once again at human capital.

Next, involving creative industries, the tendency for them to agglomerate in cities is very strong, so do the industrial sectors that were there previously specialize, are they more responsive, and what about the meshing together of economic and non-economic factors? There was lively discussion about these things, and at the same time what was stressed was that merely by agglomerating, were they only in physical proximity to each other, or was there also a perceptual or psychological closeness? Professor Lazzaretti talked about that, and then Professor Cohendet, using the term 'cognitive platform,' talked about whether the effects of agglomeration were working being based on whether people held perceptions in common with each other, and whether there were some things that they could share. The fruits of agglomeration, or the advantages if you will, are in some ways similar to those of the already existing industries, particularly the already existing manufacturing industries, but there are ways in which they are different… Professor Pratt in particular said that the industrial system itself of the creative industries is different than in other industries. Among those ways, as for advantages of industrial agglomeration talked about before, there are cost reductions, in that certain expenses are reduced, and there is a learning effect, but at the same time Professor Hanzawa pointed out in his talk about the Japanese video game industry in particular that there is redundancy and a certain amount of waste, and everyone has to struggle against that, and so not much creativity emerges. In that sense, unlike in the previously mentioned sectors, for the creative industry, the situation has emerged that there are trade-offs to made regarding the classical advantages of agglomeration.

There was also a lot of discussion about creative cities, and especially important in that was Professor Cohendet's suggestion that we see it in three layers or strata, with the all the various individuals operating in the lower layer, the 'underground,' and in the 'upperground' there are organizations for putting all that creativity to good effect, but it is the 'middleground' which is precisely the environment in the city where people either get to know and work together well or do not. How is that layer actually made up? That is one discussion, whether people mingle well together or not, when the creative class is clustered together, does that turn into a creative city or not… and then the fact that the creative city will not necessarily solve all problems, that even when there is agglomeration, it will include various culture contradictions and frictions, as Professor Pratt said. Also, and here is another promotion, in *City, Culture and Society*, Professor Edmond Preteceille of France, who came here just four years ago for the URP's foundation symposium, has an article titled, "The Fragile Urban Situation of Cultural Producers in Paris." We must not forget that that aspect will inevitably be involved. While we want to think again about urban studies, one of the keywords that Professor Lazzeretti used in her case study about lasers being used in the restoration of various cultural properties was 'cross fertilization,' whether different things mesh well together or not, and this has been part of urban studies for a very long time. That is an issue not just for creative industries but for urban studies as a whole. While saying that, just as 'Urban Studies' is deliberately written in different forms in English, there are people from a variety of different fields, and then when talking about cities their particularities inevitably are mentioned, so in the sense that we all have different backgrounds and different methods, the question of whether by mixing together we can become better or not has been a problem in urban studies both in the past and at present. Whether something is universal or situated, as Professor Pratt talked about in the discussion on creative cities, is a problem that will always arise in urban studies. Just because something works in a particular city somewhere, whether that can be applied universally or not has always been an issue in urban studies, and it became once again an issue in our discussions here.

In the midst of that, as for the prospects for our Urban Research Plaza, what is the outlook for the future, I'm thinking that we have the potential for becoming one of the hubs in Asia, even if we don't go global right away. There are two popular expressions in my field of economic geography these days, 'local buzz' and 'global pipeline.' 'Buzz' may be a bit hard for Japanese to understand, but it is like people talking together, blah blah blah, in a noisy bar. Just before now, while eating lunch, when Professor Kamo was chattering away, that might give you a hint, but whether there is an environment like that or not is extremely important in the face to face communication of the city. Talking about Osaka City University in that context, and it is true for the professors here today as well, at OCU everyone comes from different departments and has their own field of specialization, but there are really a lot of people interested in cities, both teachers and students, so in that sense, in this very local spot, there is an environment where it is easy to generate a buzz. And then, while all the teachers and students have a pipeline, at the same time, putting on conferences like this creates a global pipeline. And putting on the conference itself, while it is not of long duration, in the sense that it generates a local buzz, perhaps means that we are just such an Asian hub.

However, in considering creative cities, and Professor Sasaki has also written about this in the special supplement issue of *CITIES*, in Yokohama and Osaka, for example, and other cities where the previous mayors enthusiastically promoted the creative city and used it as a catch phrase, in each case, these are the cities whose public universities are experiencing the biggest reductions in budgets and people among all the universities in Japan. Frankly speaking, they seem to be taking a warped view that universities are not creative industries, and so, cost reductions are the most important thing. In any case, this is the sad reality, but if we look at this from a creative industry agglomeration theory perspective, the fact that many of the universities in Japan are part of a system that has forgotten tolerance is a disadvantage in trying to create a hub. And then, while universities are also a kind of creative industry in which creative talent works, they are in the kind of fragile situation that Professor Preteceille talks about, and looking at the people who are here as conference members, the people on the executive committee, except for a few faculty members, are a long list of temporary faculty or contract teachers, and this is really a severe situation. Universities to some degree have this aspect, by having tolerances, having slack and waste, actually the URP is made stronger, but I think that is hard. The reason I bring this up is that in Japan the inequality between generations and the difference in perception between generations has become a big problem, and that is true at universities too. The professors in Mizuuchi's and Okano's generation, and the ones older than that, are OK, but in my generation, first of all there aren't many people, or if there are, they have to do certain things, and they don't show up much. For people younger than me, first of all there are no full time professors, and that is particularly severe in the case of our university, but it's true elsewhere also, and in the sense of passing things down to next generation, if they don't do something about human capital in Japanese universities, if this does become the hub of Asia, a level of substance will be demanded, so what will become of people younger than me, how will they be dealt with, how will they be included and energized to do well, I think that is an issue. As for my own personal opinions, I will end them with the hope that you will be tolerant in listening to them. Thank you very much.

Masayuki Sasak: Thank you very much. I enjoyed your interesting talk. And the next speakers are Professor Wing Shing Tang and Dr. Suzy Goldsmith. Please.

Suzy Goldsmith: Hello and thank you. I have been nominated to report back on our session because Prof. Nakagawa apologizes that he cannot be here. So, first I would like to thank the organizers of this symposium for what has been a very fruitful experience for the network of Asian Sub-Centers. We might stretch it to Asia-Pacific so that Australia feels part of it, but we found it a very fruitful experience and I can honestly say with reference to the last speaker there was a buzz. And there is continuing to be a buzz, and we were just meeting over lunch with Professor Mizuuchi about where we go from here. So I just want to provide a brief reflection on the presentations that we had, which were really wide-ranging, but they do actually have some connecting themes which we are starting to draw out. I just wanted to perhaps run through them briefly in terms of a specific through to a wider systems view to show these connections a little bit, and reflect on them for those who weren't able to be there. So, we had Bussakorn Binson speaking from Bangkok, and the work that she has been doing on the individual voices that emerge particularly focusing on the arts and preserving and valuing the unique nature of art in that city. And that concept of preservation was continued by Liling Huang from Taipei who also discussed some concepts of preservation in the context of successful government-community partnership focused on city parks and reconnecting culture and art. So that was a project-type view. And, a more activist project view was presented by Jong Gyun Seo from Anyang, focusing on Anyang in the Republic of Korea. So that was a more activist intervention, trying to give small businesses a larger voice in a major redevelopment project, which tended then towards more of a discussion of a participatory process, which was a theme continued by Nikolaas Warouw from Yogyakarta. He explored processes whereby marginalized citizens gained ground through cross-class alliances, so local interests can be given greater prominence by thinking about a shared future for that particular community. And, then Ying-Fang Chen from Shanghai looked from the movement of a specific process to consider more assistance, and she was asking how the system of housing in Shanghai can work in the face of such a huge miracle, what she calls the economic miracle, and many people do, of huge growth in Shanghai. So that was an interesting characterization of the dynamic of housing exclusion and the housing estate market, how those two work together. Our own account from Western Melbourne also looked at a systems type view, but more looking at the notion of employment as an integrating theme among disparate topics in terms of social exclusion and innovation, productivity and education. And finally Wing Shing Tang used the example of pairing cities, Hong Kong and Mumbai to extend the systems view further to consider the academic system of inquiry and proposed an inside-out view. That has become a bit of mantra now with us. That is a buzz, which is perhaps a parallel with the idea of grassroots movement in citizen participation, and takes us full circle to a more grounded academic method open to fresh ways of seeing. Perhaps that is what we want to build on and what we have been discussing as a group since. As for questions of how we can build the network among the Asian-Pacific Sub-Centers, first I would like to say something for Australia here, because I am delighted and I think many Australians would be delighted to be viewed as part of an Asian network. Australia is very conscious of its location and the relevance of its Asian context. And already with the work that we have been doing with the Urban Research Plaza, the workshop that we organized when we had many visitors from this group, there has been huge enthusiasm among practitioner participants, ranging from the federal government through state, local, and also nongovernmental organizations, huge excitement about the idea of understanding and learning from the experience of other Asian cities. There is a huge interest and enthusiasm for that. I also would like to make some controversial suggestions, building on what people have been saying. One was the question of social science being less international, or Asian countries being less represented in the social sciences in the academic journals. And I wanted to just put out the suggestion that maybe, rather than jump to conclusions, maybe that the social sciences are not such a universal language as the pure sciences or medical sciences. They are more context-specific. But the further challenge then is to say, "Well, is that just about geographic context? Is it just Anglo-American versus Asian, because they are different places? Or is it maybe more about a contemporary context?" So, I am just, you know, the potential is there maybe for us to, in trying to create a new story and perhaps take a fresh view, to also provide something that is just as relevant or fresh for an Anglo-American context, as for an Asian context. So I was just trying to perhaps suggest that that might be a possibility. The sort of theme that unites us as a network... I am speaking for us all, but I think I have got it about right, and Professor Mizuuchi suggested this during yesterday's discussion as well, is the tendency of challenging the status-quo, but a static, observational description-type-model, and certainly in business this has been the context for regional development of businesses, is a passive recipient of policy. We are inclined towards a more activist, even participatory model that not only seeks to understand but also to enact, to change. And perhaps the different political contexts of our cities are actually a useful backdrop for understanding some of this participatory difference and what it is really about. In academic terms it is risky work. It is not something just laid out, just incrementally different, it is risky work. But it may well promise a new engagement among academics and practitioners or professionals. So, that fits with what Prof. Okano was just saying about the future positioning of *CCS* as a journal, and that potential for practitioners and professionals to find a site to work together. So what we propose to do, I am just going to wrap up here quickly, is focus on a couple of themes and one of those is probably the participatory nature or the interface, various forms of interfaces, and work together initially over the internet as the Asian-Pacific cities network, perhaps as a Sub-Center of this association serving creativity if it gets going. This is just a summary, thank you.

Masayuki Sasaki: Okay, the last speaker is Professor Hong Gyu Jeon

Hong Gyu Jeon: Good afternoon everyone. My name is Hong Gyu Jon and I am an associate professor of the Urban Research Plaza. This time, I was in charge of the 5th session. This was the session for presentations by our Research Plaza's doctoral research fellows. And we have established a career building program, which is the GCOE postdoctoral program. In this program we have an open recruiting system, twice a year inviting applicants from all over the world. And our GCOE program consists of four units which are urban theory unit, cultural creativity unit, social inclusion unit, and finally international promotion unit. All of the research fellows belong to one of the units to accomplish their research purposes. And the URP has provided supported for their activities. Within their relationships related to research and fieldwork activities in this supportive environment, we can achieve creative new research results. After this symposium, each of the presenters can revise their presentation paper and has a chance to submit for academic publication. For example, *CCS*, or our research documents, and our working papers series. And you can see their abstracts on the screen, and the individuals, and their topics are very different, as you know. For instance, successor training in the traditional performing arts; accounting in recycling network enterprises, social enterprises and community-based art, comparative studies between South Korea and the USA; and finally housing issues for single mother households in Japan. In spite of the differences, we can share with each other research ideas and research activities, which are very close to the society and its members. Before this symposium, most of our research fellows applied to give presentations on urban studies. And our faculty members reviewed their abstracts. By this process, five presentations were selected finally, but one of them could not join in this session because of a personal emergency. After the presentations, our guest reviewer, Dr. Hyun Bang Shin of LSE, gave some valuable comments to each of the presenters. And we hope that his comments and the discussions in this session will help the presenters to upgrade their research papers to a higher level. And our URP will continue to support their research plans and career paths more globally by supporting creative relationships internationally through this symposium. Thank you very much.

Masayuki Sasaki: We have about an hour in which we would like by all means to hear your views on what directions we can pursue in our research on this big theme of 'reconstructing the city through cultural creativity and social inclusion' to do joint research internationally, and in particular in what way our guests who have come here from overseas can contribute. For our remaining one hour, I would like to organize the discussion to be as efficient and intensive as possible, so I am asking for your kind cooperation. I will only first announce the name of the speaker. We would like to begin with Professor Andy Pratt, who also made a very great contribution to the inaugural publication of *CCS*. Well then, Professor Pratt, please.

Andy Pratt: Hi, thanks. I am not sure what you want me to say. One of the things is a reflection on the sort of discussions that we have had, and there seem to be a number of conversations going on, I think. What I have identified in hearing the discussions is that sometimes these perhaps are either not connecting, or it is difficult to make bridges across them. I think we have had this very fruitful discussion about research that is going on in Osaka, and the attempt to link that to the existing social science research on cities and creative cities, etc. Within that there seem to be a couple of tensions at work, and that is between the sorts of resolutions for social problems and the resolutions of economic problems. And I think that one of the areas that we haven't perhaps heard about is the perspective that I guess is being pursued by people like Charles Landry, which is about creative problem-solving rather than being creative in a creative practice. But actually the way I interpret that is about new and inventive ways of governance. And I think some of the discussions cutting across the debates here are about really thinking about the challenges of new forms of governance. And this is not unique to this part of the world by any means. It is a global problem of how to engage with the culturally creative activities, but how to engage with problem-solving in cities in general. And I think that is an interesting area that hasn't had that much emphasis here, that I think could supplement some of those issues. In fact, many people have referred to the challenges of solving problems in that way. I think another thing that has come out fairly strongly is the linkage between the culturally creative industries and the rest of the economy. And I think that whilst understandably people have focused on the culturally creative industries and related activities, I think the real challenge for all of us is to examine that relationship with the rest of the economy. And I think we have had some examples of that through the analysis of particular innovations, but I think more generally there are a range of issues here that are very interesting that we can explore, about how the labor market operates between the informal economy, etc. as well. So those are two related areas. There is one other issue, that is, how do you as a community of scholars relate to the knowledge that is produced in this field in the rest of the world, which means in this case the Anglo-American dominant world? And I think there is a real challenge about how to make the linkage. And I think that is the issue that you are discussing in terms of the focus of the journal, about how you link in there, it is partly about the style of journals and the style of papers, but it is also about how you link particular case studies to the particular and theoretical and conceptual debates as well, or introduce new ones to make those connections. I think there have been some really interesting tensions, and I think they are not just about what happens in Asia. I think it is a general problem with the study of cities. If I may, I would just like to add one further point about the challenge, which I think is a very interesting one, of launching a journal in this way. I just want to encourage you to think also about this issue in a very instrumental and strategic way. What I mean by this is how is it that you get a high impact factor, and that is about citations. How do you get five citations? You self-cite, or cite yourselves amongst the group. You will have to find a group of people that will cite one another in multiple papers. That is how hard scientists do it, okay? It is a game. This is not about the proper academic expertise. You have been given a very difficult task by Elsevier, to produce this, and therefore you have to play a game with it. One of the characteristics of high-citation journals is that they produce review papers. Review papers tend to get cited more than others because people like to point to that in the first part of their paper. So it is another way to get a high number of citations. A third way would be to target authors whose work is highly cited already. And the new datametrics that are provided with these journals over the citation systems, like Web of Science and SCOPUS, allow you to identify them as well. It is maybe wrong, but the point is that people who are cited get cited more. It is very difficult for people to get in at the bottom. And one of the technical indices that are produced by these journals, and we all hate them, but it is called the H-index. is of those people that have large numbers of citations associated with their work. These are the rules of the game for playing this citation game and I think personally they are very corrosive to academic work but that is the name of the game. And I think you cannot afford to not to play that game, and I think, given the task that you have been given by Elsevier, then I think you have to be very brutal with some of these approaches. So there are two things that I think were some very productive linkages in terms of the academic debate, but I think given that this journal is a platform for that productive debate, you need to attend to that platform as well, and I think this is a very difficult task. Thanks.

Masayuki Sasaki: Thank you very much. So, are there any other comments or advice? Please.

François Corbert: I keep trying, since my presentation, to find a way of defining the field that you want to get into, but I will start with the question you asked, "How to make collaborations between the Asian Region and the other regions?" I don't think that collaborations can be forced. Collaborations between researchers come about when individuals come to know each other, so this kind of conference to my mind is important, and I think that another way would be to of course to do other conferences. I don't know if every year is too soon, or if it should be every second year. I mean, it is your decision. And then it also depends on what kind of conference you would like to have. Do you want a conference like you organized right now, by inviting people, or do you want to proceed like other scientific conferences where you launch a call for papers, and you choose the best papers? That is another way. But what I think will be important is to define the field, and after having heard the syntheses this afternoon, it struck me that this network that is here right now on this floor is composed of different kinds of people. There are those who manage organizations, and if we are thinking about social inclusion, well we could discuss the management of all those organizations that focus on social inclusion in a city. That is one point. We have got here the urban sociologists, who have a different point of view, and urban geographers and urban planners, all those… and you could add to that cultural activists. So I think this is a group of people that maybe don't, are not used to, work together, but through this kind of conference could meet each other and people will fall in love with somebody else, I mean scientifically, well it could be also another way too, and then maybe do joint research. That is in response to your question, and I would like to finish with a very small element. Maybe in the journal, and the journal should proceed in the same way, and the conference can be a good way of getting good articles for the journal, and play the game that Andy just mentioned. And maybe CCS could also be a place where you can find some kind of success stories. How social inclusion was achieved, how an organization or movement was able to address the social exclusion in a city and the explanation of success stories could lead to the theorization of the field. Thank you.

Masayuki Sasaki: Thank you.

Patrick Cohendet: First I would like to thank you very much for the fruitful conference, this symposium. And my first reaction was the following, as I heard the presentations, more and more the feeling that we are talking much more about creativity in the cities than creative cities as a unique solution to solve the problems of the world. We talked a lot about creativity in cities, and I think what was very interesting in this symposium, there was a positive side and a negative side, with controversies, and I think this is extremely important. And the second point is, I think what we lack are in fact case studies. Case studies, I don't know, on Osaka? And creativity in Osaka. Not Osaka as a creative city. I don't care if Osaka is more creative than Montréal, or vice versa, but how do you play with creativity in Osaka? And I think if the journal review is good, sometimes propose a given city, and how creativity is expressed with positive and negative aspects in this city. I think this could be of huge interest, and certainly a huge attraction for quotations and citations. Maybe, concerning the journal, one thing which will be extremely difficult is to attract talented young researchers. And the reason why is, when you have a multi-disciplinary journal, you can attract the seniors who have already made a career, but it is very difficult to attract the very young talented researchers because they want to be published in a very defined discipline. And you should think about that. I think one way we, I am also an editor of a journal in international management, one way we do it is, we don't have special issues, but issues focused on methodologies, methods, measurements, and this helps a lot young researchers to come in and to try to be published. In terms of discipline, I think, I didn't see that much history. I think first historians, in the number of quotations, they are in a discipline which is more quoted, and so it is a strategic asset, okay? And there were not that many historians around, and that could be very helpful in giving one another a sense of how the city works. Thanks.

Masayuki Sasaki: Thank you very much. Okay, go ahead.

Sharon Zukin: Well first, I agree with everything the preceding speakers have said. That is very important. Second, as a member of the editorial board of several other journals, I am no stranger to impact evaluation. But you face a very difficult task in aiming specifically at a certain mathematical calculation of impact from the very beginning, and I would do everything possible hit that specific impact figure. I would also do everything possible to stimulate excitement in the articles that you publish. From that point of view, as Andy Pratt said, it is going to be very difficult to make a bridge between the social welfare dimensions of cultural policy and the industrial dimensions of cultural policy, as well as the spatial dimensions of cultural policy. I disagree with only one piece of advice that Andy gave, but of course this is the situation with all free advice, that people can disagree with it. I don't think that review articles or review essays are well cited. I speak as someone with the most downloaded but not most cited article of the year in various journals, and the most downloaded article that I have published recently was an essay reviewing the career of a distinguished urban sociologist. But even though that essay was perhaps widely read or made at least into a lot of paper copies, it is probably not as widely cited, so I am not sure that review essays in the field that the journal will cover will be widely cited. Specific articles, as Patrick just suggested, with specific information, I think will be widely cited. I have walked around this district in Osaka, which as my eyes suggested is an affluent area of Osaka, but I have walked in the Kuruma Ichiba food market and I have walked in the Shinsaibashi shopping district, and I would like to know, where are the spaces of the creative and cultural producers of this city? I think it would be very valuable to have empirical articles about the really existing creative producers of this city. And that brings me to my final piece of free advice, which is that it would be so interesting to have the journal become a hub of Asian cultural identity. Why aspire from the beginning to be an international voice? Why not aspire to be an international journal that people go to learn about Asia? Why not be a journal that brings to us Anglophone readers news about Asian cities, and why not become a published vehicle, a medium, for Asian cities? I think if you would do that, it would bring the you the attention of those of us who want to read about Asian cities. When Asian writers try to publish in Anglophone journals, they really are forced to fit what they want to say into an Anglophone framework. Not just in terms of language, but also in terms of intellectual ideas, and it would be so useful for the thousands of Asian scholars and Asian practitioners to become an Asian journal that people go to when they want to read about Asian cities and Asian culture.

Masayuki Sasaki: Thank you very much. Any other comments? Please.

Luciana Lazzeretti: Just to connect with Sharon, because my first point was to define an Asian identity. So I would like perhaps, if it is possible, to apply in this case at what we have sustained until now about creativity. We have talked about the informal environment. We have discussed about the fact that we need to find a new kind of organization. And then we want to be recognized by the mainstream. So, if we want to be recognized by the mainstream, like the English editors, we have to use their rules of the game like Andy said. In this case we have discussed about creativity and culture and so on as the other thing in the same way. We want to use a new concept, and the old editorial rules, but we can say that because we are professors, we can say that because we are invited by you from Europe in this case, but we can't do the same things for the new generations if you have to recognize an international community. So I think that we can decide not something, not everything now, but just a path for the task ahead. The first path is always, in management you define the mission, and the economists define the opposite, and the sociologists, they usually look for identity. It is the same thing. I don't know anything about Asia. I would like that local and global remain. And not for the global to also arrive here. We are in time to began a new revolution from Asia. A new revolution from the bottom, not from the top down. Because if you use the approach of the mainstream, that is top-down. If we to use the bottom-up, you need to be passionate and if you are not, you are another culture, you have different religions, and a lot of European and American people, they look at Asia to find a new piece in a way of living, a new style. So I think that you need to think about what you have. This is your most important resource, that all the Anglo-Americans and Europeans recognize as something that we have left. That was my first point. So I would like to have a journal for open discussion with an informal organization that will be recognized perhaps in the future by a network of editors and not by only one. It is a dream about, if I have to fit in every way I can dream, why not? And the second point is about the subject. There are some opportunities, and some problems. The city, as my colleagues from Canada said, are not creative cities, they are cities of art, but they are creative local systems. So the city is just one of the creative local systems. So, open space. And as Sharon said, why do we not write a book on creative spaces, so perhaps we can try to think of creative spaces and not only of creative cities. This is an opportunity which is also a problem. The problem is disciplinary. I have done this, I have taken my life in this direction, and I know the consequences in terms of the academy of multi-disciplinary activities. And we have to take care again for the new generation, because economics recognizes some criteria and some journals, and sociology other ones. Others cite others, so we need to decide what to do. If you want to do it, you don't accept some rules of the game. If you want to be other things, you need to accept in a very clear way the rules of the day, but I cannot say anymore to the PhD students to publish in the journals that are not useful for their career. In this sense I speak as a PhD advisor after 10 years of what I have seen happening to the poor PhDs all over the world. Thank you very much.

Masayuki Sasaki: Thank you very much.

Evelyn Shulz: Now, many things have already been said, and I would like to comment on, for example, what Sharon Zukin has said. I think, for example, there is really a need for comparative research on urban issues, and if you want to get some information in English written on Japanese cities or Chinese cities, it is really hard to get it. If you look for example at the Journal for Urban Studies, most of the articles focus on North America or maybe also on Europe, but, for example if you look at numbers, I mean most of the people who live in cities are in Asia, East Asia, or you also have to include India and in this respect I think there is really a need for producing knowledge written in English on this particular urban experience. And I also think Japan is a unique place because, compared to China, in Japan you already have to struggle with the problem of shrinkage. China still sticks to the pattern of growth and I think in this respect, comparative research is very important, and I really think there is a lack of information about what is going on in Asia. One more thing I would like to talk is, I mean of course to create a journal is a challenge, but on the other hand most of the established journals have an enormous pressure for publication. That means young scholars have to queue up to get published. For example in my field, Japanese studies, there is a very good established journal, the Journal of Japanese Studies. And you have to wait for two or three years to get published. And this is very frustrating for young scholars because they have to publish quite quickly because they are doing their PhD, their research. And, for example, as far as I have observed, I mean I have been coming now to Japan regularly for more than 20 years, and there is a new generation here in Japan, that means young people, that have at least spent one year abroad and who are fluent, even if it is hard for them to communicate in spoken English, they can read English or maybe write English, and they are also used to communicating in a foreign language. And for those people, not only in Japan but also in China and the Sub-Center countries, such a journal would be a great chance to become part of a wider discourse, and we too would have a chance to get published. And in this respect I think the notion of trying to create a hub of Asian cultural identity might also be the focus of this journal. Of course, one has to accept the challenge, one has to try it, but I think that it is really important to produce knowledge in the 21st century which comes very particularly from each country. For example, this morning I have been at the book store and bought a book, Tokyo Metropolizing. And in this book, it has been published in the context of the Biennale in Venice, and in this context it is also clearly written that the 20th century has been, let us say that 20th century urbanism was strictly under the influence of Western thought, but now in the 21st century, there is a return to particularism. That means each country or each region is looking for solutions that are rooted in the local conditions. And in this respect I think a journal that focuses on these topics, for example, is there shrinkage in Malaysia? Or how does Osaka deal with it?... I mean, Professor Mizuuchi has done a lot of research on how Osaka deals with poverty and things like that. I think there is huge potential, because I think from now on a lot of various issues will come up. And one more thing, actually, we have organized two conferences in Munich in 2007, a very spontaneous workshop, and this year in February we had a conference on creative cities, cultural space, and sustainability, and actually I think it was a very good opportunity also for my colleagues of Munich University, and also for people who live in Munich who participated in this conference, to get some idea about not only Asian cities but also how to communicate with each other. In our native language it is so much different, but to find a common language to try, I mean, we always have to struggle, to find a common ground where we can talk to each other, but I think this a very challenging task and I… Yes, thank you very much.

Jung Duk Lim: First of all, congratulations on successfully wrapping up of this three-day conference. I think you are on track so far from the beginning, and it seems to be time for talk about a new marketing strategy for the new product in the competitive market. So all suggestions from previous commentators were good, and I support that, but if I can repeat the strategy, that should be focused or concentrated on Asia, or Asia-specific topics, because, you know, topics related to Asian cities are relatively less developed and less discussed. And that is like a goldmine. And in addition to that, this is the time when we have to come out with a new model on urban development or urban creativity, something like that. Because, so far, we have tended to imitate the cases of advanced cities in advanced countries. So now we need to show a new model, especially to the cities in developing countries, and suggest to them not to imitate the previous cases of advanced countries, but they should say something themselves. For example, if we talk about the creative city in terms of industrial structure, we just emphasize moving towards the creative sector. And the question is then, what should you say to those cities about the manufacturing sectors, which should be the base for employment and output or everything? So, you know, we now need to give advice or a model for those cases, and then I think we would be able to succeed. And repeating my comment, this is the world we live in. And I think this is good point for the future of the journal, and I have one more thing to say about the AUC, I am not sure that the character of this organization is well set out. So I think positioning is very important. If you are to just put effort into publishing a journal, I think that would maybe redundant. So maybe you need to find a new way to just develop this kind of concept. And lastly, my reaction to the past three days is, you need to find a balance between so-called creativity, creative cities, and social inclusion. I think both are important, but you just need to have a balance. Thank you.

Masayuki Sasaki: Thank you very much.

Hyun Bang Shin: I don't want to add any more new things, given that the previous scholars have already submitted very good suggestions, just a couple of points, and to start with, the Asian young junior academics contributing papers to the journal, for when it comes to promoting this new journal in the market, I think that the key task here for *CCS* is to make *CCS* attractive to young scholars so that they feel like *CCS* is something, is a place where they have built quite a good place to publish. So to attract young scholars to *CCS* is to make *CCS* attractive, and I think that needs to wait for a least a few years until at least *CCS* is established in the market so that young scholars, everybody has been talking about how these young scholars are nowadays in the economic industry, how they try to establish themselves in the sector. But in order to become established, the key element is publishing in a good journal with a very high impact factor. But now we are talking about how to raise the impact factor of *CCS*, so I think there is a kind of, a few goals for *CCS* to achieve before attracting young scholars. But I think on the other hand, another way to proceed, if I may suggest, is there are so many academics, when you think of all the contributions to the debate and to the journal, you can think of three different groups, like one group may come from the Western academics who look at similar issues, and the second group might be these academics in Asian regions who operate in Asia or in non-Western regions, whereas the third group, mainly the group of people like me, Asians or non-Westerners who work and operate in Western institutions, and who by nature, by definition, are always forced to make comparisons and whose work usually includes research on Asian countries, for instance in my case when I look at China or South Korea. So you have this academic third group of people who may not be progressive or may not be doing interesting things, but some of them are doing interesting things and they may actually have something to say in terms of making suggestions to the way in which these questions are shaped and played out. So I think attracting this third group might be one way of proceeding, and one way of actually creating a role for *CCS*. And by attracting key players from these three groups and making them debate with each other, for instance, about certain issues, and making them become more provocative, is a suggestion for the journal. So I think the key issue for the journal, as I said from my point of view, is how provocative the journal can be in the existing world where issues which have not been addressed readily by existing journals can be addressed. But making the journal provocative must be done properly. One way to do it is to attract and invite these key players in those three groups, and make them not be intimidated when debating with each other and criticizing each other. Well I think those kinds of debate sections, by inviting key players in the field, may be one way of promoting *CCS* in the academic world. Thank you.

Hiroshi Okano: This is closely related to what Professor Shin said. At the end, when we were told that *CCS* is a very good place for young people in the middle, that's a very good thing, but it seems to me that is more of a midterm goal than a short term goal. That is to say, as Professor Jules has said, for young researchers, whether or not they will be able to pursue their careers as researchers, whether they truly will be able to or not, depends on whether they write articles that are published in the SSCI, the Social Science Citation Index. Even if they write other articles, they won't get any points for that. That means zero points. And that is also true for young Korean graduate students. They have to write for the journals that the South Korean government recognizes, ones that are in the SSCI. Regrettably, *CCS* is not yet in the SSCI. In order to get there is, as has been said, a medium or long term project, it might take ten years or more. Or, it's even possible

Hiroshi Okano

that even after 20 years, we still won't get in. Therefore, in trying to make it an attractive place for young people, really trying to raise the impact factor, for example, that's the part that is the problem. My alternate proposal, what Professor Shin said at the end, is that we need people form each of three groups, an American group, and a non-western one, and then people like Professor Shin from Asia or other places who are working at places like the University of London, and have these people talk about the core theories of *CCS* at the plenary sessions of academic association conferences like the American Sociological Association , or the European Sociology Congress, or the Cultural Economics Association. Not in the ordinary sessions that already exist in these giant conferences, but have them set up plenary sessions, and we will need the help of people like Sharon Zukin or Lily Kong, without which it will be very hard for us to set such things up in international conferences, so it is quite urgent that have a special session on *CCS* topics set up for a big international conference next year, and have people write about the results of that for publication in *CCS*. Or, have people write articles in English, not for *CCS*, but for journals that are in the Social Science Citation Index. These things are not medium term, but are short term, that is to say, since there is a possibility that our *CCS* journal may disappear because of its three-year impact factor, I really want us to do these things urgently. That was what I thought when I heard Professor Shin's words.

And then, about the AUC. For the AUC, to start with, I went ahead and wrote an example of a draft constitution, something like a set of association rules. And along with some general clauses, it would be called the Association for Urban Creativity, or Toshi Sozosei Gakkai in Japanese, and the headquarters would first be in Osaka, and it may be that we will have to set up divisional branches internationally. And then, as for its purpose, its scope, and its activities, it would be not just for academics but would also include people engaged in practical activities. And then for Article 2, membership, how should we go about making the rules for membership? And then, if one becomes a member, what benefits are there? The 'rights of members' are written down. And then, withdrawing from the association. And then, in Article 3, Organization, the terms of office, and what kind of board of directors. Or what kind of scientific committee, a committee for putting on workshops and conferences and judging papers. And a conference committee, a secretary, and their organization. And this doesn't mean only Japan, we need to have a lot of variety, from Asia, Europe, North America, South America, etc. What we are thinking about in the beginning is having two people, one as president and another as vice-president. And then a secretary general. In international academic associations, the secretary general plays a very important role. An then rules about how such officers are chosen, and what their terms of office are. About that, even in the American Accounting Society, a huge association, they still don't hold elections, if they held elections, there could be cases where the officers chosen would not match well with their mid and long term strategic direction. They have something like an advisory committee, so something like that could be created instead of having elections. What should we do about that? Then, the duties of the officers. And then, a board of directors. These are scattered in various places around the world, so how do we have a meeting of the board? For this conference, we thought about having a meeting of the recommended board members, but not all of them have come here to attend. And then there are emergency board meetings. What constitutes a quorum? That is done in a way based on Japanese academic associations. Then there are financial matters, the setting of yearly membership dues. And then, income from publications. And then, the official language. In the European Accounting Association for example, they put up yellow cards. That is to say, if the speed of English being spoken is too fast, there are yellow cards telling the speaker to slow down. In other words, it is multilingual and international group, and they are trying to prevent it from being taken over by Anglo-American native speakers of English, but, on the other hand, if they need native speakers to write articles, so that is a difficult area to deal with. And then, people who can give English language support for the English written by non-native speakers. I think we need to put even something about that into the rules. I'd like to hear what other people think.

Masayuki Sasaki: Well, I will speak in Japanese. This is nothing more than one proposal, it is certainly not something that is set in concrete. I'm thinking that, beginning now, for about a year or so we should solicit a variety of opinions, and then make a new type of association in the form of a network that is as flexible as possible, so this is no more than one way of thinking. If we were to start debating that here today, we would need an entire day, so that is just being put out today as one idea. Well, is there anything besides that?

Sharon Zukin: Certainly it is important to set up the legal forms of responsibility in every new association. And I am not familiar with the norms of the European Accounting Society, I must admit, but in sociology associations, the main goal is to be inclusive, as in the phrase social inclusion. And so, in sociology associations there is an emphasis on openness and elections. Not elections within a board, but elections from within the entire membership of the association. So, I wanted to suggest that you consider building in more openness in the elections and in the representation of the membership as a whole.

Masayuki Sasaki: Thank you very much. Any other comments or advice? Please.

Toshio Kamo: As I said before, I wasn't here to listen to the discussion yesterday or the day before, but I think that finally my head is on the same wavelength as the thrust of this conference. One of the things that really impressed me was this: Ordinarily at international symposiums, there is a tendency for things to conclude with just stopping after a lot of talking, or with the compiling of the papers that were presented at the conference into a printed volume, but at this conference, by presenting the problems involved with *CCS*, there was a lot of discussion mixed in about the problems of international academic communication, and I thought that was very interesting and stimulating. Actually, some years ago I was drafted to be a member of the Ministry of Science and Education's university evaluation committee, and at that time, for one of the standards used for evaluating the articles that Japanese researchers had written, there was a debate saying, isn't it important how these articles are evaluated internationally? And so we submitted that, and when we looked for evidence of the academic accomplishment of papers reflected in the international citation index, we saw that among the articles written by Japanese physiologists during the previous five years, there were fewer than ten that had actually been cited in the index. That is terrible, so first of all, in general, I would like to credit that criterion. Therefore, even though *CCS* has appeared, my feeling is that it isn't going to be so simple creating a situation where, using that as one of the mediums for disseminating from Japan or from Asia academic information and knowledge, you have an impact on the academic circles of the world. However, as somebody said earlier, the important thing is that disseminating a lot of multilateral academic information, a more global academic network than the one up till now will come into being. The fact that in the midst of that, the discussion related to the themes of creativity and social inclusion will de deepened, is something that I feel is very important. In that sense, I don't think we need to get too hysterical over the international competition for citations, but what I was thinking is the most important thing is to keep moving on the road to putting out information on Japanese cities as proactively as possible in English-language articles, and through *CCS*, actually getting them publicized. That is my strongest feeling. As I said at the beginning, the themes of cultural creativity and social inclusion are already more than just themes of urban studies. Probably they are themes at the level of the national government, and currently, the questions that the Democratic Party of Japan and the Liberal Democratic Party are fighting over, when seen in a larger framework, could even be read as political fights over just such issues. I think they have become themes of such enormity, so I am looking forward to your continuing to hold symposiums like the one here today, and with regard to *CCS*, I hope that through it you will continue your efforts at communication.

Masayuki Sasaki: Thank you very much. Well, I think it is now time for me to try to make a final summation of this three-day symposium. We have been preparing for this conference since about a year ago. And two years before that is when Professor Okano and I walked into the office of the social science editing branch of Elsevier, Ltd. in Oxford, and talked about trying to inaugurate the publication of a new journal from Asia with more passion and enthusiasm than ever before in my life. That is to say, there had never before been an international journal in the social sciences that one university in Asia had the editorial rights for. How can we realize something that hasn't been done before? This was precisely, in fact, a case study in creative problem-solving, and we faced up to it with tremendous ambition and hopes. Having done that, our enthusiasm succeeded in moving mountains. With that, Mr. James the said to us, "Okay, let's try it," and from there on, a big stage started moving for the preparations for today's conference. Although I already had, up till now, a network with all kinds of researchers around the world, in order to realize this huge pioneering work, I would need the support of a myriad of people, and so I have been bending my efforts towards that for about three years. With your help, we have been able to put together the first three issues already, and next week issue no. 4 will be published on the web, so we have conquered one mountain in creating our issues for the first year. Whether I will be able to continue with more of this, actually, the time for me to retire from the university is approaching, and I think I would like to pass it on to a successor, and actually I have been thinking that this conference might be the last big event in my university career, but it looks like I will have to keep on working a little longer. Today I felt, while carrying on the open discussion with all of you, that I would like to realize somehow the first, inaugural conference of the Association for Urban Creativity. Therefore, I really hope that all of you gathered here will work on even more researchers and expand our network. And again I sincerely welcome all your criticisms, your comments, and your advice. Over the course of the last three days, many stimulating discussion points have been raised, and now the question is whether we can somehow reflect that in the pages of *CCS*, and moreover achieve the high quality that will lead to worldwide approval. That is the task that is now waiting for us. To those of you who gave presentations this time, we will need your cooperation again. If you get a request from us, if you are asked, please accept it quickly and rewrite your report so that it can be submitted for publication. Also, for those of you who did not make presentations this time, I hope you will by all means make presentations next time, and we will be grateful if you make article submissions at every opportunity. And finally, I would like to express my thanks to the translators who have supported our exchange of view over the last three days. With that, I will bring this three-day symposium to a close. Thank you everybody for your cooperation.

The 1st International Roundtable Meeting: Towards the Century of Cities
International Symposium
Urban Regeneration through Cultural Creativity and Social Inclusion

Date: December 15-17, 2010
Venue: The Osaka International House

Organized by The Urban Research Plaza at Osaka City University and Osaka International House
    Foundation
Supported by The Agency for Cultural Affairs of the Ministry of Education and Science, The Japan
    Foundation and Tadao Ando Cultural Foundation
Co-sponsored by Institute of Systems Science Research

URP GCOE DOCUMENT 9
国際学術シンポジウム
文化創造と社会包摂による都市の再興

2011年6月
編集責任　佐々木雅幸、水内俊雄
編集委員　全泓奎、佐藤由美、高岡伸一、櫻田和也、堀口朋亨、雨森信、林朋子、ハンヌ・クルンサアリ、
　　　　　崔宇、北川眞也、ヒェラルド・コルナトウスキ、笹島秀晃
発　　行　大阪市立大学 都市研究プラザ

大阪市立大学 都市研究プラザ
〒558-8585
大阪市住吉区杉本 3-3-138
電話 06-6605-2071　FAX06-6605-2069
URL www.ur-plaza.osaka-cu.ac.jp／

© 2011 Urban Research Plaza, Osaka City University

ISBN978-4-88065-270-2
Printed in Japan

発売所 株式会社 水曜社
〒160-0022
東京都新宿区新宿 1-14-12
電話 03-3351-8768　FAX03-5362-7279
URL www.bookdom.net／suiyosha／